M000308819

MINNESOTA

RECIPES

*Favorite Recipes of
4-H Families and Friends*

Published by: Minnesota 4-H Foundation

Copyright by: Minnesota 4-H Foundation
340 Coffey Hall
1420 Eckles Avenue
St. Paul, Minnesota 55108
1-612-625-6250 or 1-800-444-4238

ISBN: 0-9647987-0-0

Edited, Designed and Manufactured by
Favorite Recipes® Press
P.O. Box 305142
Nashville, Tennessee 37230
1-800-358-0560

Manufactured in the United States of America
First Printing: 1995   25,000 copies

Acknowledgements

It is with sincere appreciation that we thank the 1,500 4-Hers, parents friends, families, Minnesota Adult Volunteer Association members, State Ambassador Alumni, Minnesota 4-H donors, and 4-H Clubs who submitted recipes and creative drawings for the all new Minnesota 4-H cookbook. Publication of this unique cookbook would not have been possible without the support, advice and assistance of numerous individuals.

We regret that all the recipes (2,100) and creative drawings (197) could not be used at this time, although the committee would have liked to. We did, though, try to use as many as we could within the cookbook. Generally, all published recipes were selected by the staff of Favorite Recipes® Press under their established guidelines to present a complete variety.

The actual production challenge could not have been met without the special efforts of all the 4-H Club leaders, Extension Educators, and Center for 4-H Youth Development Faculty, namely Julie Swanson, Cynthia McArthur, and Linda Bradley, who actively worked to solicit recipes and artwork for the cookbook. In addition, the efforts of the Minnesota 4-H Foundation Staff: Jim Lewis, Deb Noll, and Amy Watje, and the Cookbook Committee were invaluable in developing, publishing and marketing the cookbook. To everyone involved, we acknowledge their enthusiasm, participation and support of this special project.

Cookbook Committee

Linda Bradley
Elaine Christiansen
Molly Fischer
Dede Hard

Mary Fran Lamison
Marian Larson
Sara Thoms

Artwork

The piece of artwork on the cover of this cookbook is possible because of the enthusiasm of *Bill Svendsgaard*, Extension Educator in Hennepin County. We sincerely thank him for his input on the project. We also thank all of those who provided the artwork that appears as chapter divider pages in the book.

Foreword

The Minnesota 4-H Foundation is proud to present *Minnesota 4-H Recipes*. This collection of culinary delights represents contributions from Minnesota 4-H youth involved in a wide array of programs, parents, adult volunteers, staff, alumni and financial supporters. This book is the realization of a goal to bring youth and adults together around a project representing food and fun. It is a creation filled with love, work, family recipe treasures, and talent. As you use *Minnesota 4-H Recipes* we hope you think about the book's dedication:

Minnesota young people,
our greatest and most precious natural resource.

The Minnesota 4-H Foundation was founded in 1981. The Foundation exists to support the educational programs offered through Minnesota 4-H youth development programs. The Foundation and 4-H programs are committed to the positive development of young people. The Foundation acquires financial resources from individuals, families, businesses and other groups to support 4-H to more than 250,000 Minnesota kids each year.

Proceeds from the sale of *Minnesota 4-H Recipes* will be used to help fund the small grants program of the Minnesota 4-H Foundation. Small grants are available to all 4-H clubs and programs, counties, and clusters of counties to encourage activities that link youth and adults. The small grants program has been a part of the Minnesota 4-H Foundation since 1984. Over 260 grants ranging in size from $100 to $2,500 have been awarded. We conservatively estimate that those grants have touched the lives of more than 28,000 young people.

Enjoy the fruits of 4-H participation represented in *Minnesota 4-H Recipes*. As you discover the benefits of your investment through a feast of great foods, also know that you are benefiting the positive development of Minnesota's young people.

Mark Wilberts
Chair
Minnesota 4-H Foundation
Board of Trustees

Contents

$\mathcal{M}$innesota 4-H–
The Evolution of a Tradition

Founded in 1903, Minnesota 4-H developed from a concern and need to provide relevant hands-on learning and social development for rural youth. A central purpose of that early program was to encourage technology transfer from the University to the farm by encouraging youth to demonstrate the effectiveness of new practices to their parents. The success of those efforts are now legendary.

Since 1912, 4-H has been a part of the Minnesota Extension Service of the University of Minnesota. Our link with the University is a unique and powerful strength of 4-H. University generated knowledge and research relevant to youth and youth development provides the basis for 4-H outreach. The University of Minnesota extends the search for knowledge to the Minnesota public through an Extension Service and programs like those of 4-H.

Today we offer a bold vision for Minnesota 4-H–*that every Minnesota youth will have the opportunity to benefit from a meaningful experience with caring adults to gain life skills needed for functioning well in society.* The primary 4-H learners are children and youth ages 5 to 19; however 4-H does provide opportunities for adults, particularly parents and volunteers who work with the young people. The primary guides and teachers in 4-H are the parents and other adults and older teen volunteers who take responsibility for community clubs, project clubs, special events, and a wide range of community-based educational programming.

Young people in 4-H join voluntarily and select projects and areas of involvement based on their personal interests. Working independently or in groups, 4-H youth experiment, work, demonstrate and produce products in areas as diverse as aerospace, animal science, entomology, food preparation, creative expression, leadership and a host of other areas. Youth also work with adults in group settings to provide service to their communities in areas like pregnancy prevention, alcohol use, nutrition and fitness.

Learning in 4-H takes place in kitchens, living rooms, community centers, church basements, community parks, county fairgrounds, gymnasiums or anywhere young people and adults gather to pursue their work. Young people are encouraged to be active in the learning environment. They approach new situations and ideas by exploring, engaging with others, reflecting and questioning in order to discover answers and implications.

In 4-H we define *positive youth development* by eight features essential to the healthy development of young people. Young people benefit from opportunities to:

- feel a sense of safety and structure
- experience active participation, group membership and belonging
- develop self-worth achieved through meaningful contribution
- experiment to discover self, gain independence, and gain control over one's life
- develop significant relationships with peers and adults
- discuss conflicting values and formulate their own
- feel the pride and accountability that come with mastery
- expand the capacity to enjoy life and know that success is possible

4-H programs are conducted under the auspices of County Extension Offices located in every Minnesota county. For information about 4-H, contact your County Extension Office (see page 199 for a listing of Extension Offices).

GET READY, GET SET, COOK!

4-H FOUNDATION COOKBOOK

Mary Gillette
Sherburne County

Handwashing Rap

You **gotta'** wash your **hands**, and
You **gotta'** wash 'em **right**,
Don't **give** in to **germs**
With-**out** a **fight**.

Use **water** that's **warm**
And **lots** of soapy **bubbles**,
These are your **weapons**
For **preventing** germ **troubles**.

Don't cut your time **short**
Your **fingers** — get **between**,
It **takes** twenty **seconds**
To **make** sure they're **clean**.

Gotta' **wash** . . . gotta' **wash**
Gotta' — **wash** — your — **hands**,
Gotta' **wash** . . . gotta' **wash**
Gotta' — **wash** — your — **hands**.

NOTE: Words/syllables in heavy type carry the stronger beat.

Operation RISK: A research and outreach program of Michigan State University's College of Human Ecology and Children, Youth and Family Extension Programs.

KIDS' KITCHEN

Tressa McLouth
Kanabec County

Apple Wraps

3 tablespoons butter
2 medium apples
1/2 cup sugar
1 teaspoon cinnamon
1 (10-count) can
   buttermilk biscuits
1/2 cup orange juice

- Preheat oven to 350 degrees.
- Heat butter in saucepan until melted.
- Peel and thinly slice apples.
- Combine sugar and cinnamon in bowl; mix well.
- Dip biscuits into butter; coat with sugar and cinnamon mixture.
- Arrange 3 apple slices in center of each biscuit. Fold to enclose filling; seal edges.
- Arrange in greased 8x8-inch baking pan. Sprinkle with remaining sugar and cinnamon mixture; drizzle with orange juice.
- Bake at 350 degrees for 30 minutes. Serve warm.
- *Yield: 10 servings.*

Approx Per Serving: Cal 169; Prot 2 g; Carbo 27 g; T Fat 8 g; 37% Calories from Fat; Chol 9 mg; Fiber 1 g; Sod 335 mg

Just for Fun

Make *Edible Chocolate Fundough* by combining 1 can of chocolate frosting, 1 cup peanut butter and 1½ cups confectioners' sugar in a large bowl and mixing well. Add enough cornflakes, rice krispies or rolled oats to make a workable dough. Make into shapes and eat if desired.

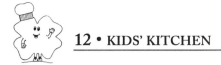

Bird Nests

3 cups crisp rice cereal
1 cup shredded coconut
³/₄ cup peanut butter
**¹/₂ cup packed brown
    sugar**
¹/₃ cup light corn syrup
1 teaspoon vanilla extract
36 to 48 jelly beans

- Combine cereal and coconut in bowl; mix well.
- Bring peanut butter, brown sugar, corn syrup and vanilla to a boil in saucepan, stirring occasionally. Pour over cereal mixture; mix well. Let stand until cool.
- Form cereal mixture into shape of bird nests; fill with 3 to 4 jelly beans.
- Ask Mom, Dad or an older brother or sister to help you remove boiling liquids from the stove top.
- *Yield: 12 servings.*

Approx Per Serving: Cal 230; Prot 5 g; Carbo 32 g; T Fat 11 g; 40% Calories from Fat; Chol 0 mg; Fiber 2 g; Sod 195 mg

Fruit Sauce Dip

1 cup sour cream
**3 tablespoons orange
    marmalade**
1 tablespoon honey
1 teaspoon vanilla extract

- Combine sour cream, orange marmalade, honey and vanilla in bowl; mix well.
- Chill, covered, until serving time.
- Serve with sliced peaches, sliced apples, pineapple chunks, strawberries or your favorite fruit.
- Do not use imitation vanilla flavoring.
- *Yield: 12 (2-tablespoon) servings.*

Approx Per Serving: Cal 59; Prot 1 g; Carbo 6 g; T Fat 4 g; 59% Calories from Fat; Chol 9 mg; Fiber <1 g; Sod 13 mg

ℳexican Roll-Ups

8 ounces cream cheese, softened
1 cup sour cream
1 envelope taco seasoning mix
1 (4-ounce) can chopped green chiles, drained
1 (4-ounce) can chopped black olives, drained
1 cup shredded Cheddar cheese
1 (10-count) package 10-inch flour tortillas

- Beat cream cheese, sour cream and seasoning mix in mixer bowl until smooth.
- Stir in green chiles, olives and Cheddar cheese.
- Spread cream cheese mixture evenly over tortillas; roll to enclose filling.
- Chill, wrapped securely in plastic wrap, for 3 hours or longer.
- Cut into 1-inch slices.
- *Yield: 80 servings.*

Approx Per Serving: Cal 49; Prot 1 g; Carbo 5 g; T Fat 3 g; 50% Calories from Fat; Chol 6 mg; Fiber <1 g; Sod 122 mg

ℕibbles

2 (11-ounce) packages oyster crackers
3/4 to 1 cup vegetable oil
1 envelope ranch salad dressing mix
1 teaspoon dillweed
1 teaspoon garlic powder

- Place oyster crackers in microwave-safe bowl.
- Combine oil, dressing mix, dillweed and garlic powder in microwave-safe bowl; mix well.
- Microwave on High for 1 minute; mix well. Pour over crackers, tossing to coat.
- Microwave on High for 3 minutes, stirring at the end of each minute.
- Let stand until cool. Store in airtight container.
- *Yield: 25 servings.*

Approx Per Serving: Cal 188; Prot 2 g; Carbo 19 g; T Fat 12 g; 56% Calories from Fat; Chol 0 mg; Fiber 1 g; Sod 402 mg

Popcorn Six Ways

Caramel Popcorn

½ cup packed brown
    sugar
½ cup butter
10 marshmallows
2 quarts warm popped
    popcorn

- Combine first 3 ingredients in saucepan. Cook over medium heat until blended, stirring constantly; do not boil. Pour over popcorn in bowl, tossing to coat.
- *Yield: 16 (½-cup) servings.*

Approx Per Serving: Cal 102; Prot 1 g; Carbo 12 g; T Fat 6 g; 51% Calories from Fat; Chol 16 mg; Fiber 1 g; Sod 63 mg

Cheese Popcorn

½ cup melted butter
½ cup grated Parmesan
    cheese
2 quarts warm popped
    popcorn

- Mix butter and cheese in bowl. Pour over popcorn in bowl, tossing to coat.
- *Yield: 16 (½-cup servings).*

Approx Per Serving: Cal 80; Prot 2 g; Carbo 3 g; T Fat 7 g; 75% Calories from Fat; Chol 18 mg; Fiber 1 g; Sod 117 mg

Chili Popcorn

¼ cup melted butter
¾ teaspoon chili powder
¼ teaspoon popcorn salt
2 quarts warm popped
    popcorn

- Combine butter, chili powder and salt in bowl; mix well. Drizzle over popcorn in bowl, tossing to coat.
- *Yield: 16 (½-cup) servings.*

Approx Per Serving: Cal 41; Prot 1 g; Carbo 3 g; T Fat 3 g; 65% Calories from Fat; Chol 8 mg; Fiber 1 g; Sod 63 mg

Italian Popcorn

¹/₄ cup melted butter
¹/₄ cup grated Parmesan
  cheese
1 teaspoon oregano
¹/₄ teaspoon popcorn salt
2 quarts warm popped
  popcorn

• Combine butter, cheese, oregano and salt in bowl; mix well. Drizzle over popcorn in bowl, tossing to coat.

• *Yield: 16 (¹/₂-cup) servings.*

Approx Per Serving: Cal 48; Prot 1 g;
  Carbo 3 g; T Fat 4 g; 65% Calories from
  Fat; Chol 9 mg; Fiber 1 g; Sod 92 mg

Onion and Garlic Popcorn

¹/₄ cup melted butter
¹/₄ teaspoon onion salt
¹/₄ teaspoon garlic salt
¹/₄ teaspoon popcorn salt
2 quarts warm popped
  popcorn

• Combine butter, onion salt, garlic salt and popcorn salt in bowl; mix well. Drizzle over popcorn in bowl, tossing to coat.

• *Yield: 16 (¹/₂-cup) servings.*

Approx Per Serving: Cal 41; Prot 1 g;
  Carbo 3 g; T Fat 3 g; 65% Calories from
  Fat; Chol 8 mg; Fiber 1 g; Sod 120 mg

Taco Popcorn

¹/₄ cup melted butter
³/₄ teaspoon taco
  seasoning mix
¹/₄ teaspoon popcorn salt
2 quarts warm popped
  popcorn

• Combine butter, seasoning mix and salt in bowl; mix well. Drizzle over popcorn in bowl, tossing to coat.

• *Yield: 16 (¹/₂-cup) servings.*

Approx Per Serving: Cal 41; Prot 1 g;
  Carbo 3 g; T Fat 03g; 64% Calories from
  Fat; Chol 8 mg; Fiber 1 g; Sod 78 mg

Spook and Crunch Snack Mix

3 tablespoons margarine
½ teaspoon apple pie
   spice
2 cups oyster crackers
4 cups popped popcorn
1 cup dry roasted peanuts
3 (1-ounce) packages
   mixed chewy fruit bits

- Heat margarine in saucepan over low heat until melted. Stir in apple pie spice.
- Pour margarine mixture over oyster crackers in bowl, stirring until coated.
- Add popcorn, peanuts and fruit bits; mix well.
- *Yield: 16 (½-cup) servings.*

Approx Per Serving: Cal 139; Prot 3 g; Carbo 14 g; T Fat 8 g; 50% Calories from Fat; Chol 0 mg; Fiber 2 g; Sod 163 mg

Witches Brew

A great Halloween treat!

1 cup blood drops or red
   hot cinnamon candies
1 cup snake eyes or
   chocolate chips
1 cup owl eyes or "M &
   M's" chocolate candies
1 cup chicken toenails or
   candy corn
1 cup ants or raisins
2 cups earthworms or
   pretzels
2 cups cobwebs or Chex
   cereal

- Combine cinnamon candies, chocolate chips, chocolate candies, candy corn, raisins, pretzels and cereal in bowl; mix well.
- Store in covered container.
- *Yield: 18 (½-cup) servings.*

Approx Per Serving: Cal 248; Prot 2 g; Carbo 51 g; T Fat 6 g; 19% Calories from Fat; Chol 0 mg; Fiber 2 g; Sod 127 mg

Pink Passion

3 cups vanilla ice cream
½ cup cranberry juice
¼ cup orange juice
½ cup 7-Up

- Combine ice cream, cranberry juice and orange juice in blender container.
- Process until smooth.
- Pour into glasses; top with 7-Up.
- May omit 7-Up.
- *Yield: 6 servings.*

Approx Per Serving: Cal 158; Prot 2 g; Carbo 22 g; T Fat 7 g; 40% Calories from Fat; Chol 29 mg; Fiber <1 g; Sod 54 mg

Strawberry Milk Shake

Great after school snack.

1 cup cold milk
1 cup any flavor ice cream
2 teaspoons strawberry gelatin

- Combine milk, ice cream and gelatin in beverage shaker; cover tightly.
- Shake vigorously until blended.
- Pour into glass.
- *Yield: 1 serving.*

Approx Per Serving: Cal 434; Prot 13 g; Carbo 47 g; T Fat 23 g; 46% Calories from Fat; Chol 91 mg; Fiber <1 g; Sod 237 mg

Just for Fun

Make your own *Bubble Stuff* by combining 2 cups liquid dish-washing detergent, 6 cups water and ¾ cup light corn syrup in a large container and mixing well. Let the mixture stand for 4 hours before using. Store the unused Bubble Stuff in the refrigerator but bring to room temperature before using.

Chunky Chicken Rice Soup

2 (13-ounce) cans
   boneless chicken
6 cups hot water
1 (16-ounce) package
   mixed vegetables,
   thawed
2 tablespoons poultry
   seasoning
Pepper to taste
2 cups uncooked instant
   rice
1 tablespoon chopped
   fresh parsley

- Heat undrained chicken in saucepan until hot, stirring constantly.
- Add hot water, mixed vegetables, poultry seasoning and pepper; mix well.
- Bring to a boil; reduce heat.
- Simmer, covered, for 5 minutes. Stir in rice and parsley.
- Let stand, covered, for 5 minutes.
- Ladle into soup bowls.
- *Yield: 6 servings.*

Approx Per Serving: Cal 371; Prot 32 g; Carbo 37 g; T Fat 10 g; 25% Calories from Fat; Chol 76 mg; Fiber 4 g; Sod 647 mg

Crunchy Cranberry Salad

4 cups cranberries
2 cups sugar
2 cups seedless red grapes
1 cup pineapple tidbits
½ to 1 cup coarsely
   chopped walnuts
1 cup whipping cream,
   whipped

- Slice cranberries into halves. Place in bowl.
- Sprinkle sugar over cranberries; stir.
- Let stand at room temperature for 8 to 10 hours; drain.
- Stir in grapes, pineapple and walnuts.
- Fold in whipped cream.
- Chill, covered, until serving time.
- *Yield: 10 servings.*

Approx Per Serving: Cal 375; Prot 3 g; Carbo 58 g; T Fat 17 g; 38% Calories from Fat; Chol 33 mg; Fiber 3 g; Sod 12 mg

Mandarin Orange Salad

1 (6-ounce) package
    orange gelatin
1 cup boiling water
1 cup orange juice
1 pint orange sherbet
1 (11-ounce) can
    mandarin oranges,
    drained

- Dissolve gelatin in boiling water in bowl; mix well. Add orange juice and sherbet, stirring until sherbet dissolves. Let stand for 1 hour or until partially set.
- Stir in mandarin oranges. Spoon into mold. Chill for 2 to 3 hours or until set.
- *Yield: 8 servings.*

Approx Per Serving: Cal 184; Prot 3 g; Carbo 43 g; T Fat 1 g; 5% Calories from Fat; Chol 2 mg; Fiber <1 g; Sod 79 mg

Honey-Glazed Chicken

3 pounds chicken pieces
$1/2$ cup flour
1 teaspoon salt
$1/2$ teaspoon cayenne
$1/3$ cup melted butter
$1/4$ cup packed brown
    sugar
$1/4$ cup honey
$1/4$ cup lemon juice
1 tablespoon soy sauce
$1^1/2$ teaspoons curry
    powder

- Preheat oven to 350 degrees.
- Rinse chicken and pat dry.
- Combine flour, salt and cayenne in sealable plastic bag, shaking to mix. Place chicken in plastic bag; seal tightly. Shake to coat.
- Arrange chicken in 9x13-inch baking pan. Drizzle with $1/2$ of the butter.
- Bake at 350 degrees for 30 minutes.
- Combine remaining ingredients in bowl; mix well. Spoon over chicken.
- Bake for 45 minutes longer, basting occasionally.
- *Yield: 6 servings.*

Approx Per Serving: Cal 419; Prot 34 g; Carbo 28 g; T Fat 19 g; 40% Calories from Fat; Chol 128 mg; Fiber <1 g; Sod 732 mg

Flowerpot Dirt Cake

1 (16-ounce) package
  chocolate sandwich
  cookies
8 ounces cream cheese,
  softened
1 cup confectioners'
  sugar
1/4 cup butter or
  margarine, softened
2 (4-ounce) packages
  vanilla instant
  pudding mix
3 1/2 cups cold milk
12 ounces whipped
  topping, thawed

- Process cookies in food processor or blender until finely crushed.
- Beat cream cheese, confectioners' sugar and butter in mixer bowl until smooth, scraping bowl occasionally.
- Combine pudding mix and milk in bowl, stirring until blended. Fold into cream cheese mixture. Fold in whipped topping.
- Layer cookie crumbs and pudding mixture alternately in new 8- or 10-inch flowerpot until all ingredients are used, ending with cookie crumbs.
- Chill for 2 to 10 hours.
- Decorate with silk flowers and gummy worms.
- *Yield: 12 servings.*

Approx Per Serving: Cal 511; Prot 6 g; Carbo 62 g; T Fat 28 g; 48% Calories from Fat; Chol 41 mg; Fiber 1 g; Sod 603 mg

Just for Fun

Make your own *Sidewalk Chalk* by mixing 1 cup plaster of paris with 1/2 cup water and adding tempra paint for the color you want. Cut the bottoms from 35mm film canisters, tape 2 together and then snap a canister top on one of the ends. Pour the plaster of paris into the mold and let it dry overnight.

Popcorn Cake

Add holiday-colored-coated chocolate candies to this cake for a special holiday treat.

14 cups popped popcorn
1 cup salted peanuts
25 caramels
1 (10-ounce) package
 miniature
 marshmallows
1 cup butter
1 cup "M & M's"
 Chocolate Candies

- Combine popcorn and peanuts in bowl; mix well.
- Heat caramels, marshmallows and butter in saucepan over low heat until smooth, stirring constantly. Pour over popcorn mixture, stirring until coated.
- Cool slightly. Stir in chocolate candies. Spoon into greased bundt or tube pan.
- Let stand for several hours before serving.
- *Yield: 16 servings.*

Approx Per Serving: Cal 342; Prot 5 g; Carbo 39 g; T Fat 20 g; 50% Calories from Fat; Chol 32 mg; Fiber 2 g; Sod 208 mg

Peanut Butter Balls

1¼ cups confectioners'
 sugar
1¼ cups nonfat dry milk
 powder
1 cup peanut butter
1 cup light corn syrup

- Combine confectioners' sugar, milk powder, peanut butter and corn syrup in bowl; mix well.
- Shape into small balls.
- Arrange on waxed paper-lined sheet.
- Chill until firm.
- *Yield: 24 (1-ball) servings.*

Approx Per Serving: Cal 138; Prot 4 g; Carbo 21 g; T Fat 5 g; 33% Calories from Fat; Chol 1 mg; Fiber 1 g; Sod 87 mg

*H*omemade Chocolate Kiss

2 (2-ounce) squares
  almond bark
2 (2-ounce) squares
  chocolate bark

- Cover small opening of ³/₄ cup funnel with foil. Set inside a cup to balance.
- Melt almond bark and chocolate bark in double boiler over hot water, stirring until smooth. Pour chocolate into funnel.
- Freeze for 45 minutes.
- Remove foil. Scrap excess chocolate off tip. Invert chocolate kiss onto foil. Wrap in foil.
- May add crushed peanuts or crisp rice cereal to melted chocolate.
- *Yield: 4 servings.*

Approx Per Serving: Cal 298; Prot 2 g;
  Carbo 35 g; T Fat 18 g; 54% Calories from
  Fat; Chol 6 mg; Fiber 2 g; Sod 21 mg

*E*asy Cookies

1 (2-layer) package
  chocolate cake mix
¹/₂ cup butter, softened
2 eggs

- Preheat oven to 350 degrees.
- Beat cake mix, butter and eggs in mixer bowl until blended. Drop by spoonfuls onto greased cookie sheet.
- Bake at 350 degrees for 15 minutes.
- Remove to wire rack to cool.
- May add chopped nuts, raisins, candied-coated chocolate candies, chocolate chips or mint chips to dough.
- *Yield: 48 (1-cookie) servings.*

Approx Per Serving: Cal 66; Prot 1 g;
  Carbo 8 g; T Fat 4 g; 49% Calories from
  Fat; Chol 14 mg; Fiber <1 g; Sod 110 mg

*C*heerio Bars

1 cup honey
¹/₂ cup sugar
1 cup peanut butter
6 cups Cheerios
1 cup raisins
¹/₂ cup chopped pecans

- Bring honey and sugar to a boil in saucepan, stirring frequently. Remove from heat.
- Stir in peanut butter.
- Add cheerios, raisins and pecans; mix well.
- Press into greased 9x13-inch dish.
- Let stand until cool. Cut into bars.
- *Yield: 36 (1-bar) servings.*

Approx Per Serving: Cal 121; Prot 3 g; Carbo 19 g; T Fat 5 g; 34% Calories from Fat; Chol 0 mg; Fiber 1 g; Sod 76 mg

*B*utter Cookies

2 cups butter, softened
1 cup packed brown
   sugar
4 cups flour

- Preheat oven to 325 degrees.
- Cream butter and brown sugar in mixer bowl until light and fluffy.
- Add flour ³/₄ cup at a time, beating well after each addition.
- Shape into ¹/₂-inch balls.
- Arrange on ungreased cookie sheet; flatten with fork.
- Bake at 325 degrees for 15 minutes.
- Remove to wire rack to cool.
- May add food coloring to dough. May decorate cookies with candy sprinkles.
- *Yield: 48 (1-cookie) servings.*

Approx Per Serving: Cal 120; Prot 1 g; Carbo 12 g; T Fat 8 g; 58% Calories from Fat; Chol 21 mg; Fiber <1 g; Sod 80 mg

Coffee Can Ice Cream

1 cup milk
1 cup half-and-half
¹/₂ cup sugar
¹/₄ cup egg substitute
1 teaspoon vanilla extract
1 gallon crushed ice
¹/₂ cup salt

- Combine milk, half-and-half, sugar, egg substitute and vanilla in bowl; mix well.
- Pour into 1 (1¹/₂-pound) metal can; seal with tightfitting lid.
- Cover bottom of 3-pound coffee can with 1 inch of crushed ice. Sprinkle with 1 tablespoon salt.
- Place small can in coffee can. Surround coffee can with alternating layers of ice and salt until all ingredients are used; seal with tightfitting lid.
- Rotate can for 10 minutes. Remove small can.
- Stir ice cream.
- Repeat process for firmer product.
- *Yield: 5 (¹/₂-cup) servings.*

Approx Per Serving: Cal 181; Prot 5 g; Carbo 24 g; T Fat 8 g; 37% Calories from Fat; Chol 25 mg; Fiber 0 g; Sod 66 mg

Just for Fun

Make *Bird Corn Bread* by combining 1 cup cornmeal, 1 cup cracked corn or sunflower seeds, 1 cup white or whole wheat flour, 2 teaspoons baking powder and 1 ground up egg shell in a large bowl. Add 1 egg, 1 cup milk and ¹/₂ cup lard or bacon drippings and mix well. Press the mixture into 8x8-inch baking pan and bake at 400 degrees for 20 minutes. Cut into cubes when cool and place on the ground or bird feeding tray.

Appetizers, Snacks & Beverages

Kelly Purdy
Freeborn County

NOTES

Cheesy Cheddar Ball

8 ounces cream cheese
1 cup shredded sharp
    Cheddar cheese
1 cup shredded mild Colby
    cheese
1/2 cup grated Parmesan
    cheese
1 tablespoon milk
1/2 teaspoon garlic powder
Salt to taste
Worcestershire sauce to taste
1/2 cup chopped pecans

- Combine cheeses in large bowl. Let stand at room temperature to warm to 60 degrees or until softened.
- Add milk, garlic powder, salt and Worcestershire sauce; mix well.
- Shape into ball or log; roll in pecans.
- Chill, covered, until serving time.
- Serve with assorted party crackers.
- *Yield: 16 (2-tablespoon) servings.*

Approx Per Serving: Cal 145; Prot 6 g; Carbo 1 g; T Fat 13 g; 79% Calories from Fat; Chol 32 mg; Fiber <1 g; Sod 187 mg

Artichoke Dip

1 (14-ounce) can artichoke
    hearts, drained, chopped
1 cup grated Parmesan
    cheese
1 cup mayonnaise
1 cup shredded mozzarella
    cheese
Garlic salt to taste

- Preheat oven to 350 degrees.
- Combine artichokes, Parmesan cheese, mayonnaise, mozzarella cheese and garlic salt in bowl; mix well.
- Spoon into baking dish.
- Bake at 350 degrees for 20 to 30 minutes or until brown and bubbly.
- Serve with water crackers.
- *Yield: 15 (2-tablespoon) servings.*

Approx Per Serving: Cal 164; Prot 5 g; Carbo 2 g; T Fat 15 g; 83% Calories from Fat; Chol 20 mg; Fiber 0 g; Sod 322 mg

Bean Chip Dip

1/2 to 2 pounds ground meat
1 green bell pepper, chopped
1 onion, chopped
2 (16-ounce) cans refried
  beans
2 (8-ounce) cans tomato
  sauce
1 envelope taco seasoning
  mix
1 teaspoon chili powder
1 teaspoon dry mustard
2 cups sour cream
1/4 cup shredded Cheddar
  cheese
1/2 teaspoon chili powder
2 cups shredded Cheddar
  cheese
1 to 2 cups shredded lettuce

• Brown ground meat with green pepper
  and onion in skillet, stirring until ground
  beef is crumbly; drain.
• Stir in refried beans, tomato sauce,
  seasoning mix, 1 teaspoon chili powder
  and dry mustard.
• Bring to a boil. Spoon into 9x13-inch
  dish.
• Let stand until cool.
• Spread with mixture of sour cream,
  1/4 cup Cheddar cheese and 1/2 teaspoon
  chili powder. Sprinkle with 2 cups
  Cheddar cheese.
• Bake in moderate oven just until heated
  through. Top with lettuce.
• Serve with tortilla chips.
• *Yield: 48 (2-tablespoon) servings.*

Approx Per Serving: Cal 111; Prot 7 g; Carbo 6 g;
  T Fat 7 g; 6% Calories from Fat; Chol 24 mg;
  Fiber 6 g; Sod 258 mg

Hot Cheese Dip

2 cups shredded mozzarella
  cheese
2 cups shredded Cheddar
  cheese
2 cups mayonnaise
1 medium onion, minced
1 (4-ounce) can green chiles,
  drained

• Preheat oven to 350 degrees.
• Combine mozzarella cheese, Cheddar
  cheese, mayonnaise, onion and chiles in
  bowl; mix well.
• Spoon into greased 9- or 10-inch round
  baking dish.
• Bake at 350 degrees for 20 minutes or
  until bubbly.
• Serve with tortilla chips.
• *Yield: 48 (2-tablespoon) servings.*

Approx Per Serving: Cal 100; Prot 2 g; Carbo 1 g;
  T Fat 10 g; 88% Calories from Fat; Chol 14 mg;
  Fiber <1 g; Sod 127 mg

*M*exican Beef Appetizers

8 ounces cream cheese,
 softened
½ (12-ounce) jar thick
 chunky picante sauce
½ (2-ounce) jar dried beef,
 chopped
8 to 10 flour tortillas
1 cup shredded Cheddar
 cheese
Paprika to taste

- Combine cream cheese, picante sauce and dried beef in bowl, stirring until mixed.
- Place 1 tortilla on serving platter. Spread with cream cheese mixture. Repeat process until all ingredients are used, ending with tortilla. Chill, covered with plastic wrap, for 8 to 10 hours.
- Sprinkle with Cheddar cheese and paprika; cut into wedges.
- Serve with sour cream, guacamole or additional picante sauce.
- *Yield: 16 servings.*

Approx Per Serving: Cal 158; Prot 5 g; Carbo 14 g; T Fat 9 g; 51% Calories from Fat; Chol 24 mg; Fiber 1 g; Sod 313 mg

*B*eef Jerky

¼ cup Worcestershire sauce
¼ cup soy sauce
2 tablespoons liquid smoke
1 teaspoon onion powder
1 teaspoon MSG
½ teaspoon seasoned salt
⅓ teaspoon garlic powder
¼ teaspoon pepper
1 (1½-pound) flank steak,
 cut into thin strips

- Combine Worcestershire sauce, soy sauce, liquid smoke, onion powder, MSG, seasoned salt, garlic powder and pepper in glass dish or crock; mix well.
- Add flank steak, turning to coat.
- Marinate in refrigerator for 24 hours, turning occasionally; drain.
- Line bottom of oven with foil.
- Arrange steak strips on oven racks.
- Bake at 200 degrees for 4 to 6 hours or until desired degree of dryness.
- Remove to wire rack to cool.
- Store in sealable plastic bag in refrigerator.
- *Yield: 48 servings.*

Approx Per Serving: Cal 19; Prot 2 g; Carbo <1 g; T Fat 1 g; 41% Calories from Fat; Chol 6 mg; Fiber 0 g; Sod 209 mg

Dried Beef Roll-Ups

1 pound Velveeta cheese, chopped
6 ounces cream cheese
1 teaspoon liquid smoke
Garlic powder to taste
8 ounces dried beef

- Combine Velveeta cheese, cream cheese, liquid smoke and garlic powder in double boiler.
- Cook over low heat until smooth, stirring constantly.
- Spread cheese mixture over dried beef; roll to enclose filling.
- Chill until serving time.
- *Yield: 40 servings.*

Approx Per Serving: Cal 67; Prot 4 g; Carbo <1 g; T Fat 5 g; 71% Calories from Fat; Chol 18 mg; Fiber 0 g; Sod 371 mg

Cheeseburger Snowball Bites

6 slices bread, crusts trimmed
8 ounces lean ground beef
2 tablespoons grated onion
1 egg yolk, beaten
1/2 teaspoon salt
Pepper to taste
24 (1/2-inch cubes) Cheddar cheese

- Roll bread to flatten; cut into 1 1/2-inch rounds with cutter.
- Combine ground beef, onion, egg yolk, salt and pepper in bowl; mix well.
- Shape into 24 balls.
- Arrange meatballs on bread rounds; make indention in center of each meatball. Fill indention with cheese cube; bread should be covered with meat mixture.
- Arrange on baking sheet.
- Broil 6 inches from heat source for 3 to 5 minutes or until cooked through.
- Garnish with ketchup, mustard, sliced green onions or sliced dill pickles.
- *Yield: 24 servings.*

Approx Per Serving: Cal 77; Prot 5 g; Carbo 3 g; T Fat 5 g; 59% Calories from Fat; Chol 26 mg; Fiber <1 g; Sod 137 mg

Cheese Puffs

1 cup water
1/2 cup butter or margarine
1 cup flour
1 teaspoon salt
4 eggs
1/2 teaspoon paprika
1 cup shredded Cheddar
    cheese

- Preheat oven to 400 degrees.
- Heat water in saucepan until hot.
- Add butter. Bring to a boil.
- Add flour all at once. Stir in salt. Cook until mixture forms ball, stirring constantly with wooden spoon.
- Remove from heat. Cool slightly.
- Add eggs 1 at a time, beating until smooth and shiny after each addition. Stir in paprika and cheese.
- Drop by teaspoonfuls 1 1/2 inches apart on lightly greased baking sheet.
- Bake at 400 degrees for 24 minutes or until puffed and golden brown. Remove to wire rack to cool.
- May freeze puffs in single layer on baking sheet for 30 minutes. Place puffs in sealable freezer bag. Freeze until serving time. Reheat in 350-degree oven for 8 to 10 minutes.
- May sprinkle with Parmesan cheese before baking.
- *Yield: 36 servings.*

Approx Per Serving: Cal 56; Prot 2 g; Carbo 3 g; T Fat 4 g; 67% Calories from Fat; Chol 34 mg; Fiber <1 g; Sod 112 mg

Prepare *Low-Fat Mock Sour Cream* by processing cottage cheese with a small amount of lemon juice or vinegar in a blender or food processor until smooth. Use as a base for dips, garnishes or in any manner sour cream could be used.

Chicken Drumettes

5 pounds chicken drumettes
3 onions, finely chopped
1/4 cup salad oil
3 cups tomato sauce
1 1/2 cups packed brown sugar
3/4 cup white vinegar
1/4 cup chili powder
3 tablespoons
   Worcestershire sauce
1 tablespoon salt
3/4 teaspoon dry mustard

- Preheat oven to 375 degrees.
- Rinse chicken and pat dry. Arrange in 9x13-inch baking pan.
- Sauté onions in oil in skillet.
- Add tomato sauce, brown sugar, vinegar, chili powder, Worcestershire sauce, salt and dry mustard; mix well.
- Simmer for 30 minutes, stirring occasionally. Pour over chicken.
- Bake at 375 degrees for 1 hour.
- *Yield: 62 servings.*

Approx Per Serving: Cal 92; Prot 8 g; Carbo 6 g; T Fat 4 g; 40% Calories from Fat; Chol 25 mg; Fiber <1 g; Sod 214 mg

Chicken Wings

4 pounds chicken wings
1 cup soy sauce
1 cup sugar
1/4 cup vegetable oil
1/4 cup frozen pineapple
   juice concentrate
1 teaspoon ginger
1 teaspoon garlic powder

- Rinse chicken wings and pat dry.
- Disjoint wings, discarding tips. Arrange in 9x13-inch baking dish.
- Pour mixture of soy sauce, sugar, oil, pineapple juice concentrate, ginger and garlic powder over chicken, turning to coat.
- Marinate in refrigerator for 8 to 10 hours, turning occasionally.
- Bake at 350 degrees for 1 1/2 hours. Serve immediately or reheat just before serving.
- May keep warm in slow-cooker for up to 2 hours.
- *Yield: 50 servings.*

Approx Per Serving: Cal 109; Prot 8 g; Carbo 5 g; T Fat 6 g; 53% Calories from Fat; Chol 23 mg; Fiber <1 g; Sod 351 mg

Caramel Corn

10 marshmallows
1/2 cup butter
1/4 cup packed brown sugar
6 quarts popped popcorn

- Heat marshmallows, butter and brown sugar in saucepan until blended, stirring constantly.
- Pour over popcorn in bowl, tossing to coat.
- Serve immediately.
- May add 1/2 cup peanuts.
- *Yield: 48 (1/2-cup) servings.*

Approx Per Serving: Cal 41; Prot 1 g; Carbo 5 g; T Fat 2 g; 45% Calories from Fat; Chol 5 mg; Fiber 1 g; Sod 21 mg

Crab-Stuffed Mushrooms

8 ounces fresh mushrooms
4 ounces soft cream cheese
8 ounces crab meat, chopped
Salt and pepper to taste
Garlic salt to taste
Lemon pepper to taste
Worcestershire sauce to taste
1 envelope hollandaise sauce
   mix, prepared

- Preheat oven to 350 degrees.
- Rinse mushrooms; discard stems.
- Beat cream cheese in mixer bowl until smooth.
- Stir in crab meat, salt, pepper, garlic salt, lemon pepper and Worcestershire sauce.
- Fill each mushroom cap with 1 teaspoon of the cream cheese mixture, rounding top. Arrange in round baking dish.
- Bake at 350 degrees for 15 to 20 minutes or until bubbly.
- Remove to serving plates; drizzle with hollandaise sauce.
- May substitute béarnaise sauce mix for hollandaise sauce mix.
- *Yield: 4 servings.*

Approx Per Serving: Cal 392; Prot 16 g; Carbo 10 g; T Fat 33 g; 74% Calories from Fat; Chol 146 mg; Fiber 1 g; Sod 615 mg

Olive Cheese Balls

8 ounces sharp Cheddar
  cheese, cubed, at room
  temperature
2 tablespoons butter,
  softened
1/2 cup flour
Cayenne to taste
25 large pitted black olives

- Preheat oven to 400 degrees.
- Combine cheese and butter in blender container.
- Process at high speed until smooth.
- Add flour and cayenne.
- Process at low speed until blended, scraping side occasionally.
- Shape 1 tablespoon cheese mixture into ball around each olive.
- Arrange on baking sheet.
- Bake at 400 degrees for 15 minutes.
- Serve immediately.
- May prepare in advance and bake just before serving.
- *Yield: 25 servings.*

Approx Per Serving: Cal 59; Prot 3 g; Carbo 2 g; T Fat 4 g; 67% Calories from Fat; Chol 12 mg; Fiber <1 g; Sod 95 mg

Pineapple Pickles

1 (29-ounce) can pineapple
  chunks
1 1/4 cups sugar
3/4 cup vinegar
6 to 8 whole cloves
1 (4-inch) cinnamon stick
Salt to taste

- Drain pineapple, reserving 3/4 cup syrup.
- Combine reserved syrup, sugar, vinegar, cloves, cinnamon stick and salt in saucepan.
- Simmer for 10 minutes, stirring occasionally. Stir in pineapple.
- Bring to a boil. Pour into bowl.
- Chill, covered, until serving time.
- Drain; serve with wooden picks.
- *Yield: 60 servings.*

Approx Per Serving: Cal 27; Prot <1 g; Carbo 7 g; T Fat <1 g; <1% Calories from Fat; Chol 0 mg; Fiber <1 g; Sod <1 mg

Pork Balls

2 eggs, beaten
1 cup cornflakes
1/3 cup catsup
2 tablespoons soy sauce
2 tablespoons onion flakes
1 tablespoon parsley flakes
1/2 teaspoon salt
1/4 teaspoon pepper
2 pounds ground pork
1 (16-ounce) can jellied
    cranberry sauce
1 cup catsup
3 tablespoons brown sugar
1 tablespoon lemon juice

- Preheat oven to 350 degrees.
- Combine eggs, cornflakes, 1/3 cup catsup, soy sauce, onion flakes, parsley flakes, salt and pepper in bowl; mix well.
- Add pork; mix well.
- Shape into seventy 1-inch meatballs. Place in 10x15-inch baking pan.
- Bake at 350 degrees for 20 to 25 minutes or until cooked through.
- Mix cranberry sauce, 1 cup catsup, brown sugar and lemon juice in saucepan.
- Cook until cranberry sauce is dissolved, stirring frequently. Stir in meatballs.
- Cook just until heated through.
- *Yield: 70 servings.*

Approx Per Serving: Cal 43; Prot 3 g; Carbo 5 g; T Fat 1 g; 25% Calories from Fat; Chol 16 mg; Fiber <1 g; Sod 115 mg

Sausage Buttons

2 (10-count) cans butter
    flake rolls
5 teaspoons prepared
    mustard
5 teaspoons barbecue sauce
1 pound smoked sausage,
    cut into 1/4-inch slices

- Preheat oven to 375 degrees.
- Separate roll dough into halves.
- Spoon mustard onto center of half the roll halves; spoon barbecue sauce onto center of remaining roll halves. Top each with sausage slice; wrap with dough to enclose.
- Arrange seam side down in baking pan.
- Bake at 375 degrees for 14 to 16 minutes or until brown.
- Serve with additional mustard and barbecue sauce.
- *Yield: 40 servings.*

Approx Per Serving: Cal 76; Prot 2 g; Carbo 8 g; T Fat 4 g; 43% Calories from Fat; Chol 4 mg; Fiber <1 g; Sod 301 mg

Vegetable Bars

3 (8-count) cans crescent
  rolls
16 ounces cream cheese,
  softened
1 cup mayonnaise-type salad
  dressing
1 envelope ranch salad
  dressing mix
1 cup finely chopped celery
1 cup finely chopped
  cauliflower
1 cup finely chopped green
  bell pepper
1 tomato, finely chopped
8 ounces Cheddar cheese,
  shredded

- Unroll crescent roll dough. Spread in 10x15-inch baking pan, pressing edges and perforations to seal.
- Bake using package directions.
- Combine cream cheese, mayonnaise-type salad dressing and salad dressing mix in bowl; mix well.
- Spread over baked layer. Sprinkle with celery, cauliflower, green pepper and tomato; top with cheese.
- Broil just until cheese melts.
- Chill in refrigerator. Cut into bars.
- *Yield: 36 servings.*

Approx Per Serving: Cal 156; Prot 4 g; Carbo 12 g; T Fat 11 g; 61% Calories from Fat; Chol 24 mg; Fiber <1 g; Sod 347 mg

Banana Milk Shake

A quick after school snack that makes use of those overripe bananas that no one seems to want.

4 cups low-fat milk
3 bananas, frozen, sliced
1/4 cup sugar
6 ice cubes, crushed
1 teaspoon vanilla extract

- Process milk, bananas, sugar, ice cubes and vanilla in blender until frothy.
- Pour into glasses. Serve immediately.
- *Yield: 4 servings.*

Approx Per Serving: Cal 247; Prot 9 g; Carbo 44 g; T Fat 5 g; 18% Calories from Fat; Chol 18 mg; Fiber 2 g; Sod 122 mg

Freeze fruit juices in ring molds, ice cube trays or other shapes. Melting juice will not dilute punch or tea.

Cider Sangria

3 cups sparkling apple cider
1/3 cup lime juice
1/2 (6-ounce) can frozen
    lemonade concentrate
1 tablespoon grenadine

- Combine apple cider, lime juice, lemonade concentrate and grenadine in pitcher; mix well.
- Pour over ice into glasses. Garnish with apple or lime slices.
- *Yield: 6 servings.*

Approx Per Serving: Cal 95; Prot <1 g; Carbo 24 g; T Fat <1 g; 2% Calories from Fat; Chol 0 mg; Fiber <1 g; Sod 5 mg

Tutti-Frutti Fizz

1 cup strawberry yogurt
1 banana, sliced
1 cup milk
1/2 cup juice-pack crushed
    pineapple

- Combine yogurt and banana in blender container.
- Add milk and pineapple.
- Process until blended.
- Pour into glasses.
- Garnish with fresh strawberries.
- *Yield: 4 servings.*

Approx Per Serving: Cal 145; Prot 5 g; Carbo 25 g; T Fat 4 g; 21% Calories from Fat; Chol 8 mg; Fiber 1 g; Sod 65 mg

Ice Cream Punch

1 (46-ounce) can pineapple
    juice, chilled
1 quart strawberry ice cream
2 1/4 cups water
3/4 cup sugar
1 (6-ounce) can frozen pink
    lemonade concentrate,
    thawed
2 1/2 quarts ginger ale

- Combine pineapple juice, ice cream, water, sugar and lemonade concentrate in punch bowl; mix well.
- Add ginger ale just before serving; mix well.
- Ladle into punch cups.
- *Yield: 30 (6-ounce) servings.*

Approx Per Serving: Cal 115; Prot 1 g; Carbo 26 g; T Fat 2 g; 12% Calories from Fat; Chol 5 mg; Fiber <1 g; Sod 17 mg

Rhubarb Punch

2 quarts cold water
5 cups chopped rhubarb
1¹/₂ cups sugar
1 (6-ounce) can frozen
    orange juice concentrate
1 (6-ounce) can frozen
    lemonade concentrate
1 quart ginger ale

- Combine cold water and rhubarb in saucepan.
- Cook over medium heat until rhubarb is tender, stirring occasionally; drain.
- Combine rhubarb and sugar in saucepan; mix well.
- Cook until sugar dissolves, stirring frequently.
- Stir in orange juice concentrate and lemonade concentrate.
- Chill until serving time.
- Stir in ginger ale just before serving.
- Ladle into punch cups.
- *Yield: 21 (6-ounce) servings.*

Approx Per Serving: Cal 105; Prot <1 g; Carbo 27 g; T Fat <1 g; 1% Calories from Fat; Chol 0 mg; Fiber 1 g; Sod 5 mg

Wassail

2 cinnamon sticks
16 whole cloves
6 cups water
1 cup sugar
2 cups cider
³/₄ cup unsweetened orange
    juice
¹/₂ cup unsweetened
    grapefruit juice
¹/₄ cup lemon juice

- Tie cinnamon sticks and cloves together in cheesecloth bag.
- Combine with 2 cups of the water and sugar in saucepan.
- Boil for 5 minutes; discard cheesecloth bag.
- Stir in remaining 4 cups water, cider, orange juice, grapefruit juice and lemon juice.
- Ladle into mugs or punch cups.
- *Yield: 12 (6-ounce) servings.*

Approx Per Serving: Cal 96; Prot <1 g; Carbo 24 g; T Fat <1 g; 1% Calories from Fat; Chol 0 mg; Fiber <1 g; Sod 2 mg

Nichole Hodapp
Nobles County

NOTES

Creamy Broccoli Soup

4 cups chopped fresh
  broccoli
1 cup chopped celery
1 cup chopped carrots
2 cups boiling water
1/2 cup chopped onion
6 tablespoons butter or
  margarine
6 tablespoons flour
3 cups chicken broth
2 cups milk
1 tablespoon minced fresh
  parsley
1 teaspoon onion salt
1/2 teaspoon garlic powder
1/2 teaspoon salt

- Cook broccoli, celery and carrots in boiling water in saucepan for 2 to 3 minutes; drain.
- Sauté onion in butter in stockpot until tender. Stir in flour. Cook until thickened, stirring constantly.
- Stir in broth and milk gradually. Boil for 1 minute, stirring constantly. Add broccoli mixture, parsley, onion salt, garlic powder and salt; reduce heat.
- Simmer, covered, for 30 to 40 minutes, stirring occasionally.
- Ladle into soup bowls.
- *Yield: 8 servings.*

Approx Per Serving: Cal 173; Prot 6 g; Carbo 13 g; T Fat 12 g; 58% Calories from Fat; Chol 32 mg; Fiber 2 g; Sod 769 mg

Golden Cauliflower Soup

2 (10-ounce) packages
  frozen cauliflower
1 cup water
1/2 cup chopped onion
1/3 cup margarine or butter
1/3 to 1/2 cup flour
1 cup water
2 cups milk
3 chicken bouillon cubes
2 cups shredded mild
  Cheddar cheese
1/8 to 1/4 teaspoon ground
  nutmeg

- Cook cauliflower in 1 cup water in saucepan until tender. Reserve 1 cup cauliflowerets. Purée remaining cauliflower with liquid.
- Sauté onion in margarine in saucepan until tender. Stir in flour. Add 1 cup water, milk and bouillon gradually. Cook until slightly thickened, stirring constantly. Add cheese, puréed cauliflower, reserved cauliflowerets and nutmeg.
- Cook until cheese melts, stirring occasionally; do not boil.
- Ladle into soup bowls.
- *Yield: 6 servings.*

Approx Per Serving: Cal 357; Prot 15 g; Carbo 18 g; T Fat 26 g; 64% Calories from Fat; Chol 51 mg; Fiber 2 g; Sod 986 mg

Chili

1 pound ground beef
1 pound ground pork
1 (32-ounce) can whole
  tomatoes, drained
2 (16-ounce) cans kidney
  beans, drained
1 (8-ounce) can tomato
  sauce
1 (6-ounce) can tomato paste
2 medium onions, chopped
1 cup chopped green bell
  pepper
1/2 cup sliced jalapeños
1/4 cup sliced black olives
1 1/2 tablespoons chili powder
1 teaspoon garlic salt
1/4 teaspoon cayenne
1/4 teaspoon paprika

- Brown ground beef and ground pork in skillet, stirring until crumbly; drain.
- Combine ground beef, ground pork, tomatoes, kidney beans, tomato sauce, tomato paste, onions, green pepper, jalapeños, olives, chili powder, garlic salt, cayenne and paprika in slow cooker; mix well.
- Cook for 10 to 12 hours or until of the desired consistency.
- Ladle into soup bowls. Serve with sour cream, shredded cheese and corn bread.
- *Yield: 12 servings.*

Approx Per Serving: Cal 263; Prot 23 g; Carbo 22 g;
  T Fat 9 g; 32% Calories from Fat; Chol 56 mg;
  Fiber 7 g; Sod 936 mg

Smoky Corn Chowder

1/2 cup chopped onion
1/4 cup butter or margarine
1/4 cup flour
1 teaspoon salt
1/8 teaspoon pepper
4 cups milk
1 (12-ounce) package
  smoked sausage links,
  sliced
1 (16-ounce) can whole
  kernel corn, drained
1 (8-ounce) can lima beans,
  drained

- Sauté onion in butter in saucepan until tender, but not brown.
- Stir in flour, salt and pepper. Add milk; mix well.
- Cook until thickened, stirring constantly.
- Stir in sausage, corn and lima beans.
- Simmer for 10 minutes, stirring occasionally.
- Ladle into soup bowls.
- *Yield: 6 servings.*

Approx Per Serving: Cal 393; Prot 16 g; Carbo 34 g;
  T Fat 0 g; 50% Calories from Fat; Chol 61 mg;
  Fiber 4 g; Sod 1246 mg

$\mathcal{N}$orthern Connection Corn Chowder

$^1/_2$ cups finely chopped celery
$^1/_4$ cup finely chopped onion
1 cup water
1 (16-ounce) can low-
    sodium chicken broth
$1^1/_4$ cups cream-style corn
1 (16-ounce) can whole
    kernel corn, drained
1 to 2 cups instant potato
    flakes
$1^1/_2$ cups skim milk
$^3/_4$ cup shredded reduced-
    fat Cheddar cheese
Pepper to taste

- Combine celery, onion and water in 2-quart microwave-safe dish. Microwave on High until tender.
- Add chicken broth, cream-style and whole kernel corn and enough potato flakes to make soup of desired thickness; mix well. Stir in milk and cheese.
- Microwave on High for 10 minutes, stirring several times. Let stand for several minutes. Microwave until heated to serving temperature. Ladle into soup bowls.
- *Yield: 6 servings.*

Approx Per Serving: Cal 225; Prot 12 g; Carbo 41 g; T Fat 4 g; 13% Calories from Fat; Chol 9 mg; Fiber 3 g; Sod 767 mg

$\mathcal{L}$entil Soup

$^3/_4$ cup lentils
5 cups water
$^1/_2$ medium onion, chopped
1 small clove of garlic,
    minced
1 (32-ounce) can tomatoes
1 cup finely chopped celery
1 cup sliced carrots
1 (6-ounce) can tomato paste
$^1/_2$ cup whole wheat macaroni
2 teaspoons parsley flakes
$^3/_4$ teaspoon salt
$^1/_4$ teaspoon basil
$^1/_4$ teaspoon oregano
$^1/_8$ teaspoon freshly ground
    pepper
Thyme to taste
1 (14-ounce) can cut green
    beans
1 tablespoon wine vinegar

- Sort and rinse lentils.
- Combine lentils, water, onion and garlic in stockpot; mix well.
- Bring to a boil; reduce heat. Simmer for 45 minutes, stirring occasionally.
- Add undrained tomatoes, celery, carrots, tomato paste, macaroni, parsley flakes, salt, basil, oregano, pepper and thyme.
- Bring to a boil; reduce heat. Simmer, covered, for 20 minutes.
- Stir in undrained green beans and vinegar.
- Simmer for 10 to 15 minutes or until of the desired consistency.
- Ladle into soup bowls.
- *Yield: 10 servings.*

Approx Per Serving: Cal 105; Prot 7 g; Carbo 21 g; T Fat 1 g; 5% Calories from Fat; Chol 0 mg; Fiber 4 g; Sod 603 mg

Fresh Fruit Soup

1 (12-ounce) can frozen
  orange juice concentrate,
  reconstituted
1/4 cup cornstarch
1 1/2 cups sugar
6 whole cloves
1 cinnamon stick
2 tablespoons lemon juice
2 cups sliced fresh
  strawberries
2 bananas, sliced
2 cups green grape halves

- Reserve 1/2 cup of the juice. Dissolve cornstarch in reserved juice; set aside.
- Bring remaining orange juice, sugar, cloves and cinnamon stick to a boil in saucepan; reduce heat. Simmer for 5 minutes.
- Stir in cornstarch mixture. Bring to a boil, stirring constantly; remove from heat. Stir in lemon juice.
- Chill, covered, until serving time. Discard cloves and cinnamon stick. Stir in strawberries, bananas and grapes.
- Ladle into soup bowls.
- *Yield: 8 servings.*

Approx Per Serving: Cal 324; Prot 2 g; Carbo 81 g; T Fat 1 g; 2% Calories from Fat; Chol 0 mg; Fiber 3 g; Sod 4 mg

French Market Soup

2 cups bean mix
3 quarts water
1 (16-ounce) can diced
  tomatoes
1 large onion, chopped
1 large green bell pepper,
  chopped
1 cup chopped celery
1 clove of garlic, finely
  chopped
2 tablespoons
  Worcestershire sauce
1 tablespoon lemon juice
1 tablespoon sugar

- Prepare bean mix by combining equal portions of green split peas, yellow split peas, black-eyed peas, pinto beans, red beans, black beans, white lima beans, Great Northern beans, navy beans, garbanzo beans, barley, soybeans and lentils.
- Sort and rinse beans.
- Combine beans and water in stockpot. Simmer for 2 hours, stirring occasionally.
- Add remaining ingredients; mix well. Simmer for 2 hours or until of the desired consistency, stirring occasionally.
- Ladle into soup bowls. Serve with hot crusty French bread.
- *Yield: 24 servings.*

Approx Per Serving: Cal 67; Prot 4 g; Carbo 12 g; T Fat 1 g; 9% Calories from Fat; Chol 0 mg; Fiber 3 g; Sod 51 mg

Cream of Potato Soup

1 cup chopped onion
1 cup sliced celery
2 tablespoons bacon
 drippings
5 large potatoes, peeled,
 sliced
1/2 cup sliced carrots
6 slices crisp-fried bacon,
 crumbled
2 cups milk
2 cups light cream or
 evaporated milk
1 1/2 teaspoons salt
1/4 teaspoon white pepper

- Sauté onion and celery in bacon drippings until tender.
- Cook potatoes and carrots in boiling water to cover in large soup pot until tender; drain. Add sautéed vegetables, bacon, milk, salt and pepper to soup pot. Simmer for 30 minutes.
- Ladle into soup bowls. Garnish with sprinkle of shredded Cheddar cheese and chopped parsley.
- *Yield: 10 servings.*

Approx Per Serving: Cal 311; Prot 6 g; Carbo 26 g; T Fat 21 g; 60% Calories from Fat; Chol 66 mg; Fiber 2 g; Sod 453 mg

Potato Wild Rice Soup

4 slices bacon, cut into
 1/2-inch pieces
2 to 3 tablespoons chopped
 onion
1 tablespoon margarine or
 butter
1 tablespoon chicken
 bouillon
1 tablespoon flour
2 cups water
1 3/4 cups milk
1 1/2 cups cooked wild rice
1 cup potato flakes
1 cup shredded American
 cheese
Sliced mushrooms to taste
Chopped almonds to taste
Salt and pepper to taste

- Fry bacon with onion in 3-quart saucepan until bacon is crisp and onion is tender. Drain, reserving 2 tablespoons pan drippings.
- Combine reserved pan drippings and margarine in same saucepan. Stir in bouillon and flour until blended.
- Cook until thickened and bubbly, stirring constantly. Stir in water gradually.
- Bring to a boil. Remove from heat.
- Stir in milk, wild rice, potato flakes, cheese, mushrooms and almonds. Bring to a boil; reduce heat.
- Simmer for 10 to 15 minutes or until thickened, stirring occasionally.
- Season with salt and pepper.
- Ladle into soup bowls.
- *Yield: 7 servings.*

Approx Per Serving: Cal 233; Prot 9 g; Carbo 17 g; T Fat 15 g; 56% Calories from Fat; Chol 31 mg; Fiber 1 g; Sod 375 mg

Venison and Vegetable Soup

1¹/₂ pounds venison
3 cups water
1 (15-ounce) can tomato
  sauce
1 (6-ounce) can whole
  kernel corn
¹/₂ cup each chopped celery,
  potato, carrot, green bell
  pepper
¹/₂ cup chopped onion
¹/₃ cup barley
1 tablespoon sugar
2 teaspoons salt
1 teaspoon Worcestershire
  sauce
¹/₈ teaspoon chili powder
Pepper to taste
5 ounces egg noodles,
  cooked

- Combine venison, water, tomato sauce, corn, celery, potato, carrot, green pepper, onion, barley, sugar, salt, Worcestershire sauce, chili powder and pepper in slow cooker; mix well.
- Cook on High for 6 to 8 hours or until venison is tender, adding noodles 30 minutes before end of cooking process.
- *Yield: 8 servings.*

Approx Per Serving: Cal 161; Prot 20 g; Carbo 31 g; T Fat 3 g; 11% Calories from Fat; Chol 87 mg; Fiber 3 g; Sod 955 mg

Wild Rice Soup

1 cup wild rice
6 cups water
Salt to taste
¹/₂ cup chopped onion
³/₄ cup butter
1 cup flour
6 cups chicken broth
2 cups milk
1 to 2 cups grated Cheddar
  cheese
1 cup chopped celery
1 cup chopped or grated
  carrot
¹/₂ cup (or more) chopped
  cooked ham
6 tablespoons chopped
  slivered almonds

- Combine wild rice, water and salt in saucepan; mix well. Simmer for 45 minutes. Drain and rinse.
- Sauté onion in butter in stockpot until tender. Stir in flour.
- Cook for 1 minute, stirring constantly.
- Add broth; mix well. Cook until slightly thickened, stirring constantly.
- Add wild rice, milk, cheese, celery, carrot, ham and almonds; mix well.
- Simmer until of the desired consistency, stirring frequently.
- *Yield: 8 servings.*

Approx Per Serving: Cal 560; Prot 22 g; Carbo 36 g; T Fat 37 g; 59% Calories from Fat; Chol 90 mg; Fiber 3 g; Sod 1100 mg

*B*roccoli Salad

1 pound bacon, crisp-fried,
   crumbled
1 large head broccoli, cut
   into bite-size pieces
1 medium red onion, sliced
   into rings
1 (8-ounce) can sliced water
   chestnuts, drained
1 cup cashews
1/2 cup raisins
1 cup mayonnaise
1/2 cup sugar
2 tablespoons vinegar

- Combine bacon, broccoli, red onion,
  water chestnuts, cashews and raisins in
  bowl; mix well.
- Combine mayonnaise, sugar and vinegar
  in small bowl; mix well.
- Stir into broccoli mixture.
- Chill, covered, for 3 to 10 hours.
- *Yield: 8 servings.*

Approx Per Serving: Cal 503; Prot 11 g; Carbo 34 g;
   T Fat 39 g; 66% Calories from Fat; Chol 31 mg;
   Fiber 4 g; Sod 450 mg

*C*hicken Salad

3 (7-ounce) cans white meat
   chicken, drained
2 tablespoons orange juice
2 tablespoons vinegar
2 tablespoons salad oil
1 teaspoon salt
3/4 (16-ounce) package
   tricolor wagon wheel
   pasta, cooked, drained
1 (20-ounce) can pineapple
   chunks, drained
1 (20-ounce) can mandarin
   oranges, drained
1 1/2 cups chopped celery
1 cup red grapes
2 cups mayonnaise-type
   salad dressing

- Combine chicken, orange juice, vinegar,
  oil and salt in bowl; mix well.
- Marinate, covered, in refrigerator.
- Stir in pasta, pineapple, mandarin
  oranges, celery and grapes.
- Chill for 1 hour before serving.
- *Yield: 8 servings.*

Approx Per Serving: Cal 638; Prot 23 g; Carbo 72 g;
   T Fat 30 g; 41% Calories from Fat; Chol 61 mg;
   Fiber 2 g; Sod 1086 mg

Serve chicken or seafood salad in avocado halves, tomato cups, melon
rings or pineapple boats.

Curried Chicken and Rice Salad

3/4 cup mayonnaise-type
   salad dressing
1 tablespoon curry powder
1 tablespoon prepared
   mustard
1 tablespoon apple cider
   vinegar
1 tablespoon honey
1 teaspoon salt
Cayenne to taste
1 (16-ounce) can garbanzo
   beans, drained
1 1/2 to 2 cups chopped
   cooked chicken
1 1/2 cups wild rice, cooked
1 cup currants
1 cup cashews
Sliced green onions to taste

- Combine salad dressing, curry powder, prepared mustard, vinegar, honey, salt and cayenne in bowl; mix well.
- Combine garbanzo beans, chicken, wild rice, currants, cashews and green onions in bowl; mix well.
- Stir in salad dressing mixture.
- Serve at room temperature.
- May substitute raisins for currants.
- *Yield: 10 servings.*

Approx Per Serving: Cal 386; Prot 17 g; Carbo 49 g; T Fat 15 g; 34% Calories from Fat; Chol 29 mg; Fiber 2 g; Sod 523 mg

Waldorf Chicken Salad

5 boneless skinless chicken
   breast halves, cooked,
   chopped
3/4 cup chopped celery
1 Granny Smith apple,
   peeled, chopped
20 seedless grapes, cut into
   halves
1/2 cup plain nonfat yogurt
2 tablespoons nonfat
   mayonnaise
2 teaspoons instant chicken
   broth mix
2 teaspoons sunflower seeds

- Combine chicken, celery, apple and grapes in bowl; mix well.
- Combine yogurt, mayonnaise and chicken broth in small bowl; mix well.
- Stir into chicken mixture.
- Sprinkle with sunflower seeds.
- Chill, covered, until serving time.
- *Yield: 8 servings.*

Approx Per Serving: Cal 126; Prot 18 g; Carbo 7 g; T Fat 3 g; 18% Calories from Fat; Chol 46 mg; Fiber 1 g; Sod 392 mg

Cordella Salad

1 bunch broccoli, cut into
    bite-size pieces
1 head cauliflower, cut into
    bite-size pieces
6 large carrots, sliced
2 cups frozen peas, thawed
20 (or more) green grapes
20 (or more) purple grapes
3 stalks celery, sliced
1/2 small onion, chopped
1 cup mayonnaise-type salad
    dressing
1/2 cup milk
2 tablespoons vinegar
1 tablespoon sugar
1/2 cup mixed nuts
1/2 cup sunflower seeds

• Combine broccoli, cauliflower, carrots,
  peas, grapes, celery and onion in bowl;
  mix well.
• Combine salad dressing, milk, vinegar
  and sugar in small bowl; mix well.
• Stir into broccoli mixture.
• Chill until serving time. Sprinkle with
  mixed nuts and sunflower seeds just
  before serving.
• May substitute fruits and vegetables with
  your favorite choices.
• *Yield: 12 servings.*

Approx Per Serving: Cal 227; Prot 6 g; Carbo 24 g;
    T Fat 14 g; 51% Calories from Fat; Chol 6 mg;
    Fiber 6 g; Sod 215 mg

Luscious Lemon Salad

2 (3-ounce) packages lemon
    gelatin
2 cups boiling water
1 (12-ounce) can Mountain
    Dew
1 (21-ounce) can lemon pie
    filling
1 (15-ounce) can crushed
    pineapple, drained
2 cups miniature
    marshmallows
8 ounces whipped topping,
    thawed

• Combine gelatin and boiling water in
  bowl; mix until gelatin is completely
  dissolved.
• Add Mountain Dew, stirring until
  blended. Stir in 1/2 of the pie filling.
• Spoon into 2-quart shallow dish. Stir
  in pineapple and marshmallows. Chill
  until set.
• Combine remaining pie filling and
  whipped topping in bowl; mix well.
  Spread over chilled layer. Chill until
  serving time.
• *Yield: 12 servings.*

Approx Per Serving: Cal 340; Prot 4 g; Carbo 66 g;
    T Fat 8 g; 21% Calories from Fat; Chol 65 mg;
    Fiber <1 g; Sod 88 mg

Frozen Tropical Treat

2 (20-ounce) cans crushed
    pineapple
2 (11-ounce) cans mandarin
    oranges
2 (10-ounce) packages
    frozen strawberries,
    thawed
1 (12-ounce) can frozen
    orange juice concentrate,
    thawed
1/2 cup lemon juice
6 bananas, quartered, sliced

- Combine undrained pineapple, oranges and strawberries in large bowl.
- Add orange juice concentrate and lemon juice; mix gently. Stir in bananas.
- Spoon into 3-ounce paper cups; place on tray.
- Freeze. Store in plastic bags if desired.
- Let stand at room temperature for 30 minutes before serving.
- *Yield: 18 servings.*

Approx Per Serving: Cal 139; Prot 1 g; Carbo 36 g; T Fat <1 g; 2% Calories from Fat; Chol 0 mg; Fiber 2 g; Sod 4 mg

Pineapple and Cheese Picnic Salad

1 (20-ounce) can crushed
    pineapple
1 (8-ounce) can crushed
    pineapple
2 (3-ounce) packages lime
    gelatin
1 (3-ounce) package lemon
    gelatin
8 ounces cream cheese,
    softened
1 cup sour cream
1 1/2 cups shredded Cheddar
    cheese
1 1/2 cups cottage cheese

- Chill mixer bowl and beaters in freezer.
- Drain pineapple, reserving syrup. Combine reserved syrup with enough water to measure 4 cups.
- Bring 2 cups of the liquid to a boil in saucepan. Pour over lime gelatin and lemon gelatin in bowl, stirring until gelatin dissolves.
- Add hot gelatin mixture to cream cheese in bowl; mix well. Stir in remaining 2 cups liquid. Chill until partially set.
- Beat sour cream in mixer bowl with beaters for 5 minutes or until doubled.
- Add Cheddar cheese, cottage cheese and pineapple to gelatin mixture. Fold in sour cream. Spoon into 9x13-inch dish. Chill.
- *Yield: 16 servings.*

Approx Per Serving: Cal 242; Prot 8 g; Carbo 26 g; T Fat 12 g; 45% Calories from Fat; Chol 36 mg; Fiber <1 g; Sod 236 mg

$\mathscr{R}$aspberry Salad with Raspberry Vinaigrette

1 cup raspberry wine vinegar
  (page 57)
$^{1}/_{2}$ cup canola oil
$^{1}/_{4}$ cup sugar
2 tablespoons poppy seeds,
  lightly toasted
Grated rind and juice of 1
  lemon
$^{1}/_{2}$ teaspoon lemon pepper
3 cups torn green leaf lettuce
3 cups torn spinach
12 green onions, sliced
1 (11-ounce) can mandarin
  oranges, drained
1 (8-ounce) can water
  chestnuts, drained
12 slices crisp-fried bacon,
  crumbled
$^{1}/_{2}$ cup sliced almonds,
  toasted
2 cups fresh raspberries

- Process raspberry wine vinegar, canola oil, sugar, poppy seeds, lemon rind, lemon juice and lemon pepper in food processor for 1 minute or until blended.
- May store in refrigerator for up to 3 weeks.
- Toss leaf lettuce and spinach together in salad bowl. Add green onions, mandarin oranges, water chestnuts, bacon and almonds in salad bowl; mix well.
- Pour raspberry vinaigrette over salad just before serving, tossing to coat. Sprinkle with raspberries.
- *Yield: 12 servings.*

Approx Per Serving: Cal 218; Prot 4 g; Carbo 18 g; T Fat 15 g; 59% Calories from Fat; Chol 5 mg; Fiber 3 g; Sod 154 mg

$\mathscr{S}$auerkraut Salad

$1^{1}/_{2}$ cups sugar
$^{2}/_{3}$ cup cider vinegar
1 (29-ounce) can
  sauerkraut, drained,
  rinsed
1 cup chopped green bell
  pepper
1 cup chopped celery
$^{1}/_{2}$ cup chopped onion
1 (2-ounce) jar chopped
  pimento

- Bring sugar and vinegar to a boil in saucepan.
- Boil until clear, stirring frequently.
- Let stand until cool.
- Combine sauerkraut, green pepper, celery, onion and pimento in bowl; mix well. Stir in sugar mixture.
- Marinate in refrigerator for 24 hours.
- Store, covered, in refrigerator up to 1 week.
- *Yield: 8 servings.*

Approx Per Serving: Cal 179; Prot 1 g; Carbo 46 g; T Fat <1 g; 1% Calories from Fat; Chol 0 mg; Fiber 3 g; Sod 694 mg

Quick and Easy Strawberry Salad

2 (4-ounce) packages
 tapioca pudding mix
1 (4-ounce) package vanilla
 pudding and pie filling
 mix
1 (6-ounce) package
 strawberry gelatin
4 cups water
1¹/₂ cups sliced fresh or
 frozen strawberries
8 ounces whipped topping

- Combine tapioca pudding mix, vanilla pudding mix, gelatin and water in saucepan; mix well.
- Cook over medium-high heat for 5 minutes or until mixture begins to boil, stirring constantly.
- Let stand until cool.
- Stir in strawberries. Fold in ³/₄ of the whipped topping.
- Spoon into 9x13-inch dish.
- Chill until set. Spread with remaining whipped topping.
- Chill until serving time.
- *Yield: 10 servings.*

Approx Per Serving: Cal 277; Prot 2 g; Carbo 56 g; T Fat 6 g; 19% Calories from Fat; Chol 0 mg; Fiber 1 g; Sod 270 mg

Snickers Salad

2 (4-ounce) packages vanilla
 instant pudding mix
3 cups milk
12 ounces whipped topping
1¹/₂ cups miniature
 marshmallows
3 or 4 Granny Smith apples,
 cut into bite-size pieces
5 or 6 (2-ounce) Snickers
 candy bars, cut into
 bite-size pieces

- Combine pudding mix and milk in bowl; mix well.
- Let stand until thickened.
- Fold in whipped topping and marshmallows.
- Stir in apples.
- Chill until serving time.
- Fold in candy bars just before serving.
- *Yield: 10 servings.*

Approx Per Serving: Cal 431; Prot 6 g; Carbo 63 g; T Fat 19 g; 38% Calories from Fat; Chol 14 mg; Fiber 2 g; Sod 424 mg

Spinach and Mushroom Salad

4 to 5 tablespoons olive oil
2 tablespoons lemon juice
2 tablespoons egg substitute
1 clove of garlic, minced
1 teaspoon sugar
3/4 teaspoon salt
1/4 teaspoon freshly ground
    pepper
1/8 teaspoon dry mustard
1 pound fresh spinach, torn
    into bite-size pieces
4 ounces fresh mushrooms,
    sliced
8 slices crisp-fried bacon,
    crumbled
3 hard-cooked eggs, sliced
2 green onions, chopped

- Combine olive oil, lemon juice, egg substitute, garlic, sugar, salt, pepper and dry mustard in jar with lid; shake to mix well.
- Combine spinach, mushrooms, bacon, eggs and green onions in salad bowl; mix well.
- Drizzle dressing over spinach mixture just before serving, tossing to coat.
- *Yield: 8 servings.*

Approx Per Serving: Cal 164; Prot 7 g; Carbo 4 g; T Fat 14 g; 74% Calories from Fat; Chol 85 mg; Fiber 2 g; Sod 377 mg

Strawberry Delight Salad

3/4 cup mayonnaise
1/3 cup sugar
2 tablespoons vinegar
2 tablespoons poppy seeds
1 head romaine, torn into
    bite-size pieces
16 ounces fresh
    strawberries, sliced
1/2 red onion, thinly sliced

- Whisk mayonnaise, sugar, vinegar and poppy seeds together in bowl.
- Combine romaine, strawberries, and red onion in salad bowl; toss lightly. Toss with dressing just before serving.
- *Yield: 15 servings.*

Approx Per Serving: Cal 116; Prot 1 g; Carbo 8 g; T Fat 9 g; 71% Calories from Fat; Chol 7 mg; Fiber 1 g; Sod 65 mg

Romaine lettuce dates back to Roman times and is the basis for Caesar salads. It has long narrow leaves and a sweet flavor.

Tabouli

2 cups boiling water
1 cup bulgur
1 cup finely chopped parsley
1 tomato, chopped
1/4 cup finely chopped fresh
    mint
1/4 cup lemon juice
1/4 cup olive oil
1 green onion, chopped
1/2 teaspoon salt
Coarsely ground pepper to
    taste

• Pour boiling water over bulgar in bowl.
  Let stand until water is absorbed.
• Stir in parsley, tomato, mint, lemon
  juice, olive oil, green onion, salt and
  pepper.
• Chill until serving time.
• Spoon onto lettuce-lined salad plates.
  Garnish with thin lemon slices, kalamata
  olives, additional mint and/or feta cheese.
• May add 1 chicken bouillon cube to
  mixture.
• *Yield: 6 servings.*

Approx Per Serving: Cal 171; Prot 3 g; Carbo 20 g;
    T Fat 9 g; 47% Calories from Fat; Chol 0 mg;
    Fiber 5 g; Sod 190 mg

Tortellini Salad

1 (7-ounce) package cheese
    tortellini
3 or 4 artichoke hearts or
    bottoms, chopped
2 to 3 tablespoons chopped
    pimentos
1/4 cup mayonnaise
1/4 cup grated Parmesan
    cheese
2 tablespoons chopped fresh
    basil or 1/2 teaspoon dried
    basil
2 tablespoons chopped fresh
    parsley
2 teaspoons Dijon mustard
Salt to taste
White pepper to taste

• Cook tortellini using package directions.
  Drain and rinse with cold water; drain.
• Combine tortellini, artichoke hearts and
  pimento in bowl; mix well.
• Combine mayonnaise, cheese, basil,
  parsley, Dijon mustard, salt and white
  pepper in small bowl; mix well.
• Stir into tortellini mixture.
• Chill, covered, until serving time.
• *Yield: 6 servings.*

Approx Per Serving: Cal 202; Prot 8 g; Carbo 19 g;
    T Fat 11 g; 49% Calories from Fat; Chol 25 mg;
    Fiber 2 g; Sod 313 mg

Tossed Salad with Nectarines

1/3 cup sugar
3 tablespoons vinegar
1 teaspoon finely chopped
    onion
1/2 teaspoon salt
1/2 teaspoon dry mustard
1/2 cup vegetable oil
2 teaspoons poppy seeds
2 teaspoons lemon juice
2 cups sliced nectarines
3 cups torn leaf lettuce
3 cups torn spinach
1/4 cup slivered almonds,
    toasted

- Process sugar, vinegar, onion, salt and dry mustard in blender or food processor until blended.
- Add oil in fine stream, processing constantly until thick and smooth. Add poppy seeds. Process just until mixed.
- Sprinkle lemon juice over nectarines in bowl; reserve 1/2 cup.
- Combine remaining nectarines, leaf lettuce and spinach in salad bowl, tossing lightly.
- Arrange reserved nectarines over top; sprinkle with almonds.
- Serve poppy seed dressing with salad.
- To toast almonds spread in single layer on baking sheet. Bake at 350 degrees for 5 to 10 minutes or until brown, stirring occasionally.
- *Yield: 8 servings.*

Approx Per Serving: Cal 209; Prot 2 g; Carbo 15 g; T Fat 17 g; 68% Calories from Fat; Chol 0 mg; Fiber 2 g; Sod 152 mg

Wild Rice Salad

1 (7-ounce) package long
    grain and wild rice mix
1 cup chopped carrot
1 cup chopped green bell
    pepper
1 cup chopped celery
1 cup chopped cucumber
1 cup cashews
1 cup mayonnaise
1 teaspoon seasoned salt
1/8 teaspoon lemon pepper

- Prepare rice using package directions, omitting butter. Let stand until cool.
- Combine rice, carrot, green pepper, celery, cucumber and cashews in salad bowl; mix well.
- Stir in mayonnaise, salt and lemon pepper.
- Garnish with cherry tomatoes.
- *Yield: 8 servings.*

Approx Per Serving: Cal 390; Prot 6 g; Carbo 28 g; T Fat 30 g; 67% Calories from Fat; Chol 16 mg; Fiber 2 g; Sod 764 mg

Coleslaw Dressing

1 egg
1/4 cup sugar
1 cup milk
1 tablespoon butter
2 teaspoons cornstarch
1 teaspoon flour
1 teaspoon dry mustard
1 teaspoon salt
1/2 cup vinegar

• Beat egg and sugar in mixer bowl until blended.
• Bring milk and butter to a boil in saucepan, stirring frequently. Pour over egg mixture; mix well.
• Combine cornstarch, flour, dry mustard and salt in bowl; mix well. Stir in vinegar until blended. Stir vinegar mixture into egg mixture in saucepan gradually.
• Cook over low heat until thickened, stirring constantly. Chill until serving time.
• Combine with your favorite coleslaw ingredients. Store leftover dressing in refrigerator.
• *Yield: 16 (2-tablespoon) servings.*

Approx Per Serving: Cal 36; Prot 1 g; Carbo 5 g; T Fat 2 g; 38% Calories from Fat; Chol 17 mg; Fiber <1 g; Sod 152 mg

Potato Salad Dressing

6 eggs
1/2 cup sugar
1/2 cup vinegar
1 tablespoon prepared mustard
1/2 teaspoon salt
1 cup (or more) mayonnaise
Whipping cream to taste

• Combine eggs, sugar, vinegar, mustard and salt in bowl. Beat with rotary beater until blended. Spoon into double boiler.
• Cook over hot water until thickened, stirring constantly. Cool slightly.
• Stir in mayonnaise. Add whipping cream, stirring until of the desired consistency.
• Combine with chopped cooked potatoes, chopped onion, chopped celery and chopped hard-cooked eggs or your favorite potato salad ingredients.
• *Yield: 16 servings.*

Approx Per Serving: Cal 153; Prot 3 g; Carbo 7 g; T Fat 13 g; 75% Calories from Fat; Chol 88 mg; Fiber <1 g; Sod 181 mg

*R*aspberry Wine Vinegar

4 cups cider vinegar
2 cups dry red wine
2 cups fresh raspberries

- Combine cider vinegar, red wine and raspberries in nonmetallic bowl; mix well. Let stand, covered, at room temperature for 8 to 10 hours.
- Bring vinegar mixture to a boil in stainless steel or enamel saucepan; reduce heat. Cook for 3 minutes. Let stand until cool.
- Strain, discarding raspberries. Pour into sterilized bottle with tightfitting lid. Let stand for 2 to 4 weeks before using. Store in cool dark environment.
- *Yield: 96 (1-tablespoon) servings.*

Approx Per Serving: Cal 6; Prot <1 g; Carbo 1 g; T Fat <1 g; 2% Calories from Fat; Chol 0 mg; Fiber <1 g; Sod <1 mg

*A*ntipasto Submarines

This recipe was awarded second place in the Minnesota Beef Cook-off.

1 (18-inch) loaf soft crust French bread
1 pound thinly sliced Italian or Cajun deli roast beef
6 ounces hot pepper cheese, thinly sliced
1/2 to 1 small red onion, thinly sliced, separated into rings
1/2 to 1 cup artichoke salad
Freshly ground pepper to taste

- Preheat oven to 350 degrees.
- Slice loaf lengthwise into halves. Hollow out soft bread carefully, leaving 1/2-inch shell on both halves. Discard extra bread or save for another use.
- Arrange 1/2 of the roast beef on bread bottom. Top with cheese and red onion. Spread with artichoke salad; sprinkle with pepper. Top with remaining roast beef and bread top. Wrap securely in foil
- Bake at 350 degrees for 25 to 30 minutes or until heated through. Cut into 2-inch portions. Arrange on lettuce-lined platter.
- *Yield: 4 servings.*

Approx Per Serving: Cal 734; Prot 58 g; Carbo 64 g; T Fat 27 g; 33% Calories from Fat; Chol 147 mg; Fiber 5 g; Sod 1175 mg

Best Barbecued Beef Sandwich

1 (3- to 4-pound) chuck
  roast, trimmed
1½ cups catsup
1 envelope onion soup mix
3 tablespoons vinegar
2 tablespoons
  Worcestershire sauce
1 tablespoon chili powder
2 teaspoons prepared
  mustard
¼ teaspoon garlic powder
24 small sandwich buns

- Preheat oven to 350 degrees.
- Place chuck roast in roasting pan.
- Combine catsup, soup mix, vinegar, Worcestershire sauce, chili powder, mustard and garlic powder in small bowl; mix well. Pour over roast.
- Bake, covered, for 3 hours or until tender, turning 1 or 2 times. Remove roast from sauce; skim fat.
- Shred roast with fork. Stir into sauce; mix well. Spoon about ¼ cup shredded meat with sauce on each bun.
- *Yield: 24 servings.*

Approx Per Serving: Cal 260; Prot 18 g; Carbo 28 g;
  T Fat 8 g; 29% Calories from Fat; Chol 47 mg;
  Fiber 1 g; Sod 514 mg

French Dip

1 (5- to 6-pound) chuck
  roast
2 envelopes onion soup mix
1 to 2 cups water
2 (2-ounce) jars sliced
  mushrooms
15 sandwich buns

- Preheat oven to 300 degrees.
- Place chuck roast in roasting pan; sprinkle with soup mix.
- Bake, covered, at 300 degrees for 3½ to 4 hours or until tender.
- Remove roast to platter; cut into bite-size pieces.
- Skim fat from pan drippings. Add water, stirring until of the desired consistency.
- Add roast and undrained mushrooms; mix well.
- Simmer just until heated through.
- Spoon beef and juice onto buns.
- *Yield: 15 servings.*

Approx Per Serving: Cal 401; Prot 37 g; Carbo 24 g;
  T Fat 16 g; 38% Calories from Fat; Chol 113 mg;
  Fiber 1 g; Sod 445 mg

Picnic Loaf

1 round loaf sourdough
  bread
1/3 cup Italian salad dressing
6 to 8 spinach leaves
1/2 cup shredded mozzarella
  cheese
1 small red onion, thinly
  sliced
6 to 8 (2-ounce) slices
  cooked turkey breast
1 medium tomato, thinly
  sliced
1/2 small cucumber, peeled,
  thinly sliced
1/2 cup shredded mozzarella
  cheese

- Preheat oven to 350 degrees.
- Cut top from loaf, reserving top. Remove center carefully, leaving 1/2-inch shell. Brush with salad dressing.
- Layer spinach, 1/2 cup cheese, red onion, turkey, tomato, cucumber and 1/2 cup cheese in shell; top with reserved bread top.
- Wrap in foil.
- Bake at 350 degrees for 45 minutes. Cool for 10 minutes.
- Cut into wedges.
- *Yield: 6 servings.*

Approx Per Serving: Cal 482; Prot 33 g; Carbo 44 g; T Fat 19 g; 35% Calories from Fat; Chol 69 mg; Fiber 3 g; Sod 688 mg

Broiled Sandwiches

1 (12-ounce) can Spam
12 ounces Cheddar cheese,
  chopped
1 onion, coarsely chopped
1 (10-ounce) can cream of
  mushroom soup
8 sandwich buns

- Process Spam, cheese and onion in food processor until ground, scraping bowl occasionally.
- Add soup.
- Process until blended
- Spread Spam mixture on cut sides of buns. Arrange on baking sheet.
- Broil until brown and bubbly.
- *Yield: 8 servings.*

Approx Per Serving: Cal 476; Prot 21 g; Carbo 28 g; T Fat 31 g; 59% Calories from Fat; Chol 45 mg; Fiber 1 g; Sod 1385 mg

Tuna Burgers

1 tablespoon chopped onion
1 tablespoon butter or
  margarine
1½ cups Velveeta cheese
  cubes
1 (6-ounce) can water-pack
  tuna, drained
½ teaspoon Worcestershire
  sauce
Pepper to taste
6 sandwich buns

- Sauté onion in butter in saucepan.
- Add cheese and tuna; mix well. Cook until cheese melts, stirring constantly.
- Add Worcestershire sauce and pepper; mix well.
- Spread tuna mixture on cut sides of buns. Arrange on baking sheet.
- Broil for 2 to 3 minutes or until brown.
- Serve with chips, carrot sticks and fruit.
- *Yield: 6 servings.*

Approx Per Serving: Cal 310; Prot 19 g; Carbo 23 g; T Fat 15 g; 45% Calories from Fat; Chol 47 mg; Fiber 1 g; Sod 872 mg

Vegetarian's Delight

This recipe won third place in the 1995 McLeod County Foods Review.

1½ cups bean sprouts
⅓ cup low-fat Italian salad
  dressing
1 medium cucumber
4 (6-inch) pitas
10 ounces sharp Cheddar
  cheese, cut into bite-size
  pieces
1 large carrot, shredded
1 medium tomato, chopped
4 large lettuce leaves

- Toss bean sprouts with salad dressing in bowl. Marinate at room temperature for 30 minutes.
- Slice unpeeled cucumber lengthwise into halves; scoop out seeds. Cut into bite-size pieces
- Cut an X through top layer of each pita with kitchen shears, cutting to outer edge.
- Stir cucumber, cheese, carrot and tomato into bean sprout mixture.
- Pull up cut sides of pita; line bottom of pita with lettuce. Fill pitas with bean sprout mixture. Serve sandwiches with knife and fork.
- *Yield: 4 servings.*

Approx Per Serving: Cal 511; Prot 26 g; Carbo 44 g; T Fat 27 g; 46% Calories from Fat; Chol 75 mg; Fiber 4 g; Sod 936 mg

Scott R. Woizeschke
Cottonwood County

NOTES

*S*picy Beef with Black Bean Salsa

1 tablespoon chili powder
1 teaspoon salt
1 teaspoon ground cumin
1/2 teaspoon ground red
 pepper
1 (3-pound) beef tip roast

- Preheat grill.
- Combine chili powder, salt, cumin and red pepper in small bowl; mix well. Reserve 2 teaspoons of the mixture for salsa. Sprinkle remaining seasoning mixture over roast.
- Grill roast over hot coals for 12 to 18 minutes on each side for medium-rare or until done to taste.
- Let roast stand for 10 minutes for easier slicing. Slice thinly across the grain.
- Arrange slices on serving platter. Spoon salsa over slices. Garnish with fresh cilantro sprigs.

Black Bean Salsa

1 (15-ounce) can black
 beans, drained
2 tomatoes, chopped
1 tomatilla, chopped
1/2 red onion, finely chopped
3 tablespoons finely
 chopped celery
3 tablespoons chopped fresh
 cilantro
1 teaspoon lemon juice

- Combine beans, tomatoes, tomatillo, onion, celery, cilantro, lemon juice and reserved seasoning mixture in bowl; mix well. Chill until serving time.
- *Yield: 6 servings.*

Approx Per Serving: Cal 330; Prot 44 g; Carbo 16 g; T Fat 10 g; 27% Calories from Fat; Chol 108 mg; Fiber 4 g; Sod 734 mg

Fast Corned Beef and Cabbage Sauté

2 tablespoons cider vinegar
1 tablespoon sugar
1 teaspoon caraway seeds
1/4 teaspoon salt
12 ounces lean corned beef,
    sliced
1 medium red onion
1 tablespoon vegetable oil
1 (16-ounce) package
    shredded cabbage and
    carrot mix
2 tablespoons vegetable oil
4 servings hot cooked rice
1 cup plain yogurt

- Combine first 4 ingredients in small bowl. Cut corned beef slices crosswise into halves; set aside.
- Cut onion into 8 wedges. Stir-fry onion in 1 tablespoon oil in 12-inch skillet over high heat for 2 minutes; remove with slotted spoon.
- Stir-fry cabbage mixture in 2 tablespoons oil in same skillet for 5 minutes or until tender-crisp. Add vinegar mixture, corned beef and onion. Cook until heated through, stirring constantly.
- Spoon rice onto plates, cover with corned beef mixture and top with yogurt.
- *Yield: 4 servings.*

Approx Per Serving: Cal 530; Prot 22 g; Carbo 46 g; T Fat 29 g; 49% Calories from Fat; Chol 91 mg; Fiber 4 g; Sod 1158 mg

Beef and Potato Loaf

6 cups thinly sliced peeled
    potatoes
1 1/2 tablespoons grated
    onion
1 1/2 teaspoons parsley flakes
1 1/2 teaspoons salt
1/4 teaspoon pepper
1 1/2 pounds lean ground beef
1 cup plus 2 tablespoons
    evaporated milk
3/4 cup rolled oats
6 tablespoons chopped
    onion
6 tablespoons catsup
1 1/4 teaspoons salt
1/8 teaspoon pepper

- Preheat oven to 350 degrees.
- Arrange potato slices evenly in greased 2-quart baking dish. Sprinkle with onion, parsley, 1 1/2 teaspoons salt and 1/4 teaspoon pepper.
- Combine ground beef, evaporated milk, oats, onion, catsup, 1 1/2 teaspoons salt and 1/8 teaspoon pepper in bowl; mix well. Spread evenly over potato layer.
- Bake, uncovered, at 350 degrees for 1 to 1 1/4 hours until potatoes are tender and ground beef mixture is cooked through.
- *Yield: 6 servings.*

Approx Per Serving: Cal 484; Prot 33 g; Carbo 43 g; T Fat 20 g; 37% Calories from Fat; Chol 98 mg; Fiber 3 g; Sod 1364 mg

Ground Beef and Cabbage Casserole Olé

1¹/₂ cups shredded peeled
   potatoes
¹/₂ cup shredded Cheddar
   cheese
¹/₄ teaspoon pepper
¹/₈ teaspoon salt
1 pound ground beef
1¹/₂ cups shredded cabbage
1 (4-ounce) can chopped
   green chiles, drained
¹/₂ cup taco sauce
¹/₄ teaspoon pepper
¹/₈ teaspoon salt
1 cup shredded Cheddar
   cheese

- Preheat oven to 350 degrees.
- Toss first 4 ingredients in bowl until well mixed. Press over bottom and sides of greased shallow baking dish.
- Bake at 350 degrees for 20 minutes.
- Brown ground beef in skillet, stirring until crumbly; drain well and set aside.
- Stir-fry cabbage in skillet over high heat for 2 to 3 minutes. Mix in ground beef and remaining ingredients except cheese. Spoon into potato crust.
- Bake for 20 minutes. Top with cheese. Bake for 2 to 3 minutes longer.
- *Yield: 4 servings.*

Approx Per Serving: Cal 532; Prot 39 g; Carbo 26 g; T Fat 31 g; 51% Calories from Fat; Chol 129 mg; Fiber 3 g; Sod 928 mg

Chimichangas

1 pound ground beef
¹/₄ onion, chopped
1 envelope taco seasoning
   mix
³/₄ cup water
¹/₄ to ¹/₂ cup shredded
   Cheddar cheese
8 (8-inch) flour tortillas,
   warmed
Oil for frying

- Brown ground beef with onion in skillet, stirring until crumbly; drain. Add taco seasoning mix and water. Simmer for 20 minutes. Stir in cheese.
- Place 2 tablespoons mixture on each tortilla, fold tortilla over filling, fold sides toward center and roll up; secure with toothpick.
- Preheat about 1 inch oil in heavy skillet.
- Fry chimichangas in hot oil until lightly browned; drain on paper towels.
- *Yield: 8 servings.*

Approx Per Serving: Cal 289; Prot 18 g; Carbo 24 g; T Fat 13 g; 41% Calories from Fat; Chol 50 mg; Fiber 1 g; Sod 679 mg
Nutritional information does not include oil for frying.

Spanish Rice

³/₄ cup uncooked rice
2 tablespoons vegetable oil
1 pound ground beef
¹/₄ cup chopped celery
¹/₄ cup chopped onion
2¹/₂ cups canned tomatoes
1 cup beef bouillon
1 teaspoon soy sauce
1 teaspoon sugar
Salt to taste

- Sauté rice in oil in large skillet for 5 minutes or until brown.
- Add ground beef, celery and onion. Cook until brown and crumbly, stirring frequently.
- Add undrained tomatoes, bouillon, soy sauce, sugar and salt; mix well. Simmer, covered, for 45 minutes or until rice is tender.
- *Yield: 6 servings.*

Approx Per Serving: Cal 319; Prot 20 g; Carbo 24 g; T Fat 16 g; 44% Calories from Fat; Chol 56 mg; Fiber 2 g; Sod 396 mg

Mexican Lasagna

1¹/₂ pounds ground beef
1 (16-ounce) can chopped tomatoes
1 tablespoon chili powder
1¹/₂ teaspoons ground cumin
1 teaspoon salt
1 teaspoon black pepper
¹/₄ teaspoon red pepper
¹/₄ teaspoon garlic powder
10 to 12 corn tortillas
2 cups small curd cottage cheese, drained
1 cup shredded Monterey Jack cheese with jalapeños
1 egg, beaten
¹/₂ cup shredded Cheddar cheese
2 cups shredded lettuce
¹/₂ cup chopped tomatoes
3 green onions, chopped
¹/₄ cup sliced black olives

- Preheat oven to 350 degrees.
- Brown ground beef in skillet, stirring until crumbly; drain. Add tomatoes, chili powder, cumin, salt, peppers and garlic powder; mix well. Simmer until heated through.
- Line lightly greased 9x13-inch baking dish with half the tortillas. Spoon ground beef mixture into prepared dish and top with remaining tortillas.
- Combine cottage cheese, Monterey Jack cheese and egg in bowl; mix well. Spoon over tortillas.
- Bake at 350 degrees for 30 minutes.
- Sprinkle Cheddar cheese, lettuce, chopped tomatoes, green onions and olives in diagonal rows across casserole.
- *Yield: 6 servings.*

Approx Per Serving: Cal 609; Prot 47 g; Carbo 36 g; T Fat 31 g; 46% Calories from Fat; Chol 157 mg; Fiber 5 g; Sod 1152 mg

𝒱ersatile Lasagna

The flavor improves if prepared a day ahead to allow the flavors to blend.

1 pound ground beef
1 (28-ounce) can tomato
    purée
1 tablespoon parsley flakes
1 tablespoon dried basil
1 clove of garlic, minced
1 (9-ounce) package frozen
    chopped spinach, thawed
9 lasagna noodles
24 ounces cottage cheese
2 eggs, beaten
¹/₂ cup grated Parmesan
    cheese
2 tablespoons parsley flakes
1 teaspoon pepper
¹/₂ teaspoon salt
1 pound mozzarella cheese,
    thinly sliced

- Preheat oven to 375 degrees.
- Brown ground beef in skillet, stirring until crumbly; drain. Add tomatoes, 1 tablespoon parsley, basil and garlic; mix well. Simmer, uncovered, for 40 to 50 minutes or until thickened, stirring occasionally.
- Drain spinach well and squeeze dry; set aside.
- Cook lasagna noodles using package directions, rinse with cold water and pat dry.
- Combine cottage cheese, eggs, Parmesan cheese, 2 tablespoons parsley, pepper and salt in bowl; mix well.
- Ladle in just enough of the ground beef mixture to cover bottom of 9x13-inch baking pan. Layer half the noodles, half the cottage cheese mixture, all the spinach and half the mozzarella in the prepared pan. Add layers of half the ground beef mixture, remaining noodles, cottage cheese mixture, ground beef mixture and mozzarella.
- Bake at 375 degrees for 30 minutes or until bubbly. Let stand for 20 minutes before serving.
- If using fresh basil, be sure to increase to 2 tablespoons.
- *Yield: 12 servings.*

Approx Per Serving: Cal 371; Prot 29 g; Carbo 22 g; T Fat 19 g; 45% Calories from Fat; Chol 105 mg; Fiber 3 g; Sod 847 mg

Quick Lasagna

1 pound ground beef
1 large onion, chopped
1 (14-ounce) can crushed
  tomatoes
2 tablespoons tomato paste
1 beef bouillon cube
1 teaspoon dried basil
1/8 teaspoon garlic powder
Salt and pepper to taste
1 tablespoon butter
3 tablespoons flour
2 cups milk
1 1/2 cups shredded
  mozzarella cheese
1/2 teaspoon nutmeg
Salt and pepper to taste
10 to 12 uncooked lasagna
  noodles
1/2 cup (or more) grated
  Parmesan cheese

- Preheat oven to 400 degrees.
- Brown ground beef with onion in large skillet stirring until crumbly; drain. Add tomatoes, tomato paste, bouillon cube, basil, garlic powder, salt and pepper; mix well. Simmer for 20 minutes, stirring occasionally.
- Melt butter in saucepan. Add flour; blend well. Whisk in milk gradually. Cook until thickened, whisking constantly. Add mozzarella. Cook until cheese melts and sauce is smooth, stirring constantly. Stir in seasonings.
- Pour half the white sauce into 8x12-inch lasagna dish. Arrange half the noodles over white sauce; cover with half the ground beef sauce. Add layers of the remaining white sauce, noodles and ground beef sauce. Top with Parmesan cheese.
- Bake at 400 degrees for 20 minutes. Let stand for several minutes before serving.
- *Yield: 6 servings.*

Approx Per Serving: Cal 547; Prot 35 g; Carbo 45 g; T Fat 25 g; 41% Calories from Fat; Chol 101 mg; Fiber 3 g; Sod 656 mg

When browning ground beef, invert a metal colander over the skillet. This will allow steam to escape but reduces spattering. Brown 5 or more pounds of ground beef at one time; drain and cool. Freeze in the quantities needed for your favorite recipes.

Quick and Easy Taco Baked Potatoes

4 large baking potatoes
1 pound ground beef
1/2 cup chopped onion
1 envelope taco seasoning
    mix
3/4 cup water
1 cup taco sauce
1/2 cup shredded Monterey
    Jack cheese with jalapeños

- Scrub potatoes; pierce in several places with fork or sharp knife. Microwave on High for 14 to 17 minutes or until potatoes are cooked through, turning and rearranging once. Let stand for 2 minutes.
- Brown ground beef with onion in skillet, stirring until crumbly; drain. Add taco seasoning mix and water. Simmer for 15 minutes, stirring occasionally. Stir in taco sauce.
- Cut X in each potato to within 1/2 inch of bottom; squeeze to open and fluff potato pulp with fork.
- Spoon ground beef mixture over potatoes; sprinkle with cheese.
- *Yield: 4 servings.*

Approx Per Serving: Cal 572; Prot 35 g; Carbo 61 g; T Fat 22 g; 34% Calories from Fat; Chol 97 mg; Fiber 4 g; Sod 1278 mg

Use-Your-Imagination Sauce

1 1/2 pounds ground beef
1 to 2 onions, chopped
1 (46-ounce) can tomato
    juice
1 (15-ounce) can tomato
    sauce
1 (12-ounce) can tomato
    paste
1 tablespoon vinegar
1 tablespoon sugar
1 tablespoon chili powder
1 teaspoon garlic powder
1 teaspoon dried thyme
1 teaspoon dried oregano
Salt and pepper to taste

- Brown ground beef with onion in large skillet or saucepan until ground beef in brown and crumbly; drain.
- Add tomato juice, sauce and paste; mix well. Add vinegar, sugar and seasonings; mix well. Simmer for 2 to 3 hours or to desired consistency, stirring occasionally.
- Serve sauce over hot cooked pasta of choice or use for lasagna. Cook to thicker consistency and ladle over hot dogs to make Coney Islands.
- *Yield: 20 (1/2-cup) servings.*

Approx Per Serving: Cal 113; Prot 9 g; Carbo 9 g; T Fat 5 g; 38% Calories from Fat; Chol 25 mg; Fiber 2 g; Sod 517 mg

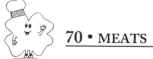
Spaghetti Pie

6 ounces uncooked spaghetti
1/3 cup grated Parmesan
   cheese
2 tablespoons margarine
2 eggs, beaten
2 pounds ground beef
1/2 cup chopped onion
1/4 cup chopped green pepper
1 (8-ounce) can tomato
   sauce
1 (6-ounce) can tomato paste
1 teaspoon dried oregano
1/2 teaspoon garlic salt
1 cup cottage cheese
1/2 cup shredded Cheddar
   cheese

- Preheat oven to 350 degrees.
- Cook spaghetti using package directions; drain well. Add Parmesan cheese and margarine; toss until well mixed. Add eggs; mix well. Line bottom and sides of 2 pie plates to form crust.
- Brown ground beef with onion and green pepper in skillet stirring until ground beef is crumbly; drain. Add tomato suace and paste, oregano and garlic salt; mix well. Simmer until heated through.
- Divide cottage cheese between pie plates; spread evenly over spaghetti. Ladle ground beef mixture over cottage cheese.
- Bake at 350 degrees for 10 minutes.
- Sprinkle with Cheddar cheese. Bake for 10 minutes longer.
- Let stand for several minutes before serving.
- *Yield: 12 servings.*

Approx Per Serving: Cal 318; Prot 25 g; Carbo 16 g; T Fat 17 g; 48% Calories from Fat; Chol 101 mg; Fiber 1 g; Sod 538 mg

Have planned-overs instead of leftovers:

- A meat loaf can be cut into cubes and added to spaghetti sauce;
- Added to a vegetable stir-fry; used as a filling for a frittata or omelet;
- Crumbled over corn tortillas, heated and topped with salsa;
- Crumbled into a cheese sauce for baked potatoes;
- Stuffed into a pita round with tomatoes, onions and dilled yogurt;
- Crumbled over a pizza;
- Added to vegetable soup; or used in quick chili.

Quick Cheeseburger Pie

This recipe can be even quicker if you use a frozen pie crust.

Pat-in-the-Pan Pastry
   (recipe below)
1 pound ground beef
1/2 to 3/4 cup finely chopped
   onion
1 clove of garlic, finely
   chopped
1/4 cup flour
1/2 teaspoon salt
1/3 cup dill pickle liquid
1/3 cup milk
1/2 cup chopped dill pickles
2 cups shredded American
   or Swiss cheese

- Preheat oven to 425 degrees
- Bake pastry at 425 degrees for 15 minutes.
- Brown ground beef with onion and garlic in skillet stirring until ground beef is crumbly; drain. Sprinkle with flour and salt; mix well.
- Stir in pickle liquid, milk, pickles and 1 cup cheese. Spoon into partially baked pastry shell.
- Bake at 425 degrees for 15 minutes. Sprinkle with remaining 1 cup cheese.
- Bake for 5 minutes longer or until crust is golden brown.

Pat-in-the-Pan Pastry

1 1/3 cups flour
1/2 teaspoon salt
1/2 cup shortening
3 to 4 tablespoons cold water

- Mix flour and salt in bowl. Cut in shortening until crumbly.
- Add water 1 tablespoon at a time, mixing with fork until mixture almosts forms a ball.
- Pat over bottom and side of pie plate or 8-inch round baking pan.
- *Yield: 6 servings.*

Approx Per Serving: Cal 597; Prot 29 g; Carbo 29 g; T Fat 40 g; 61% Calories from Fat; Chol 94 mg; Fiber 1 g; Sod 1149 mg

Make *Delicious Porcupine Meatballs* by mixing 1 1/2 pounds ground beef with 1/2 cup uncooked rice, 1/2 cup minced onion, 1 teaspoon each salt and Worcestershire sauce and 1/2 teaspoon each poultry seasoning and pepper. Shape into balls, brown on all sides in skillet and add a can of cream of mushroom soup and 2 soup cans water. Simmer, covered, for 1 1/2 hours.

Popover Pizza

1½ pounds ground beef
1 medium onion, chopped
1 envelope spaghetti sauce
    mix
1 (15-ounce) can tomato
    sauce
½ cup water
2 cups shredded mozzarella
    cheese
2 eggs
1 cup milk
1 tablespoon vegetable oil
1 cup flour
½ teaspoon salt
¼ cup (or more) grated
    Parmesan cheese

- Preheat oven to 400 degrees.
- Brown ground beef with onion in large skillet stirring until ground beef is crumbly; drain. Add spaghetti sauce mix, tomato sauce and water; mix well.
- Simmer for 10 minutes, stirring occasionally. Spoon into greased 9x13-inch baking pan. Sprinkle with mozzarella cheese.
- Beat eggs in medium bowl. Add milk, oil, flour and salt; beat until well mixed. Pour over ground beef mixture. Sprinkle with Parmesan cheese.
- Bake at 400 degrees for 30 minutes or until golden brown and firm.
- Invert onto serving platter.
- *Yield: 8 servings.*

Approx Per Serving: Cal 425; Prot 31 g; Carbo 23 g; T Fat 23 g; 49% Calories from Fat; Chol 145 mg; Fiber 2 g; Sod 1139 mg

French Meat Pie

1 large onion, thinly sliced
2 tablespoons vegetable oil
1 pound ground beef
1 pound ground pork
1 cup mashed potatoes
2 teaspoons allspice
1 teaspoon salt
1/4 teaspoon pepper
1 recipe 2-crust pie pastry

- Preheat oven to 375 degrees.
- Sauté onion in oil in skillet.
- Cook ground beef and pork in skillet until brown and crumbly; drain. Combine with onion, potatoes and seasonings in bowl; mix well.
- Spoon into pastry-lined pie plate; top with remaining pastry, sealing edge and cutting vents. Brush with beaten egg.
- Bake at 375 degrees for 30 to 35 minutes or until golden brown.
- *Yield: 6 servings.*

Approx Per Serving: Cal 654; Prot 39 g; Carbo 34 g; T Fat 40 g; 55% Calories from Fat; Chol 112 mg; Fiber 2 g; Sod 836 mg

Sesame Pork Loin

1 (5-pound) boneless pork
  loin
1/2 cup soy sauce
3 tablespoons sugar
3 tablespoons minced onion
2 cloves of garlic, minced
2 tablespoons oil
2 teaspoons ginger
3/4 cup sesame seeds

- Place pork loin in sealable plastic bag.
- Combine soy sauce, sugar, onion, garlic, oil and ginger in small bowl; mix well. Stir in sesame seeds. Pour marinade over pork loin; seal bag tightly. Turn bag to coat loin with marinade. Marinate in refrigerator for 3 hours to overnight, turning occasionally.
- Preheat oven to 325 degrees.
- Place loin with marinade in shallow baking pan. Roast, uncovered, for 1 1/2 hours or to 160 degrees on meat thermometer. Let stand for several minutes before slicing.
- *Yield: 10 servings.*

Approx Per Serving: Cal 449; Prot 42 g; Carbo 6 g;
  T Fat 29 g; 57% Calories from Fat; Chol 127 mg;
  Fiber 1 g; Sod 923 mg

South-of-the-Border Pork Chops

8 (1/2 inch thick) loin pork
  chops
2 tablespoons vegetable oil
Seasoned salt and pepper to
  taste
1 1/4 cups uncooked long
  grain rice
2 cups water
1 (8-ounce) can tomato
  sauce
1 (14-ounce) can stewed
  tomatoes
1/2 envelope taco seasoning
  mix
1 medium green bell pepper,
  chopped
1 cup shredded Cheddar
  cheese

- Preheat oven to 350 degrees.
- Brown chops on both sides in oil in skillet. Sprinkle with seasoned salt and pepper.
- Combine rice, water, tomato sauce, stewed tomatoes and seasoning mix in greased 9x13-inch baking pan; mix well. Arrange chops over rice mixture. Sprinkle with green pepper.
- Bake, covered, at 350 degrees for 1 1/2 hours.
- Uncover; sprinkle with cheese. Bake, uncovered, until cheese melts.
- *Yield: 8 servings.*

Approx Per Serving: Cal 392; Prot 30 g; Carbo 31 g;
  T Fat 16 g; 37% Calories from Fat; Chol 86 mg;
  Fiber 2 g; Sod 661 mg

$\mathscr{T}$asty Pork Chops

6 ($^1/_2$ inch thick) pork chops
$^1/_2$ teaspoon seasoned salt
1 large onion
1 (6-ounce) can frozen
    orange juice concentrate,
    thawed
$^3/_4$ cup water
$^1/_4$ cup packed brown sugar
3 tablespoons lemon juice
$^1/_2$ teaspoon allspice
6 orange sections

- Cook chops in greased skillet over medium heat until brown on both sides; drain. Sprinkle with seasoned salt. Slice onion into 6 slices; place slice on each chop.
- Combine orange juice concentrate, water, brown sugar, lemon juice and allspice in bowl; mix well. Pour over chops.
- Bring to a boil; reduce heat. Simmer, covered, for 25 minutes or until chops are tender.
- Top each chop with orange segment.
- *Yield: 6 servings.*

Approx Per Serving: Cal 259; Prot 24 g; Carbo 23 g; T Fat 8 g; 27% Calories from Fat; Chol 71 mg; Fiber 1 g; Sod 169 mg

$\mathscr{H}$am Balls

1 pound ground pork
1$^1/_2$ cups ground ham
$^1/_2$ pound ground beef
1$^1/_2$ cups graham cracker
    crumbs
1 cup milk
2 eggs
1 (10-ounce) can tomato
    soup
$^3/_4$ cup packed brown sugar
$^1/_4$ cup vinegar
1 tablespoon dry mustard

- Preheat oven to 350 degrees.
- Combine ground pork, ham and beef in large bowl. Add crumbs, milk and eggs; mix well.
- Shape into meatballs of desired size; arrange on large shallow baking sheet.
- Bake at 350 degrees for 1 hour; drain well.
- Combine soup, brown sugar, vinegar and dry mustard in saucepan; mix well. Heat until well blended, stirring frequently. Serve over ham balls.
- *Yield: 8 servings.*

Approx Per Serving: Cal 430; Prot 32 g; Carbo 41 g; T Fat 15 g; 32% Calories from Fat; Chol 134 mg; Fiber 1 g; Sod 835 mg

$\mathscr{L}$eg of Lamb Southwest-Style

1 leg of lamb, boned, rolled
2 cloves of garlic, slivered
1 medium onion, chopped
1 cup dry red wine
1/2 cup orange juice
2 tablespoons olive oil
1 tablespoon chili powder
1 teaspoon ground cumin
1 teaspoon salt

- Cut slits in lamb; insert garlic slivers. Place in glass dish. Sprinkle with onion. Pour mixture of remaining ingredients over lamb. Marinate, covered, in refrigerator for 24 hours, turning occasionally.
- Preheat oven to 450 degrees.
- Drain lamb, reserving marinade. Place on rack in roasting pan.
- Roast at 450 degrees for 15 minutes. Reduce oven temperature to 325 degrees. Baste with reserved marinade.
- Roast for 30 minutes per pound or to 140 degrees on meat thermometer for rare, basting occasionally with marinade.
- *Yield: 10 servings.*

Approx Per Serving: Cal 162; Prot 17 g; Carbo 3 g; T Fat 7 g; 41% Calories from Fat; Chol 51 mg; Fiber <1 g; Sod 261 mg

$\mathscr{H}$earty Microwave Lamb Stew

1 1/4 pounds (3/4-inch pieces) lamb leg or shoulder
12 pearl onions
2 cloves of garlic, minced
1 (15-ounce) can stewed tomatoes
1 cup burgundy
2 small potatoes
2 carrots, chopped
1 stalk celery, chopped
2 bay leaves
1/2 teaspoon dried thyme leaves
Salt and pepper to taste
1 tablespoon cornstarch
1/4 cup water

- Combine lamb, onions and garlic in 2 1/2-quart glass casserole. Microwave, covered, on High for 8 to 10 minutes or until lamb is brown, stirring twice; drain.
- Add undrained tomatoes, wine, potatoes, carrots, celery, bay leaves, thyme, salt and pepper; mix well.
- Microwave, covered, on Medium for 60 to 65 minutes or until lamb is tender, stirring often.
- Stir in cornstarch dissolved in water. Microwave, covered, on High for 1 1/2 minutes or until thickened. Discard bay leaves.
- *Yield: 4 servings.*

Approx Per Serving: Cal 304; Prot 27 g; Carbo 25 g; T Fat 7 g; 20% Calories from Fat; Chol 76 mg; Fiber 4 g; Sod 462 mg

Baked Chicken with Rhubarb Sauce

1 (3-pound) chicken, cut up
4 teaspoons butter
1/4 teaspoon salt
Rhubarb Sauce
    (recipe below)
1/2 teaspoon cinnamon
1/2 teaspoon nutmeg

- Preheat oven to 375 degrees.
- Arrange chicken in baking pan. Melt butter; brush over chicken. Sprinkle with salt.
- Bake at 375 degrees for 30 minutes.
- Spoon Rhubarb Sauce over chicken. Sprinkle with spices.
- Bake for 20 minutes longer.
- Serve chicken with sauce over hot cooked rice.

Rhubarb Sauce

1/3 cup sugar
1 1/2 tablespoons cornstarch
1/8 teaspoon salt
2 cups chopped fresh
    rhubarb
1 1/2 cups water
2 teaspoons lemon juice

- Combine sugar, cornstarch and salt in saucepan. Stir in rhubarb and water. Bring to a boil over medium heat, stirring constantly. Cook for 2 minutes or until clear and thickened, stirring constantly.
- Remove from heat. Stir in lemon juice. Let stand until cool.
- *Yield: 4 servings.*

Approx Per Serving: Cal 446; Prot 50 g; Carbo 22 g; T Fat 17 g; 34% Calories from Fat; Chol 161 mg; Fiber 2 g; Sod 388 mg

Enjoy *Campfire Chicken Delight* by mixing two or three (5-ounce) cans of chicken with one (16-ounce) can of undrained French-style green beans and 1 can cream of mushroom soup in a heavy kettle and heating over an open fire, stirring occasionally. Serve over chow mein noodles.

Chicken Cacciatore

1 (3-pound) chicken, cut up
1/3 cup flour
1 teaspoon salt
1/4 teaspoon pepper
1/4 cup margarine
1 cup chopped onion
1 small green bell pepper,
    chopped
10 ounces fresh mushrooms,
    chopped
1 (14-ounce) can tomatoes
1 (8-ounce) can tomato
    sauce
1 teaspoon sugar
1 bay leaf
1/2 teaspoon dried oregano
1/4 teaspoon garlic powder
1/4 teaspoon dried thyme
1/4 teaspoon dried basil
1/4 cup grated Parmesan
    cheese

- Shake 2 or 3 chicken pieces at a time in a mixture of flour, salt and pepper in plastic bag until coated.
- Melt margarine in heavy skillet. Brown chicken several pieces at a time on all sides in margarine; remove.
- Add onion and green pepper to skillet. Sauté until tender. Add a small amount of additional margarine if necessary.
- Add mushrooms, tomatoes, tomato sauce, sugar, bay leaf and remaining seasonings; mix well. Return chicken to skillet. Sprinkle with Parmesan cheese.
- Simmer, covered, for 35 to 40 minutes or until chicken is tender.
- Discard bay leaf.
- *Yield: 4 servings.*

Approx Per Serving: Cal 569; Prot 57 g; Carbo 25 g; T Fat 27 g; 42% Calories from Fat; Chol 156 mg; Fiber 4 g; Sod 1438 mg

Hawaiian Chicken

1 small onion, chopped
1/2 cup butter
1/4 cup flour
2 cups pineapple juice
1 (14-ounce) bottle of catsup
1 cup packed brown sugar
1/2 cup cider vinegar
3 tablespoons lemon juice
2 tablespoons
    Worcestershire sauce
1 teaspoon ground cloves
1 teaspoon salt
1/2 teaspoon garlic salt
1/2 teaspoon pepper
1 (3-pound) chicken, cut up

- Preheat oven to 400 degrees.
- Sauté onion in butter in skillet until tender. Stir in flour.
- Add next 10 ingredients; mix well. Bring to a simmer.
- Arrange chicken pieces in 9x13-inch baking pan. Spoon sauce over chicken.
- Bake, uncovered, at 400 degrees for 2 hours.
- *Yield: 4 servings.*

Approx Per Serving: Cal 918; Prot 52 g; Carbo 100 g; T Fat 36 g; 35% Calories from Fat; Chol 213 mg; Fiber 2 g; Sod 2448 mg

Chicken Monterey

3 whole chicken breasts
3/4 teaspoon salt
2 tablespoons vegetable oil
1 medium green onion,
    chopped
3 tablespoons flour
2 cups milk
1 cup water
3 tablespoons catsup
3/4 teaspoon salt
1/2 teaspoon rosemary
1 chicken bouillon cube,
    crushed
1 (9-ounce) package frozen
    artichoke hearts, thawed
1 (9-ounce) package frozen
    green beans, thawed

- Preheat oven to 350 degrees.
- Cut chicken breasts into halves. Rinse and pat dry. Rub with 3/4 teaspoon salt.
- Brown chicken in oil in 12-inch skillet over medium-high heat. Remove to 3-quart baking dish.
- Sauté green onion in 2 tablespoons drippings in skillet over medium heat. Sprinkle with flour; mix well. Stir in milk and water gradually. Cook until thickened, stirring constantly.
- Add catsup, 3/4 teaspoon salt, rosemary and bouillon cube. Cook until bouillon dissolves, stirring constantly. Pour sauce over chicken.
- Bake, covered, at 350 degrees for 30 minutes.
- Drain artichoke hearts and green beans. Stir into baking dish.
- Bake for 20 minutes longer or until chicken is tender. Skim sauce before serving if necessary.
- *Yield: 6 servings.*

Approx Per Serving: Cal 285; Prot 32 g; Carbo 16 g;
    T Fat 11 g; 34% Calories from Fat; Chol 84 mg;
    Fiber 4 g; Sod 947 mg

For *Quick Chicken Cordon Bleu,* pound boneless skinless chicken breasts between waxed paper, top each with slices of ham and Swiss cheese and roll up. Dip into melted butter, coat with crushed seasoned croutons and bake at 350 degrees for 30 minutes. Serve over rice with a sauce of 1 can cream of mushroom soup, 1/2 cup milk and a container of sour cream and chives heated to serving temperature.

*Ch*icken Dijon Fettucini

2 pounds boneless skinless
   chicken breasts
1¹/₂ teaspoons salt
¹/₄ teaspoon pepper
¹/₄ cup margarine
2 cups whipping cream
¹/₃ cup Dijon mustard
¹/₄ cup chopped fresh parsley
2 tablespoons minced fresh
   chives
9 ounces uncooked fettucini

- Rinse chicken; pat dry. Cut into 1-inch pieces. Sprinkle with salt and pepper.
- Sauté chicken in margarine in large heavy skillet for 4 to 7 minutes or until no longer pink. Remove chicken from skillet.
- Stir cream and mustard into pan drippings. Bring to a boil, stirring constantly; reduce heat. Simmer for 8 minutes or until slightly thickened.
- Return chicken to skillet. Add parsley and chives. Heat to serving temperature; do not boil.
- Cook fettucini using package directions; drain well. Toss chicken mixture with hot fettucini. Serve immediately.
- *Yield: 6 servings.*

Approx Per Serving: Cal 709; Prot 43 g; Carbo 35 g;
   T Fat 0 g; 44% Calories from Fat; Chol 205 mg;
   Fiber 1 g; Sod 1095 mg

*Ea*sy Company Chicken

8 boneless skinless chicken
   breasts
8 (1-ounce) slices Swiss
   cheese
1 (14-ounce) package
   stuffing mix
2 cans cream of celery soup
¹/₂ cup butter

- Preheat oven to 350 degrees.
- Rinse chicken; pat dry. Arrange in greased 9x13-inch baking pan. Place cheese slice on each piece. Cover chicken and cheese with stuffing mix. Spoon soup over stuffing.
- Melt butter in saucepan. Drizzle over top.
- Bake, covered, at 350 degrees for 1 hour.
- Bake, uncovered, for 15 minutes longer.
- *Yield: 8 servings.*

Approx Per Serving: Cal 588; Prot 41 g; Carbo 44 g;
   T Fat 28 g; 42% Calories from Fat; Chol 139 mg;
   Fiber <1 g; Sod 1620 mg

Design-Your-Own Chicken Nuggets

1 pound boneless skinless
   chicken breasts
2/3 cup fine dry bread crumbs
1/4 cup grated Parmesan
   cheese
1/2 to 1 teaspoon Italian
   herbs
1/4 teaspoon pepper
1/4 cup buttermilk
3 tablespoons melted butter

- Preheat oven to 450 degrees.
- Rinse chicken; pat dry. Cut chicken into bite-size pieces.
- Combine crumbs, Parmesan cheese, herbs and pepper in plastic bag; shake to mix.
- Beat buttermilk with margarine in shallow bowl.
- Dip 3 or 4 chicken pieces at a time into buttermilk mixture; drain slightly. Shake in crumb mixture until coated. Place on lightly greased baking sheet.
- Bake at 450 degrees for 4 minutes. Turn pieces over using tongs. Bake for 4 to 5 minutes longer or until golden brown.
- **Variations:**
- Substitute cornflake crumbs or instant mashed potato flakes for bread crumbs.
- Substitute chili powder, onion powder or garlic powder for Italian herbs.
- Substitute plain yogurt or low-fat sour cream for buttermilk.
- *Yield: 4 servings.*

Approx Per Serving: Cal 316; Prot 32 g; Carbo 13 g; T Fat 15 g; 42% Calories from Fat; Chol 101 mg; Fiber 1 g; Sod 427 mg

Make effortless *Chicken and Rice* by layering 1 cup uncooked rice, favorite chicken pieces and 1 package dry onion soup mix in baking dish. Pour 4 cups chicken broth over top and bake at 375 degrees for 1 hour.

Crunchy Parmesan Chicken

4 boneless skinless chicken
  breasts
1/4 cup fine dry bread crumbs
1/4 cup wheat germ
1/4 cup grated Parmesan
  cheese
1 teaspoon dried oregano
1 teaspoon parsley flakes
1 egg, beaten
1/4 teaspoon salt
1/4 teaspoon pepper

- Preheat oven to 325 degrees.
- Rinse chicken; pat dry.
- Combine crumbs, wheat germ, cheese, oregano and parsley flakes in plastic bag; shake until well mixed.
- Beat egg with salt and pepper in shallow bowl.
- Dip chicken into egg mixture; shake in crumb mixture to coat. Place in greased baking dish.
- Bake at 325 degrees for 25 minutes or until golden brown and crisp.
- *Yield: 4 servings.*

Approx Per Serving: Cal 235; Prot 33 g; Carbo 8 g; T Fat 7 g; 28% Calories from Fat; Chol 131 mg; Fiber 1 g; Sod 383 mg

Chicken and Green Beans

5 chicken breasts
1 (10-ounce) can cream of
  chicken soup
1 (10-ounce) can cream of
  mushroom soup
2 (16-ounce) cans French-
  cut green beans, drained
2 cups shredded Cheddar
  cheese
1 (4-ounce) can onion rings

- Rinse chicken. Cook as desired. Bone and cut into cubes.
- Preheat oven to 350 degrees.
- Combine soups in bowl; mix well.
- Layer green beans, chicken and soup in greased 9x13-inch baking pan. Sprinkle with cheese and onion rings.
- Bake, covered with foil, at 350 degrees for 1 hour.
- *Yield: 8 servings.*

Approx Per Serving: Cal 386; Prot 28 g; Carbo 17 g; T Fat 23 g; 54% Calories from Fat; Chol 79 mg; Fiber 3 g; Sod 1200 mg

Sour Cream Chicken Enchiladas

4 chicken breasts, cooked,
    chopped
2 (10-ounce) cans cream of
    chicken soup
1 cup sour cream
1 (4-ounce) can chopped
    green chiles
1 bunch green onions,
    chopped
4 cups shredded Cheddar
    cheese
12 whole wheat flour tortillas

- Preheat oven to 325 degrees.
- Combine chicken, 1 can soup, sour cream, chiles, green onions and half the cheese in bowl; mix well.
- Spoon chicken mixture onto tortillas; roll up to enclose filling. Arrange seam side down in 9x13-inch baking pan.
- Spoon remaining can soup over top. Sprinkle with remaining cheese.
- Bake at 325 degrees for 30 minutes.
- *Yield: 6 servings.*

Approx Per Serving: Cal 729; Prot 47 g; Carbo 53 g; T Fat 42 g; 52% Calories from Fat; Chol 153 mg; Fiber 5 g; Sod 1896 mg

Grilled Turkey Steaks

1¹/₂ pounds (³/₄ to 1 inch
    thick) turkey breast steaks
¹/₂ cup soy sauce
¹/₄ cup canola oil
2 teaspoons sugar
1 teaspoon ginger
1 teaspoon dry mustard
2 cloves of garlic minced or
    ¹/₂ teaspoon garlic juice

- Rinse turkey steaks; pat dry. Place in shallow dish.
- Combine soy sauce, oil, sugar, ginger, dry mustard and garlic in bowl; mix well. Pour over turkey, turning to coat with marinade. Marinate, covered, in refrigerator for 2 hours to overnight, turning occasionally.
- Preheat grill.
- Drain turkey, reserving marinade. Place on grill over medium coals.
- Grill for 5 to 8 minutes per side or until no longer pink in center, basting occasionally with reserved marinade.
- *Yield: 6 servings.*

Approx Per Serving: Cal 267; Prot 26 g; Carbo 4 g; T Fat 16 g; 55% Calories from Fat; Chol 61 mg; Fiber <1 g; Sod 1419 mg

Baked Turkey Rotini

1 pound ground turkey
1 (28-ounce) can tomatoes
1 (6-ounce) can tomato paste
1 medium onion, chopped
2 (4-ounce) cans sliced
    mushrooms
1/2 teaspoon basil leaves
1/4 teaspoon oregano leaves
8 ounces uncooked rotini
3 cups shredded mozzarella
    cheese

- Preheat oven to 350 degrees.
- Brown turkey in skillet, stirring until crumbly.
- Add tomatoes, tomato paste, onion, mushrooms, basil and oregano; mix well. Bring to a boil; reduce heat. Simmer for 20 minutes.
- Cook rotini using package directions; drain. Stir into turkey mixture.
- Layer rotini mixture and cheese 1/2 at a time in greased 3-quart baking dish.
- Bake at 350 degrees for 20 to 30 minutes or until bubbly.
- *Yield: 6 servings.*

Approx Per Serving: Cal 499; Prot 35 g; Carbo 44 g; T Fat 21 g; 38% Calories from Fat; Chol 102 mg; Fiber 5 g; Sod 873 mg

Hot Turkey Salad

4 cups chopped cooked
    turkey
4 cups chopped celery
1 cup chopped mushrooms
1 cup slivered almonds
4 tablespoons grated onion
1 cup mayonnaise
1/4 cup lemon juice
2 cups shredded Cheddar
    cheese
1 (8-ounce) can shoe string
    potatoes

- Preheat oven to 350 degrees.
- Combine turkey, celery, mushrooms, almonds and onion in large bowl; mix well.
- Blend mayonnaise and lemon juice in small bowl. Add to turkey mixture; mix well. Spoon into greased 9x13-inch baking pan.
- Bake, covered, at 350 degrees for 40 minutes.
- Sprinkle cheese and shoestring potatoes over top.
- Bake, uncovered, for 5 minutes longer.
- *Yield: 6 servings.*

Approx Per Serving: Cal 925; Prot 45 g; Carbo 32 g; T Fat 70 g; 67% Calories from Fat; Chol 132 mg; Fiber 5 g; Sod 824 mg

Vegetarian Lasagna

1¹/₂ cups chopped onions
6 ounces fresh mushrooms, chopped
2 cloves of garlic, minced
3 tablespoons sherry
1 tablespoon butter
2 stalks broccoli, chopped
8 ounces fresh spinach, chopped
¹/₂ teaspoon salt
Cayenne, savory, thyme, basil, mace and sage to taste
16 ounces cottage cheese
4 ounces mozzarella cheese, shredded
4 ounces Parmesan cheese, grated
2 eggs, beaten
¹/₄ cup chopped parsley
12 to 16 lasagna noodles
3 cups tomato sauce

- Preheat oven to 350 degrees
- Sauté onions, mushrooms and garlic in sherry and butter in skillet until tender. Add broccoli, spinach and seasonings. Simmer for 5 minutes.
- Mix cheeses, eggs and parsley in bowl.
- Cook noodles for 4 layers; drain well.
- Ladle enough tomato sauce into 9x13-inch baking dish to cover bottom. Alternate layers of noodles, cheese mixture, vegetable mixture and tomato sauce in baking dish, ending with cheese.
- Bake at 350 degrees for 30 to 40 minutes or until bubbly. Let stand for 10 minutes.
- *Yield: 12 servings.*

Approx Per Serving: Cal 272; Prot 17 g; Carbo 31 g; T Fat 9 g; 30% Calories from Fat; Chol 58 mg; Fiber 4 g; Sod 863 mg

Vegetarian Thanksgiving Loaf

1¹/₂ cups sunflower seeds
³/₄ cup sesame seeds
2 cups cooked brown rice
1 cup cooked lentils
¹/₂ cup grated carrots
¹/₂ cup chopped walnuts
¹/₂ cup chopped celery
¹/₂ cup chopped parsley
3 tablespoons chopped onion
2 eggs, lightly beaten
1 tablespoon cider vinegar
2 teaspoons lemon juice
Sea salt and sage to taste

- Preheat oven to 325 degrees.
- Process sunflower and sesame seeds in blender until finely ground. Combine with next 7 ingredients in large bowl; mix well.
- Add eggs, vinegar, lemon juice, sea salt and sage; mix well. Spoon into greased casserole.
- Bake at 325 degrees for 40 minutes. Serve hot.
- *Yield: 6 servings.*

Approx Per Serving: Cal 525; Prot 22 g; Carbo 35 g; T Fat 37 g; 59% Calories from Fat; Chol 71 mg; Fiber 8 g; Sod 49 mg

Elizabeth Peeters
age 11

Elizabeth Peeters
Otter Tail County

Thai Peanut Dip

2 cups peanut butter
1/4 cup dark soy sauce
1/4 cup lime juice
1/4 cup peanut oil
3 tablespoons honey
2 tablespoons crushed red
    pepper
2 cloves of garlic, minced
2 or 3 drops of Tabasco
    sauce

- Combine peanut butter, soy sauce, lime juice and peanut oil in bowl; blend well. Add honey, red pepper, garlic and Tabasco sauce; mix well.
- Spoon into small bowl. Place in center of large serving platter. Surround bowl with assorted bite-size fresh vegetables for dipping.
- May use either smooth or chunky peanut butter.
- *Yield: 30 (1-tablespoon) servings.*

Approx Per Serving: Cal 125; Prot 4 g; Carbo 6 g; T Fat 10 g; 70% Calories from Fat; Chol 0 mg; Fiber 1 g; Sod 218 mg

Ground Beef Enchiladas

1 pound ground beef
1 (15-ounce) can tomato
    sauce
2/3 cup water
1 tablespoon chili powder
1/2 teaspoon dried oregano
1/4 teaspoon ground cumin
1 clove of garlic, minced
1/3 cup chopped green bell
    pepper
2 cups shredded Cheddar
    cheese
1 1/2 cups shredded
    Monterey Jack cheese
12 (8-inch) flour tortillas

- Preheat oven to 350 degrees.
- Brown ground beef in skillet, stirring until crumbly; drain well.
- Combine tomato sauce, water, chili powder, oregano and cumin in saucepan; mix well. Add garlic and green pepper. Simmer for several minutes.
- Place desired amount of ground beef and cheese in center of 1 tortilla. Add 1 tablespoon sauce. Roll to enclose filling; place seam side down in 9x13-inch baking dish. Repeat with remaining ingredients.
- Spoon remaining sauce over enchiladas; top with remaining cheese.
- Bake at 350 degrees for 20 minutes or until bubbly. Let stand for 5 to 10 minutes before serving.
- *Yield: 4 servings.*

Approx Per Serving: Cal 1019; Prot 61 g; Carbo 70 g; T Fat 55 g; 49% Calories from Fat; Chol 182 mg; Fiber 6 g; Sod 1807 mg

Sauerbraten

1 (3-pound) beef bottom
  round roast
3¹/₂ cups water
³/₄ cup red wine vinegar
2 small onions, sliced
2 tablespoons pickling spices
2 tablespoons brown sugar
2 teaspoons seasoned salt
1¹/₂ teaspoons pepper
2 bay leaves
¹/₂ cup crushed gingersnaps
¹/₂ cup sour cream

- Trim roast if necessary. Place in large glass bowl.
- Combine water, vinegar, onions, pickling spices, brown sugar, seasoned salt, pepper and bay leaves in bowl; mix well. Pour over roast, turning to coat with marinade.
- Marinate roast, covered, in refrigerator for 1 to 3 days, turning occasionally.
- Drain, reserving marinade. Pat roast dry with paper towels.
- Sear roast on all sides in large Dutch oven sprayed with nonstick cooking spray. Add reserved marinade.
- Bring to a boil; reduce heat. Simmer, covered, for 3 hours or until tender.
- Remove roast to serving platter. Strain pan juices. Return 2¹/₂ cups juices to Dutch oven.
- Bring juices to a boil. Whisk in gingersnap crumbs. Cook until smooth and thickened, whisking constantly; reduce heat.
- Add sour cream. Heat to serving temperature; do not boil.
- Slice roast. Serve with sauce and your choice of dumplings, boiled potatoes or noodles.
- *Yield: 8 servings.*

Approx Per Serving: Cal 282; Prot 33 g; Carbo 10 g; T Fat 12 g; 39% Calories from Fat; Chol 103 mg; Fiber <1 g; Sod 421 mg

Prepare *Homemade Seasoned Salt* by mixing ¹/₂ cup salt with 1 teaspoon paprika and 1 tablespoon each pepper, celery salt and onion salt. Use as you would commercial seasoned salt.

Sweet and Sour Pork

1¹/₂ to 2 pounds lean
    boneless pork shoulder
2 tablespoons vegetable oil
1 (20-ounce) can juice-pack
    pineapple chunks
³/₄ cup water
¹/₄ cup white vinegar
1 tablespoon soy sauce
¹/₄ cup packed brown sugar
¹/₂ teaspoon salt
2 tablespoons cornstarch
2 tablespoons water
³/₄ cup 1-inch green bell
    pepper pieces
¹/₃ cup 1-inch onion pieces
1 fresh tomato, cut into
    pieces

- Cut pork into 1-inch cubes.
- Heat oil to 275 to 300 degrees in wok or heavy skillet. Stir-fry pork in hot oil.
- Drain pineapple, reserving juice. Add mixture of juice and next 5 ingredients to wok. Simmer, covered, until tender.
- Stir in cornstarch dissolved in 2 tablespoons water. Cook until thickened, stirring constantly. Add pineapple, green pepper and onion. Cook, covered, for 10 minutes. Add tomato. Cook for 5 minutes longer.
- Serve over hot cooked rice.
- *Yield: 6 servings.*

Approx Per Serving: Cal 381; Prot 31 g; Carbo 28 g; T Fat 16 g; 38% Calories from Fat; Chol 107 mg; Fiber 1 g; Sod 451 mg

Manicotti

1 pound ground lamb
¹/₄ cup chopped onion
3 slices bread, torn
¹/₂ cup milk
1 egg, beaten
Salt and pepper to taste
1 (8-ounce) package
    manicotti shells
1 (4-ounce) can mushrooms
1 (15-ounce) can tomato
    sauce
1 (12-ounce) can tomato paste
¹/₄ cup chopped onion
¹/₄ teaspoon each garlic
    powder, salt and pepper
4 cups water
1¹/₂ cups shredded
    mozzarella cheese

- Preheat oven to 375 degrees.
- Brown lamb with ¹/₄ cup onion in skillet; drain. Mix with bread, milk, egg and salt and pepper to taste in bowl.
- Stuff into uncooked manicotti shells; arrange in 9x13-inch baking pan.
- Heat undrained mushrooms and remaining ingredients except cheese in saucepan.
- Simmer for 5 minutes. Pour over manicotti. Sprinkle with cheese.
- Bake, covered, at 375 degrees for 1¹/₂ hours.
- *Yield: 6 servings.*

Approx Per Serving: Cal 484; Prot 34 g; Carbo 55 g; T Fat 15 g; 27% Calories from Fat; Chol 115 mg; Fiber 5 g; Sod 1293 mg

*T*andoori Chicken

1 (3-pound) chicken
1 teaspoon water
¹/₂ teaspoon dry mustard
1 cup plain yogurt
¹/₄ cup lemon juice
1 teaspoon crushed garlic
1 teaspoon salt
¹/₂ teaspoon ground
   cardamom
¹/₂ teaspoon ground ginger
¹/₂ teaspoon ground cumin
¹/₂ teaspoon black pepper
¹/₄ teaspoon cayenne

- Cut chicken into pieces as desired. Skin chicken pieces, rinse and pat dry.
- Blend water with dry mustard in large bowl. Add yogurt, lemon juice, garlic, salt and remaining spices; mix well.
- Add chicken pieces; mix until coated with yogurt mixture. Marinate, covered, in refrigerator for 12 to 24 hours, turning occasionally.
- Preheat grill.
- Place chicken pieces on grill. Cook until tender, turning as necessary.
- *Yield: 6 servings.*

Approx Per Serving: Cal 245; Prot 34 g; Carbo 3 g; T Fat 10 g; 37% Calories from Fat; Chol 106 mg; Fiber <1 g; Sod 471 mg

*C*hicken Teriyaki

6 boneless skinless chicken
   breasts
1 cup soy sauce
1 cup pineapple juice
1 cup sugar
¹/₄ cup water
¹/₄ cup vegetable oil
1 teaspoon onion salt
1 teaspoon garlic powder
1 teaspoon ginger

- Rinse chicken and pat dry. Place in shallow dish.
- Combine remaining ingredients in bowl; mix well. Pour over chicken. Marinate, covered, in refrigerator for 4 to 6 hours.
- Preheat grill.
- Remove chicken from marinade; place on grill. Grill over medium coals until tender, turning as necessary.
- Suggestion: For fast summer meals, combine family-size portions of chicken breasts and marinade in tightly sealed freezer bags. Store in freezer. Thaw in refrigerator for 24 hours.
- *Yield: 6 servings.*

Approx Per Serving: Cal 400; Prot 29 g; Carbo 43 g; T Fat 12 g; 27% Calories from Fat; Chol 73 mg; Fiber <1 g; Sod 3068 mg

Chicken Fajitas

4 boneless skinless chicken
    breasts
2 teaspoons chili powder
1 teaspoon ground cumin
1 teaspoon salt
1/4 teaspoon hot red pepper
    sauce
1 large clove of garlic,
    minced
1 large onion, sliced
1 large green bell pepper,
    sliced
3 tablespoons vegetable oil
8 (6-inch) flour tortillas,
    warmed

- Rinse chicken; pat dry. Cut into strips; place in bowl. Add chili powder, cumin, salt, pepper sauce and garlic; toss until coated. Set aside.
- Sauté onion and green pepper in 2 table-spoons oil in 12-inch skillet until lightly browned. Remove to bowl.
- Stir-fry chicken in remaining 1 table-spoon oil in skillet for 4 minutes or until lightly browned. Add onion and green pepper. Spoon onto warm tortillas.
- Garnish with sour cream, salsa, chopped tomatoes, shredded cheese, chopped olives and/or guacamole.
- *Yield: 4 servings.*

Approx Per Serving: Cal 396; Prot 32 g; Carbo 35 g; T Fat 14 g; 32% Calories from Fat; Chol 73 mg; Fiber 3 g; Sod 852 mg

Egg Foo Yung

2 tablespoons soy sauce
2 tablespoons cornstarch
1/2 teaspoon sugar
1 beef bouillon cube
2 cups boiling water
6 eggs
1 (16-ounce) can bean
    sprouts, rinsed, drained
1 cup cooked shrimp
1/2 cup chopped green onions
1 teaspoon salt
1 tablespoon (or more)
    shortening

- Blend soy sauce, cornstarch and sugar in saucepan. Stir in bouillon cube dissolved in water. Cook for 10 minutes or until thickened, stirring constantly.
- Beat eggs in medium bowl. Add well-drained bean sprouts, shrimp, green onions and salt; mix well.
- Melt shortening in hot skillet over medium heat. Pour 1/4 cup egg mixture into skillet. Cook until brown on both sides, turning once.
- Serve with sauce.
- *Yield: 12 servings.*

Approx Per Serving: Cal 74; Prot 7 g; Carbo 3 g; T Fat 4 g; 46% Calories from Fat; Chol 132 mg; Fiber 1 g; Sod 536 mg

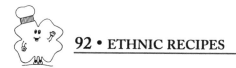

Finnish Squeaky Cheese

The squeak comes when the cheese squeaks against the teeth.

1 gallon whole milk
1 rennet tablet, crushed
2 tablespoons cold water

- Heat milk to 98 to 100 degrees in large saucepan.
- Dissolve rennet tablet in cold water. Stir into warm milk. Let milk mixture stand for 30 to 40 minutes.
- Check for curd development by placing tip of spoon into milk mixture at an angle and lifting slowly. If curd breaks "clean" over spoon, curd is ready for cutting. If curd does not seem firm, let stand for 10 to 15 minutes longer.
- Cut through curd in parallel lines 1/2 inch apart; turn saucepan 90 degrees and repeat. Make additional cuts at 45-degree angle to saucepan; turn saucepan 90 degrees and repeat cuts.
- Place saucepan over low heat. Increase temperature gradually until curd begins to cook and individual curds start to look like scrambled eggs, stirring constantly. Do not warm too fast or curd will become tough. This step may take from 20 to 40 minutes.
- Line a colander with cheesecloth; allow several inches of cheesecloth to extend over edge. Place colander in sink. Pour cheese curds and whey into colander.
- Fold cheesecloth over curds. Roll back and forth in cheesecloth to facilitate whey draining. Place cheese ball on lightly buttered broiler pan or baking pan; remove cheesecloth.
- Broil or bake until cheese is golden brown.
- *Yield: variable.*

Nutritional information for this recipe is not available.

Red Cabbage (Rote Kraut)

8 ounces bacon, finely
   chopped
1 onion, chopped
1 head red cabbage, grated
1 tablespoon vinegar
1/2 teaspoon salt
1/4 teaspoon pepper
2 apples, grated
2 tablespoons currant jelly
1 bay leaf

- Sauté bacon and onion in large skillet until onion is tender.
- Add cabbage. Cook, covered, for 10 minutes or until cabbage wilts.
- Add vinegar, salt and pepper; mix well. Stir in apples, jelly and bay leaf.
- Cook, covered, over low heat for 1 hour. Discard bay leaf.
- Serve with sauerbraten, potato dumplings and rye bread.
- *Yield: 8 servings.*

Approx Per Serving: Cal 113; Prot 4 g; Carbo 15 g; T Fat 5 g; 34% Calories from Fat; Chol 7 mg; Fiber 3 g; Sod 291 mg

Czech Potato Dumplings (Knedliky)

2 cups mashed cooked
   potatoes
1 egg
1 egg yolk
2 tablespoons farina
1 1/4 teaspoons salt
1 1/4 cups flour

- Combine potatoes, egg, egg yolk, farina and salt in bowl; mix well. Add flour; mix well. Shape into 9 dumplings.
- Bring large pan half filled with water to a full rolling boil. Add dumplings 1 at a time.
- Cook for 10 minutes or until dumplings are cooked through.
- Serve as a side dish or with butter and sugar as a main dish.
- *Yield: 9 servings.*

Approx Per Serving: Cal 123; Prot 4 g; Carbo 24 g; T Fat 2 g; 11% Calories from Fat; Chol 48 mg; Fiber 1 g; Sod 453 mg

Bagels

1 envelope dry yeast
1 cup warm water
1¹/₂ cups flour
2 eggs, beaten
¹/₄ cup honey
2 tablespoons sugar
2 tablespoons vegetable oil
1¹/₂ teaspoons salt
1³/₄ cups flour
³/₄ cup rolled oats
2 quarts water
2 tablespoons sugar

- Dissolve yeast in warm water in large bowl. Mix in 1¹/₂ cups flour, eggs, honey, sugar, oil and salt. Add remaining 1³/₄ cups flour and oats; mix well.
- Knead on floured surface until smooth and elastic. Place in greased bowl, turning to coat surface. Let rise, covered, in warm place until doubled in bulk.
- Divide into 16 portions. Roll each into rope; shape into ring, sealing ends together. Let rise, covered, until almost doubled in bulk. Place on lightly floured surface.
- Preheat oven to 375 degrees.
- Bring 2 quarts water with 2 tablespoons sugar to a boil in large saucepan. Add bagels. Simmer for 2 minutes on each side. Remove to baking sheet.
- Bake at 375 degrees for 20 to 35 minutes or until brown.
- *Yield: 16 (1-bagel) servings.*

Approx Per Serving: Cal 155; Prot 4 g; Carbo 28 g; T Fat 3 g; 17% Calories from Fat; Chol 27 mg; Fiber 1 g; Sod 209 mg

Enjoy bagels in many ways:

- A breakfast bagel is a good low-fat, high energy start to the day.
- A snack or lunchtime bagel with a flavored cream cheese or favorite sandwich filling is satisfying and healthy.
- Make mini pizzas with the addition of sauce, cheese and other toppings.
- Slice thinly and toast until very crisp to serve with salads and soups.

𝒯raditional Jewish Challah

2 tablespoons dry yeast
1 tablespoon salt
1³/₄ cups warm water
³/₄ cup honey
2 cups unbleached flour
1¹/₄ cups vegetable oil
3 eggs
5 to 6 cups unbleached flour
1 egg, beaten
Poppy seeds or sesame seeds

- Combine dry yeast and salt in large bowl. Add warm water and honey; mix well. Add 2 cups flour; mix well. Stir in oil and eggs.
- Add 4 cups remaining flour gradually. Knead on floured surface until smooth and elastic, adding remaining flour as necessary; do not underknead. Place in greased bowl, turning to coat surface. Let rise, covered, in a warm place for 1 hour.
- Punch dough down; knead several times. Divide into 6 portions. Roll each into rope. Braid 3 ropes together, seal ends and tuck under to form loaf. Place on greased baking sheet. Repeat. Let rise, covered, for 30 minutes.
- Preheat oven to 350 degrees.
- Brush with beaten egg; sprinkle with poppy or sesame seeds.
- Bake at 350 degrees for 40 to 50 minutes or until golden brown.
- *Yield: 24 (1-slice) servings.*

Approx Per Serving: Cal 280; Prot 5 g; Carbo 37 g; T Fat 13 g; 41% Calories from Fat; Chol 35 mg; Fiber <1 g; Sod 279 mg

Challah is the traditional Jewish bread usually reserved for the Sabbath in European countries. Each country has its own variation in shaping or decorating. The modern American version is usually sweeter than traditional loaves and may be enhanced with saffron, raisins or other additions.

Norwegian Cinnamon Twists (Kringers)

2 tablespoons dry yeast
1/2 cup lukewarm water
1 cup milk
1/2 cup water
1 egg, beaten
3/4 cup vegetable oil
1/2 cup sugar
1 teaspoon salt
7 cups sifted flour
1/2 cup (about) melted butter
1 cup (about) cinnamon-
    sugar

• Dissolve yeast in lukewarm water. Heat milk and 1/2 cup water to lukewarm in saucepan. Pour into large bowl. Add egg, oil, sugar and salt. Stir in yeast.
• Mix enough flour to make a smooth medium dough. Let rise, covered, in warm place until doubled in bulk.
• Punch dough down. Let rise again.
• Divide dough into 30 portions. Roll each into 6-inch rope. Fold in half and twist. Dip one side into melted butter then into cinnamon-sugar. Place sugared side up on lightly greased baking sheet. Let rise, loosely covered, in warm place until doubled in bulk.
• Preheat oven to 350 degrees. Bake at 350 degrees for 15 to 20 minutes or until golden brown.
• *Yield: 30 servings.*

Approx Per Serving: Cal 221; Prot 3 g; Carbo 31 g; T Fat 9 g; 38% Calories from Fat; Chol 16 mg; Fiber <1 g; Sod 109 mg

Another traditional Norwegian bread is *Lefse*. The basis of the bread is cold mashed potatoes mixed with enough flour to make a dough that can be rolled into thin saucer-size circles. It is baked on an ungreased griddle and usually buttered, sugared and folded into fourths. It is a holiday staple.

English Muffins

1 envelope dry yeast
2 tablespoons warm water
1 cup warm water
1/2 cup milk, scalded
2 teaspoons sugar
1 teaspoon salt
2 cups flour
3 tablespoons butter,
    softened
2 cups flour

- Dissolve yeast in 2 tablespoons warm water. Combine 1 cup warm water, milk, sugar and salt in large bowl. Cool to lukewarm. Add yeast. Mix in 2 cups flour gradually.
- Let stand, covered, in warm place for 1 to 1 1/2 hours or until sponge rises and collapses back into bowl.
- Beat in softened butter and 2 cups flour.
- Fill greased muffin rings on greased baking sheet half full. Let rise until doubled in bulk.
- Preheat oven to 425 degrees.
- Bake for 30 to 40 minutes or until golden brown. Remove to wire rack. Cool slightly; remove rings. Split muffins when cool.
- *Yield: 8 (1-muffin) servings.*

Approx Per Serving: Cal 282; Prot 7 g; Carbo 50 g; T Fat 5 g; 18% Calories from Fat; Chol 14 mg; Fiber 2 g; Sod 320 mg

Dutch Pancake (Pannekokken)

1 1/2 tablespoons butter
3/4 cup flour
3/4 cup milk
3 eggs
Cinnamon or nutmeg to
    taste

- Preheat oven to 450 degrees.
- Place butter in 9-inch round baking dish. Place in oven. Heat until butter melts; remove from oven.
- Beat flour, milk and eggs in bowl until smooth. Pour into melted butter in baking dish. Sprinkle with cinnamon.
- Bake on middle oven rack at 450 degrees for 15 minutes or until golden brown.
- *Yield: 4 servings.*

Approx Per Serving: Cal 207; Prot 9 g; Carbo 21 g; T Fat 10 g; 43% Calories from Fat; Chol 177 mg; Fiber 1 g; Sod 114 mg

Soft Pretzels

Pretzels came originally from Germany, where the monks would give them to the children as a reward for learning prayers.

1 tablespoon yeast
1/2 cup warm water
1 teaspoon honey
1 1/3 cups (or more) flour
1 egg, beaten
Coarse salt to taste

- Preheat oven to 425 degrees.
- Dissolve yeast in warm water in bowl.
- Add honey; mix well. Add enough flour to make nonsticky dough; do not add too much flour.
- Divide dough into 20 portions. Roll each into long rope. Bend into traditional pretzel shape or create your own design such as stars, letters or hearts. Place on lightly greased baking sheet.
- Brush with beaten egg; sprinkle with coarse salt.
- Bake at 425 degrees for 10 minutes or until golden brown.
- *Yield: 20 (1-pretzel) servings.*

Approx Per Serving: Cal 36; Prot 1 g; Carbo 7 g; T Fat <1 g; 9% Calories from Fat; Chol 11 mg; Fiber <1 g; Sod 4 mg

Whole Wheat Swedish Flat Bread

2 1/2 cups all-purpose flour
1 1/2 cups whole wheat flour
1 cup rye flour
1/2 cup sugar
1 teaspoon baking soda
1 teaspoon salt
3/4 cup butter
1 1/2 cups buttermilk

- Preheat oven to 350 degrees.
- Combine flours, sugar, baking soda and salt in bowl; mix well.
- Cut in butter until crumbly. Add buttermilk; mix well.
- Roll on lightly floured surface using regular rolling pin. Roll with flat bread rolling pin. Place on lightly greased baking sheets.
- Bake at 350 degrees until light brown.
- *Yield: 25 servings.*

Approx Per Serving: Cal 155; Prot 3 g; Carbo 23 g; T Fat 6 g; 34% Calories from Fat; Chol 15 mg; Fiber 2 g; Sod 191 mg

Whole Wheat Tortillas

3 cups whole wheat flour
1/4 teaspoon salt
1/8 teaspoon baking powder
3 tablespoons butter
1 cup lukewarm water

- Combine flour, salt and baking powder in large bowl; mix well. Cut in butter until crumbly.
- Add water all at once; mix until mixture forms ball, adding a small amount of additional water if necessary. Knead until smooth and elastic.
- Divide into 12 portions. Roll thinly on lightly floured surface.
- Preheat griddle until drop of water dances on surface.
- Place tortilla on hot griddle. Bake until small bubbles appear; turn over. Bake until lightly browned.
- *Yield: 12 (1-tortilla) servings.*

Approx Per Serving: Cal 127; Prot 4 g; Carbo 22 g; T Fat 3 g; 23% Calories from Fat; Chol 8 mg; Fiber 4 g; Sod 79 mg

Danish Apple Dessert

1 (1-pound) loaf cinnamon bread
1/2 cup butter
1 (50-ounce) jar applesauce
1 cup (or more) whipped cream

- Toast cinnamon bread. Cool and crush into crumbs.
- Melt butter in large skillet. Add crumbs. Cook over low heat, stirring constantly.
- Alternate layers of crumbs and applesauce in glass bowl, beginning and ending with crumbs.
- Refrigerate, covered, overnight.
- Spread whipped cream over top. Garnish with maraschino cherries.
- May serve warm with whipped cream and cherries if desired.
- *Yield: 10 servings.*

Approx Per Serving: Cal 354; Prot 4 g; Carbo 52 g; T Fat 16 g; 39% Calories from Fat; Chol 41 mg; Fiber 3 g; Sod 279 mg

*C*zech Berry Dessert (Bublania)

3 eggs
3/4 cup sugar
1 cup milk
13/4 cups flour
1 tablespoon baking powder
1/2 teaspoon salt
1/4 cup butter
3 cups fresh raspberries
1/4 to 1/2 cup sugar

- Preheat oven to 375 degrees.
- Beat eggs in bowl. Beat in 3/4 cup sugar. Add milk gradually, beating until well blended.
- Sift flour, baking powder and salt together. Add to egg mixture; mix well.
- Melt butter; cool. Beat into batter. Pour into greased 9x13-inch baking pan. Place raspberries in single layer over batter. Sprinkle with 1/4 to 1/2 cup sugar.
- Bake at 375 degrees for 20 to 25 minutes.
- *Yield: 18 servings.*

Approx Per Serving: Cal 152; Prot 3 g; Carbo 26 g; T Fat 4 g; 24% Calories from Fat; Chol 44 mg; Fiber 1 g; Sod 158 mg

*A*ustralian Pavlova

4 egg whites
1 cup sugar
1 tablespoon cornstarch
1 teaspoon vinegar
1/2 teaspoon vanilla extract
2 cups whipped cream
2 or 3 kiwifruit, peeled,
    sliced

- Preheat oven to 400 degrees.
- Combine egg whites and 1/2 cup sugar in mixer bowl. Beat until soft peaks form. Add remaining 1/2 cup sugar gradually, beating until stiff peaks form. Fold in cornstarch, vinegar and vanilla.
- Shape into 4 inch high circle on greased baking sheet.
- Reduce oven temperature to 250 degrees. Place Pavlova in oven. Bake for 11/2 hours. Let stand on baking sheet in closed oven until cooled.
- Place on serving plate. Cover with whipped cream and fresh kiwifruit slices. Cut into wedges with sharp knife.
- *Yield: 8 servings.*

Approx Per Serving: Cal 229; Prot 3 g; Carbo 31 g; T Fat 11 g; 43% Calories from Fat; Chol 41 mg; Fiber 1 g; Sod 40 mg

$\mathcal{N}$orwegian Cream Cake (Flotekake)

1/2 cup egg yolks
1/2 cup cold water
11/2 cups sugar
1/2 teaspoon vanilla extract
3/4 cup egg whites
3/4 teaspoon cream of tartar
11/2 cups cake flour, sifted
1/4 teaspoon salt
1 (4-ounce) package vanilla
　　instant pudding mix
2 cups milk
2 bananas, sliced
2 cups sliced strawberries
2 cups whipping cream,
　　whipped

- Preheat oven to 325 degrees.
- Beat egg yolks and water in mixer bowl until thick. Beat in sugar gradually. Beat in vanilla.
- Combine egg whites and cream of tartar in large mixer bowl. Beat until very stiff peaks form. Fold in mixture of cake flour and salt alternately with egg yolk mixture.
- Pour batter into 2 ungreased 9-inch round cake pans.
- Bake at 325 degrees for 25 minutes or until cake springs back when lightly touched.
- Cool in pans on wire rack. Remove from pans. Split each layer into 2 layers.
- Prepare pudding mix with milk using package directions.
- Alternate layers of cake, pudding, bananas and strawberries on serving plate. Frost top and side of cake with whipped cream. Garnish with additional whole strawberries.
- Chill for 2 hours before serving.
- *Yield: 16 servings.*

Approx Per Serving: Cal 300; Prot 4 g; Carbo 38 g; T Fat 15 g; 45% Calories from Fat; Chol 125 mg; Fiber 1 g; Sod 201 mg

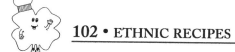

$\mathscr{K}$rumkake

½ cup butter, softened
½ cup sugar
2 eggs
½ teaspoon vanilla extract
1 cup milk
1½ cups flour

- Preheat krumkake iron over medium heat on top of stove.
- Cream butter and sugar in bowl until light and fluffy. Beat in eggs and vanilla.
- Add milk and flour alternately, beating well after each addition.
- Place rounded teaspoonful of dough on preheated krumkake iron; close gently.
- Bake for 15 seconds on each side or until lightly browned. Remove and roll up on krumkake roller or wooden dowel.
- Fill krumkake with whipped cream or sprinkle with sugar just before serving.
- *Yield: 50 (1-krumkake) servings.*

Approx Per Serving: Cal 44; Prot 1 g; Carbo 5 g; T Fat 2 g; 46% Calories from Fat; Chol 14 mg; Fiber <1 g; Sod 24 mg

$\mathscr{S}$wedish Spritz

1 cup butter, softened
1 cup flour
¾ cup sugar
1 egg
½ teaspoon baking powder
⅛ teaspoon salt
1 teaspoon vanilla extract
1 teaspoon almond extract
1½ cups flour

- Preheat oven to 375 degrees.
- Beat butter in mixer bowl for 30 seconds. Add 1 cup flour, sugar, egg, baking powder and salt; beat well. Add flavorings and 1½ cups flour; mix well.
- Press dough through cookie press or drop by teaspoonfuls onto ungreased cookie sheet.
- Bake at 375 degrees for 8 minutes or until edges are firm but not brown. Cool for 1 minute. Remove to wire rack to cool completely.
- *Yield: 36 (1-cookie) servings.*

Approx Per Serving: Cal 95; Prot 1 g; Carbo 11 g; T Fat 5 g; 50% Calories from Fat; Chol 20 mg; Fiber <1 g; Sod 66 mg

Brunches, Breakfasts & Breads

4-H

Gets Crackin'

Heather Smith
Becker County

Bacon and Egg Bake

3 cups unflavored croutons
1½ cups shredded Cheddar
   cheese
1 (4-ounce) can sliced
   mushrooms, drained
⅓ cup crumbled crisp-fried
   bacon
2 tablespoons finely
   chopped green bell pepper
1 tablespoon finely chopped
   onion
2 tablespoons butter
5 eggs
2 cups milk
¼ teaspoon dry mustard
¼ teaspoon pepper
⅛ teaspoon garlic powder

- Preheat oven to 325 degrees.
- Toss croutons with 1 cup cheese. Place in ungreased 8-inch square baking pan. Add layers of mushrooms and bacon.
- Sauté green pepper and onion in butter in skillet until tender but not brown.
- Beat eggs with milk, seasonings and sautéed vegetables. Pour over layers.
- Bake at 325 degrees for 1 hour or until set in center.
- Sprinkle with remaining ½ cup cheese around edge of baking pan. Let stand for 10 minutes before serving.
- *Yield: 6 servings.*

Approx Per Serving: Cal 331; Prot 18 g; Carbo 17 g; T Fat 21 g; 58% Calories from Fat; Chol 229 mg; Fiber 1 g; Sod 531 mg

Breakfast Pizza

1 pound pork sausage
1 (8-count) package
   refrigerator crescent rolls
1 cup frozen loose-pack
   hashed brown potatoes,
   thawed
1 cup shredded Cheddar
   cheese
5 eggs, beaten
¼ cup milk
½ teaspoon salt
⅛ teaspoon pepper
2 tablespoons grated
   Parmesan cheese

- Preheat oven to 375 degrees.
- Brown sausage in skillet, stirring until crumbly; drain.
- Separate roll dough into triangles. Arrange in 12-inch pizza pan with points to center; press to seal edges and form rim. Sprinkle sausage, potatoes and Cheddar cheese over dough.
- Blend eggs with milk, salt and pepper. Pour over layers. Sprinkle with Parmesan cheese.
- Bake at 375 degrees for 25 to 30 minutes or until eggs are set.
- *Yield: 6 servings.*

Approx Per Serving: Cal 426; Prot 21 g; Carbo 25 g; T Fat 27 g; 57% Calories from Fat; Chol 232 mg; Fiber 0 g; Sod 1191 mg

Cheese Strata

12 slices white bread
12 ounces sharp process
  cheese, sliced
1 (10-ounce) package frozen
  chopped broccoli,
  cooked, drained
2 cups chopped cooked ham
6 eggs, beaten
3¹/₂ cups milk
2 tablespoons dried minced
  onion
¹/₂ teaspoon salt
¹/₄ teaspoon dry mustard

- Trim crusts from bread; discard crusts or reserve for another purpose. Cut bread slices with doughnut cutter; set doughnut circles and holes aside. Fit bread scraps into bottom of greased 9x13-inch baking pan.
- Layer cheese, broccoli and ham over bread scraps. Arrange doughnut circles and holes on top.
- Combine eggs with milk, onion, salt and dry mustard in bowl. Pour over layers. Refrigerate, covered, for 6 hours or longer.
- Preheat oven to 325 degrees.
- Bake, uncovered, at 325 degrees for 55 minutes or until set in center. Let stand for 10 minutes before serving.
- *Yield: 12 servings.*

Approx Per Serving: Cal 284; Prot 20 g; Carbo 16 g; T Fat 16 g; 50% Calories from Fat; Chol 155 mg; Fiber 1 g; Sod 976 mg

Egg and Hashed Brown Brunch

2 pounds frozen loose-pack
  hashed brown potatoes
12 eggs
1 cup milk
2 cups shredded Cheddar
  cheese
Salt and pepper to taste

- Spread potatoes in 9x13-inch baking pan sprayed with nonstick cooking spray.
- Beat eggs with milk in bowl. Stir in cheese, salt and pepper. Pour over potatoes.
- Refrigerate, covered, overnight if desired.
- Preheat oven to 350 degrees.
- Bake, covered, at 350 degrees for 45 minutes. Bake, uncovered, for 15 minutes longer.
- *Yield: 12 servings.*

Approx Per Serving: Cal 224; Prot 13 g; Carbo 15 g; T Fat 12 g; 50% Calories from Fat; Chol 235 mg; Fiber 0 g; Sod 206 mg

Hashed Brown Quiche

4 cups loose-pack frozen
  hashed brown potatoes,
  thawed
1½ teaspoons Mrs. Dash
  seasoning
1½ cups shredded
  Monterey Jack cheese
  with jalapeños
1 cup chopped cooked ham
1½ cups shredded Swiss
  cheese
3 eggs, beaten
²/₃ cup half-and-half
½ cup chopped cooked ham

- Preheat oven to 425 degrees.
- Press potatoes over bottom and up side of greased 10-inch pie plate to form crust. Sprinkle with seasoning.
- Bake at 425 degrees for 20 to 25 minutes or until slightly crisp around edge. Reduce oven temperature to 350 degrees.
- Layer Monterey Jack cheese, 1 cup ham and Swiss cheese over potato crust.
- Blend eggs with half-and-half. Pour over layers. Sprinkle remaining ½ cup ham on top.
- Bake at 350 degrees for 20 minutes or until knife inserted in center comes out clean. Let stand for 10 minutes.
- *Yield: 6 servings.*

Approx Per Serving: Cal 448; Prot 30 g; Carbo 27 g; T Fat 24 g; 49% Calories from Fat; Chol 185 mg; Fiber 0 g; Sod 759 mg

Sunday Morning Brunch

1 pound pork sausage
8 slices of bread, cubed
2 cups shredded Cheddar
  cheese
1 (4-ounce) can sliced
  mushrooms, drained
12 eggs
1 cup milk
1 teaspoon salt
1 teaspoon dry mustard
1 (10-ounce) can cream of
  mushroom soup
²/₃ cup milk

- Brown sausage in skillet, stirring until crumbly; drain. Layer bread cubes, sausage, cheese and mushrooms in greased 9x13-inch baking pan.
- Beat eggs with 1 cup milk, salt and dry mustard in medium bowl. Mix soup with ²/₃ cup milk. Stir into egg mixture. Pour egg mixture over layers. Refrigerate overnight.
- Preheat oven to 350 degrees.
- Bake, uncovered, at 350 degrees for 45 minutes or until set.
- *Yield: 8 servings.*

Approx Per Serving: Cal 477; Prot 27 g; Carbo 22 g; T Fat 31 g; 59% Calories from Fat; Chol 378 mg; Fiber 1 g; Sod 1419 mg

Salsa Surprise

3 tablespoons vegetable oil
3 cups loose-pack hashed
   brown potatoes
5 eggs, beaten
1 cup shredded Cheddar
   cheese
1/2 cup salsa

- Preheat skillet.
- Pour oil into hot skillet. Add potatoes. Cook for 5 minutes or until brown on bottom. Turn potatoes over.
- Pour eggs over potatoes. Cook for 5 minutes. Turn potatoes over.
- Sprinkle with cheese. Cook, covered, until cheese melts.
- Serve with salsa spooned over top or on the side.
- *Yield: 4 servings.*

Approx Per Serving: Cal 436; Prot 19 g; Carbo 32 g; T Fat 28 g; 56% Calories from Fat; Chol 295 mg; Fiber 0 g; Sod 406 mg

Little-Bit-of-Everything Granola

6 cups rolled oats
1 1/2 cups wheat germ
1 1/2 cups dry milk powder
1 cup whole wheat flour
1 cup sunflower seeds
1 cup Grapenuts
1/2 cup buckwheat
1 cup vegetable oil
1/2 cup honey
2 tablespoons molasses
1 teaspoon vanilla extract
2 cups raisins
1 cup chopped prunes
1 cup chopped dates
1 cup chopped dried apricots

- Preheat oven to 300 degrees.
- Combine oats, wheat germ, dry milk powder, whole wheat flour, sunflower seeds, Grapenuts and buckwheat in large heavy roaster; mix well.
- Combine oil, honey, molasses and vanilla in saucepan. Heat until well blended, stirring frequently. Pour over oats mixture; mix well.
- Bake at 300 degrees for 45 to 60 minutes, stirring every 15 minutes. Let stand until cool.
- Add raisins, prunes, dates and apricots; mix well.
- Store in airtight container.
- *Yield: 30 (1/2-cup) servings.*

Approx Per Serving: Cal 337; Prot 8 g; Carbo 55 g; T Fat 12 g; 55% Calories from Fat; Chol 1 mg; Fiber 6 g; Sod 49 mg

African Pancake

2 tablespoons butter
2 eggs, beaten
1/2 cup milk
1/2 cup flour

- Preheat oven to 425 degrees.
- Melt butter in 9-inch pie plate in oven.
- Mix eggs with milk and flour until smooth. Pour into prepared pie plate.
- Bake at 425 degrees for 20 minutes.
- Serve with favorite pancake toppings.
- *Yield: 4 servings.*

Approx Per Serving: Cal 164; Prot 6 g; Carbo 14 g; T Fat 9 g; 52% Calories from Fat; Chol 126 mg; Fiber <1 g; Sod 105 mg

Spiced Apple Pancakes

1 egg
1 cup buttermilk
2 tablespoons vegetable oil
1 cup flour
1 tablespoon sugar
1 teaspoon baking powder
1/2 teaspoon baking soda
1/2 teaspoon salt
1/4 teaspoon cinnamon
1/2 cup grated apple

- Preheat griddle.
- Beat egg with buttermilk and oil in medium bowl. Add flour, sugar, baking powder, baking soda, salt and cinnamon; mix well. Stir in apple.
- Ladle 1/4 cup batter at a time onto hot greased griddle. Bake until golden brown on both sides, turning once.
- Serve with Cider Sauce.

Cider Sauce

1 cup sugar
2 tablespoons cornstarch
1/2 teaspoon pumpkin pie spice
2 cups apple cider
2 tablespoons lemon juice
1/4 cup butter

- Mix sugar, cornstarch and spice in saucepan. Stir in cider and lemon juice gradually. Cook over medium heat until mixture thickens and comes to a boil, stirring constantly. Boil for 1 minute; remove from heat.
- Blend in butter.
- *Yield: 12 (1-pancake) servings.*

Approx Per Serving: Cal 206; Prot 2 g; Carbo 34 g; T Fat 7 g; 30% Calories from Fat; Chol 29 mg; Fiber 1 g; Sod 218 mg

Fresh Peach Pancakes

4 eggs
³/₄ cup flour
³/₄ cup milk
¹/₂ teaspoon salt
¹/₄ cup butter
2 cups thinly sliced peaches
¹/₄ cup sugar
¹/₄ teaspoon cinnamon

- Preheat oven to 400 degrees.
- Preheat two 9-inch baking pans in oven.
- Beat eggs with flour, milk and salt in mixer bowl for 1 minute.
- Place 2 tablespoons butter in each hot pan; rotate to coat bottoms and sides.
- Arrange peach slices in pans. Pour batter over slices. Sprinkle mixture of sugar and cinnamon over batter.
- Bake at 400 degrees for 20 to 25 minutes or until puffed and golden.
- May substitute apples, pears or other fresh fruit for peaches. Sprinkle a mixture of brown sugar and cinnamon over top if desired.
- *Yield: 4 servings.*

Approx Per Serving: Cal 374; Prot 11 g; Carbo 43 g; T Fat 18 g; 44% Calories from Fat; Chol 249 mg; Fiber 2 g; Sod 470 mg

Chocolate Ecstasy Waffles

2 eggs, lightly beaten
³/₄ cup milk
6 tablespoons sugar
¹/₂ teaspoon vanilla extract
¹/₂ cup chocolate syrup
¹/₄ cup butter, melted
1¹/₂ cups cake flour, sifted
1 tablespoon baking powder
¹/₂ teaspoon salt

- Preheat waffle iron.
- Combine eggs, milk, sugar and vanilla in bowl. Blend chocolate syrup and butter in small bowl; cool.
- Combine flour, baking powder and salt in medium bowl. Add egg mixture and chocolate mixture; mix until smooth.
- Bake on hot waffle iron according to manufacturer's instructions.
- *Yield: 5 (1-waffle) servings.*

Approx Per Serving: Cal 377; Prot 6 g; Carbo 54 g; T Fat 17 g; 39% Calories from Fat; Chol 115 mg; Fiber 1 g; Sod 683 mg

Three-Grain Belgian Waffles

2 egg whites
1¼ cups flour
1 cup yellow cornmeal
½ cup oat bran
¼ cup sugar
1 envelope dry yeast
2 egg yolks
⅓ cup vegetable oil
1¾ cups warm milk
1 teaspoon vanilla extract
Apricot Syrup (recipe below)

- Beat egg whites in mixer bowl until soft peaks form; set aside.
- Combine flour, cornmeal, oat bran, sugar and dry yeast in bowl. Beat egg yolks with oil, milk and vanilla. Add to dry ingredients; beat until smooth. Fold in beaten egg whites. Batter will be thin.
- Let stand at room temperature for 1 hour. Batter will thicken while standing.
- Preheat waffle iron.
- Ladle ¾ to 1 cup batter onto waffle iron. Bake until golden brown.
- Serve with Apricot Syrup.

Apricot Syrup

1 cup apricot nectar
⅓ cup coarsely chopped
   dried apricots
2 to 3 tablespoons honey
2 teaspoons cornstarch

- Combine apricot nectar, apricots, honey and cornstarch in saucepan; mix well.
- Cook over medium heat until mixture thickens and comes to a boil, stirring constantly.
- *Yield: 6 (1-waffle) servings.*

Approx Per Serving: Cal 459; Prot 9 g; Carbo 76 g; T Fat 15 g; 28% Calories from Fat; Chol 71 mg; Fiber 5 g; Sod 26 mg

Substitute applesauce for butter or margarine to reduce fat, calories and cholesterol in recipes. Applesauce adds moisture and stability when used as a fat substitute in recipes containing other moist ingredients such as skim milk or fresh fruit.

Sour Cream Apple Coffee Cake

1 cup sugar
1/2 cup butter, softened
2 eggs
1 cup sour cream
1 teaspoon vanilla extract
2 cups flour
1 teaspoon baking powder
1 teaspoon baking soda
1/8 teaspoon salt
1 large apple, peeled,
    chopped
2/3 cup packed brown sugar
2 tablespoons flour
1 teaspoon cinnamon
2 tablespoons butter

- Preheat oven to 350 degrees.
- Cream first 2 ingredients in mixer bowl. Beat in eggs, sour cream and vanilla. Stir in mixture of flour, baking powder, baking soda and salt. Stir in apple.
- Mix brown sugar, 2 tablespoons flour and cinnamon in small bowl. Cut in 2 tablespoons butter until crumbly.
- Layer batter and brown sugar mixture half at a time in greased and floured 8-inch square baking pan.
- Bake at 350 degrees for 50 to 60 minutes or until coffee cake tests done.
- *Yield: 6 servings.*

Approx Per Serving: Cal 658; Prot 8 g; Carbo 93 g; T Fat 29 g; 40% Calories from Fat; Chol 139 mg; Fiber 2 g; Sod 482 mg

Lacy Apple Scones

1 1/4 cups flour
3 tablespoons brown sugar
1 teaspoon baking powder
1/4 teaspoon baking soda
1/4 teaspoon salt
1/4 cup butter
1/4 cup light sour cream or
    plain yogurt
1 egg, beaten
1 cup finely chopped apples
1/3 cup chopped pecans
1 tablespoon light sour
    cream or plain yogurt
1 tablespoon brown sugar
1 1/2 teaspoons cinnamon

- Preheat oven to 400 degrees.
- Combine first 5 ingredients in bowl. Cut in butter until crumbly.
- Add sour cream and egg; mix well. Add apples and pecans. Turn onto lightly floured surface. Knead lightly 5 times.
- Pat into circle on greased baking sheet. Cut into 8 wedges with floured knife; do not separate.
- Brush with 1 tablespoon sour cream; sprinkle with mixture of brown sugar and cinnamon.
- Bake at 400 degrees for 15 minutes.
- *Yield: 8 servings.*

Approx Per Serving: Cal 210; Prot 4 g; Carbo 25 g; T Fat 11 g; 47% Calories from Fat; Chol 46 mg; Fiber 1 g; Sod 206 mg

Lazy Lady Doughnuts

3 cups flour
1 cup sugar
2 teaspoons baking powder
1/2 teaspoon salt
1/2 teaspoon nutmeg
2 eggs
1 cup milk
Oil for deep frying

- Sift flour, sugar, baking powder, salt and nutmeg into bowl. Beat eggs with milk. Add to dry ingredients; mix well.
- Preheat oil to 375 degrees.
- Drop batter by teaspoonfuls into hot deep oil. Fry for 3 to 5 minutes or until golden brown on all sides, turning as necessary; drain on paper towels.
- Toss cooled doughnuts in confectioners' sugar or granulated sugar to coat.
- *Yield: 48 (1-doughnut) servings.*

Approx Per Serving: Cal 51; Prot 1 g; Carbo 10 g; T Fat <1 g; 8% Calories from Fat; Chol 10 mg; Fiber <1 g; Sod 41 mg
Nutritional information does not include oil for deep frying.

Honey Cinnamon French Toast

1/4 cup butter
2 tablespoons honey
1 teaspoon cinnamon
3 eggs, beaten
1/2 cup orange juice
6 bread slices

- Preheat oven to 400 degrees.
- Melt butter in 9x13-inch baking pan in oven. Drizzle honey over butter; sprinkle with cinnamon.
- Mix eggs with orange juice in shallow dish. Dip bread slices in egg mixture; arrange in prepared baking pan. Drizzle remaining egg mixture over bread.
- Bake at 400 degrees for 20 minutes or until browned.
- Invert slices onto plates. Serve with honey-marbled yogurt.
- *Yield: 6 (1-slice) servings.*

Approx Per Serving: Cal 201; Prot 6 g; Carbo 20 g; T Fat 11 g; 50% Calories from Fat; Chol 128 mg; Fiber 1 g; Sod 253 mg

Garlic Cheese Bread

2½ cups milk
½ cup packed brown sugar
1 tablespoon salt
2 teaspoons garlic powder
¼ cup olive oil
4 teaspoons dry yeast
1 teaspoon sugar
1 cup warm water
4 eggs
7½ to 8½ cups flour
4 cups shredded Cheddar
   cheese
2 cups shredded Monterey
   Jack cheese
1 egg yolk, beaten

- Heat milk in medium saucepan until foamy; remove from heat. Add brown sugar, salt, garlic powder and olive oil; mix until brown sugar dissolves. Pour into large bowl. Let stand until cooled to lukewarm.
- Dissolve yeast and sugar in warm water in bowl. Let stand for 5 to 7 minutes.
- Beat eggs 1 at a time into cooled milk mixture. Add 4 cups flour and yeast mixture; mix until smooth. Add cheeses; mix well.
- Add enough remaining flour gradually to make a soft dough. Turn onto floured surface.
- Knead for 12 to 15 minutes, adding flour as necessary. Shape into ball; place in greased bowl, turning to coat surface.
- Let rise, covered, in warm place for 1½ hours or until doubled in bulk.
- Punch dough down. Knead for 5 minutes. Divide into 2 portions. Divide each portion into 3 portions. Roll each into 1-inch diameter rope. Braid 3 ropes together; seal ends together and place on greased baking sheet.
- Let rise, loosely covered, for 30 to 40 minutes or almost doubled in bulk.
- Preheat oven to 350 degrees.
- Brush loaves with egg yolk. Bake at 350 degrees for 15 minutes. Cover with foil.
- Reduce oven temperature to 325 degrees. Bake at 325 degrees for 30 minutes. Remove to wire racks to cool.
- *Yield: 24 (1-slice) servings.*

Approx Per Serving: Cal 330; Prot 13 g; Carbo 40 g; T Fat 13 g; 35% Calories from Fat; Chol 75 mg; Fiber 1 g; Sod 444 mg

Oat Corn Bread

1³/4 cups flour
1 cup cornmeal
1 cup rolled oats
1 tablespoon sugar
2 teaspoons baking powder
1¹/2 teaspoons baking soda
¹/2 teaspoon salt
2 cups buttermilk
2 eggs, beaten
¹/4 cup vegetable oil
1 teaspoon shortening

- Preheat oven to 375 degrees. Place heavy 10-inch ovenproof skillet in oven.
- Combine flour, cornmeal, oats, sugar, baking powder, baking soda and salt in bowl; mix well. Stir in buttermilk, eggs and oil.
- Melt 1 teaspoon shortening in hot skillet, tilting to coat bottom and side of skillet. Pour batter into hot skillet.
- Bake at 375 degrees for 30 to 35 minutes or until corn bread tests done.
- *Yield: 8 servings.*

Approx Per Serving: Cal 317; Prot 10 g; Carbo 46 g; T Fat 10 g; 30% Calories from Fat; Chol 55 mg; Fiber 3 g; Sod 451 mg

Apricot Bread

1 cup chopped dried apricots
³/4 cup hot water
1 cup sugar
2 tablespoons butter, softened
1 egg
2 cups flour
1 teaspoon salt
1 teaspoon baking powder
¹/4 teaspoon baking soda
¹/2 cup orange juice
¹/2 cup chopped pecans

- Preheat oven to 350 degrees.
- Place apricots in small bowl. Pour hot water over apricots. Let stand for 30 minutes to soften. Drain, reserving ¹/4 cup liquid.
- Combine sugar, butter and egg in mixer bowl; beat until well mixed. Mix flour, salt, baking powder and baking soda. Add flour mixture alternately with reserved apricot liquid and orange juice to sugar mixture, mixing well after each addition. Stir in apricots and pecans. Pour into greased and floured 5x9-inch loaf pan.
- Bake at 350 degrees for 55 to 60 minutes or until loaf tests done. Remove from pan to wire rack to cool.
- *Yield: 18 (1-slice) servings.*

Approx Per Serving: Cal 169; Prot 3 g; Carbo 32 g; T Fat 4 g; 21% Calories from Fat; Chol 15 mg; Fiber 2 g; Sod 167 mg

Maple Syrup Egg Bread

4 teaspoons dry yeast
2¼ cups warm water
⅓ cup maple syrup
3 tablespoons butter,
    softened
1½ teaspoons salt
1 egg, lightly beaten
2 tablespoons wheat germ
½ cup nonfat dry milk
    powder
2¾ to 3 cups bread flour
2¾ to 3 cups whole wheat
    flour

- Dissolve yeast in warm water in large bowl. Add maple syrup. Let stand for 5 minutes. Add butter, salt, egg and wheat germ; mix well. Beat in milk powder and bread flour.
- Add enough whole wheat flour to make a medium dough; mix well. Turn onto floured pastry cloth; dough may be sticky. Cover with oiled bowl. Let rest for 10 minutes.
- Knead for 5 minutes. Place in oiled bowl, turning to coat surface.
- Let rise, covered with damp cloth, in warm place for 30 to 45 minutes or until doubled in bulk.
- Punch dough down. Shape into 2 loaves; place in greased 5x9-inch loaf pans.
- Let rise for 15 minutes or until almost doubled in bulk.
- Preheat oven to 375 degrees.
- Bake at 375 degrees for 35 to 45 minutes or until loaves sound hollow when tapped. Remove to wire racks to cool. Brush tops with butter if desired.
- Loaves will slice best if an electric knife is used.
- *Yield: 24 (1-slice) servings.*

Approx Per Serving: Cal 143; Prot 5 g; Carbo 27 g; T Fat 2 g; 13% Calories from Fat; Chol 13 mg; Fiber 3 g; Sod 160 mg

Bake bread or rolls until almost done but not yet starting to brown and cool on wire rack. Store in plastic bags in refrigerator for up to 1 week. Brown in oven at serving time.

Swedish Rye Bread

1 envelope dry yeast
1/2 cup warm water
2 cups sifted rye flour
2 teaspoons salt
3/4 cup molasses
1/3 cup shortening
2 cups boiling water
6 to 6 1/2 cups sifted
    all-purpose flour
1 egg, slightly beaten

- Dissolve yeast in warm water in bowl.
- Combine rye flour, salt, molasses and shortening in a large bowl. Add boiling water; mix well. Let stand until cooled to lukewarm.
- Add dissolved yeast; mix well. Add enough all-purpose flour to make a soft dough, mixing well.
- Turn onto a floured surface. Let rest, covered, for 10 minutes.
- Knead for 10 minutes or until smooth and elastic. Place in a greased bowl, turning to coat surface.
- Let rise, covered, in a warm place for 1 1/2 to 2 hours or until doubled in bulk.
- Punch dough down.
- Let rise, covered, in a warm place for 30 minutes or until almost doubled in bulk.
- Turn onto a lightly floured surface. Divide into 3 portions. Shape each portion into a ball. Let rest for 15 minutes.
- Shape each ball into a round loaf. Place on lightly greased baking sheets.
- Let rise, covered, for 1 hour or until almost doubled in bulk.
- Preheat oven to 350 degrees.
- Brush loaves with beaten egg. Bake at 350 degrees for 35 to 40 minutes or until loaves test done.
- *Yield: 36 (1-slice) servings.*

Approx Per Serving: Cal 136; Prot 3 g; Carbo 26 g; T Fat 2 g; 16% Calories from Fat; Chol 6 mg; Fiber 2 g; Sod 123 mg

Microwave Shortcut Banana Bread

2 cups baking mix
1/2 cup packed brown sugar
3 tablespoons flour
2 teaspoons instant coffee
    powder
1/4 cup milk
1 egg, beaten
2/3 cup mashed banana
1/2 cup snipped dates
1/3 cup chopped walnuts

- Grease 5x9-inch glass loaf pan; line bottom with waxed paper.
- Combine baking mix, brown sugar and flour in bowl; mix well.
- Dissolve coffee powder in milk in small bowl. Add egg and banana; mix well.
- Add to dry ingredients all at once; mix well. Stir in dates and walnuts. Pour into prepared loaf pan.
- Microwave on Medium for 12 minutes turning pan once.
- Microwave on High for 2 minutes or until wooden pick inserted in center comes out clean.
- Let stand for 10 minutes. Remove from pan to wire rack to cool completely.
- *Yield: 12 (1-slice) servings.*

Approx Per Serving: Cal 179; Prot 3 g; Carbo 30 g; T Fat 6 g; 28% Calories from Fat; Chol 19 mg; Fiber 1 g; Sod 253 mg

Fat-Free Bran Muffins

1 1/4 cups oat bran
1 cup flour
1 tablespoon baking powder
1/4 cup packed brown sugar
2 tablespoons corn syrup
2 egg whites
1 1/4 cups skim milk
1/2 cup chopped dried
    apricots

- Preheat oven to 425 degrees.
- Combine oat bran, flour, baking powder and brown sugar in a mixer bowl.
- Add corn syrup, egg whites and skim milk. Beat at low speed until well blended.
- Stir in apricots.
- Spoon into greased muffin cups.
- Bake at 425 degrees for 13 to 15 minutes or until golden brown.
- *Yield: 12 (1-muffin) servings.*

Approx Per Serving: Cal 123; Prot 5 g; Carbo 29 g; T Fat 1 g; 6% Calories from Fat; Chol <1 mg; Fiber 3 g; Sod 137 mg

Peanut Butter Bran Muffins

1 cup flour
1/3 cup packed light brown
  sugar
2 teaspoons baking powder
1/2 teaspoon salt
1 cup bran cereal
1 cup raisins
1 egg, beaten
1 cup milk
1/2 cup chunky peanut butter
3 tablespoons vegetable oil

- Preheat oven to 400 degrees.
- Combine flour, brown sugar, baking powder and salt in bowl. Add bran cereal and raisins; mix well.
- Blend egg with milk in small bowl. Add peanut butter and oil; mix well. Add to dry ingredients; mix just until moistened.
- Fill greased muffin cups 2/3 full.
- Bake at 400 degrees for 15 minutes or until muffins test done. Remove to wire rack to cool.
- *Yield: 12 (1-muffin) servings.*

Approx Per Serving: Cal 225; Prot 6 g; Carbo 31 g; T Fat 10 g; 38% Calories from Fat; Chol 20 mg; Fiber 4 g; Sod 252 mg

Chocolate Chipper Muffins

1 cup flour
2/3 cup uncooked chocolate
  Malt-O-Meal cereal
1/2 cup packed brown sugar
1 tablespoon baking powder
1/2 teaspoon salt
1 egg, beaten
1/2 cup milk
1/4 cup vegetable oil
1/2 cup chocolate chips

- Preheat oven to 375 degrees.
- Combine flour, cereal, brown sugar, baking powder and salt in bowl; mix well.
- Blend egg with milk and oil. Add to dry ingredients; mix just until moistened. Stir in chocolate chips.
- Spoon into paper-lined muffin cups.
- Bake at 375 degrees for 15 to 18 minutes or until muffins test done.
- Serve as muffins or as cupcakes.
- *Yield: 12 (1-muffin) servings.*

Approx Per Serving: Cal 192; Prot 3 g; Carbo 29 g; T Fat 8 g; 35% Calories from Fat; Chol 19 mg; Fiber 1 g; Sod 189 mg

Caramel Rolls

2 envelopes dry yeast
1/4 cup lukewarm water
2 cups milk, scalded
1/3 cup shortening
1/2 cup sugar
2 eggs, beaten
7 cups flour
1 teaspoon salt
1 cup packed brown sugar
1/3 cup butter
2 tablespoons light corn
   syrup
1 tablespoon water
1/4 cup (or more) butter,
   softened
1/2 cup (or more) packed
   brown sugar
Cinnamon to taste

- Dissolve yeast in lukewarm water.
- Combine hot milk and shortening in large bowl. Add sugar. Let stand until cooled to lukewarm.
- Add eggs, yeast and half the flour; beat until smooth and elastic. Add salt and enough remaining flour to make a medium dough. Let rest for 10 minutes.
- Turn onto floured surface. Knead until smooth and elastic. Place in greased bowl, turning to coat surface. Let rise, covered, in warm place until doubled in bulk.
- Combine 1 cup brown sugar, 1/3 cup butter, corn syrup and 1 tablespoon water in saucepan. Bring to a boil, stirring constantly. Boil for no more than 1 minute. Divide between 2 buttered 9x13-inch baking pans. Set aside.
- Divide dough into 2 portions. Roll 1 portion into rectangle. Spread with half the softened butter. Sprinkle with half the mixture of 1/2 cup brown sugar and a generous amount of cinnamon. Roll as for jelly roll. Cut into 3/4-inch slices. Arrange in one of the prepared baking pans. Repeat with remaining dough, butter and brown sugar mixture. Let rise, covered, until doubled in bulk.
- Preheat oven to 350 degrees.
- Bake at 350 degrees for 20 to 25 minutes or until golden brown. Invert onto serving platters or baking sheets.
- *Yield: 30 (1-roll) servings.*

Approx Per Serving: Cal 225; Prot 4 g; Carbo 36 g; T Fat 7 g; 28% Calories from Fat; Chol 26 mg; Fiber 1 g; Sod 126 mg

VEGETABLES & SIDE DISHES

Gretchen M. Klaus
Olmsted County

Baked Pinto Beans

4 cups dried pinto beans
1 pound bacon, crisp-fried,
  crumbled
2 (10-ounce) cans tomato
  soup
2 cups water
1 cup catsup
1 medium onion, chopped
1/2 cup packed brown sugar
1/4 cup molasses
1/4 cup white vinegar
2 teaspoons salt
1 teaspoon pepper

- Sort and rinse beans.
- Soak in enough water to cover in stockpot for 8 to 12 hours; drain.
- Combine beans with enough water to cover in stockpot.
- Cook over medium heat for 2 hours, stirring occasionally. Drain and rinse.
- Preheat oven to 325 degrees.
- Combine beans, bacon, tomato soup, 2 cups water, catsup, onion, brown sugar, molasses, vinegar, salt and pepper in bowl; mix well. Spoon into baking pan.
- Bake at 325 degrees for 2 hours.
- *Yield: 16 servings.*

Approx Per Serving: Cal 284; Prot 14 g; Carbo 47 g; T Fat 5 g; 16% Calories from Fat; Chol 7 mg; Fiber 11 g; Sod 858 mg

Broccoli Casserole

2 tablespoons finely
  chopped onion
2 tablespoons butter
1 tablespoon flour
1/4 cup water
1 (10-ounce) package frozen
  chopped broccoli, thawed
4 ounces Cheez Whiz
1 egg, beaten
2 or 3 slices crisp-fried
  bacon, crumbled
1/2 cup toasted croutons
2 tablespoons butter

- Preheat oven to 350 degrees.
- Sauté onion in 2 tablespoons butter in saucepan until tender. Add flour, stirring until mixed. Stir in water.
- Cook until thickened, stirring constantly.
- Add broccoli and Cheez Whiz; mix well.
- Cook until broccoli is tender.
- Add egg and bacon; mix well.
- Spoon into baking dish. Sprinkle with croutons; dot with 2 tablespoons butter.
- Bake at 350 degrees for 30 minutes.
- *Yield: 4 servings.*

Approx Per Serving: Cal 274; Prot 11 g; Carbo 11 g; T Fat 22 g; 69% Calories from Fat; Chol 104 mg; Fiber 2 g; Sod 632 mg

*M*icrowave Broccoli and Carrot Casserole

1¹/₂ cups sliced carrots
1 medium onion, sliced
1 (10-ounce) package frozen
   broccoli
3 tablespoons butter
3 tablespoons flour
¹/₄ teaspoon salt
Pepper to taste
1¹/₂ cups milk
1 cup shredded American
   cheese
1 (6-ounce) can
   French-fried onions

- Combine carrots, onion and several tablespoons water in glass baking dish.
- Microwave, covered, on High for 6 to 8 minutes or until tender; drain.
- Microwave broccoli with a small amount of water in glass baking dish, covered, on High for 5 minutes; drain.
- Microwave butter in glass baking dish on High until melted. Blend in flour, salt and pepper. Stir in milk gradually. Microwave on High for 3 to 4 minutes or until thickened, stirring 3 to 4 times.
- Blend in cheese. Layer carrot mixture, cheese mixture and broccoli in lightly greased 7x11-inch glass baking dish; top with onions.
- Microwave on High for 5 minutes.
- *Yield: 4 servings.*

Approx Per Serving: Cal 563; Prot 16 g; Carbo 35 g;
   T Fat 40 g; 64% Calories from Fat; Chol 63 mg;
   Fiber 4 g; Sod 976 mg

*B*roccoli-Cauliflower-Bean Medley

1 (10-ounce) package frozen
   broccoli
1 (10-ounce) package frozen
   cauliflower
1 (10-ounce) package frozen
   green beans
1 (10-ounce) can cream of
   mushroom soup
1 (8-ounce) jar Cheez Whiz
1 cup bread crumbs

- Place broccoli, cauliflower and green beans in colander. Let stand until partially thawed.
- Place in baking dish. Toss vegetables lightly to mix.
- Spread with mixture of soup and Cheez Whiz; sprinkle with bread crumbs.
- Bake at 350 degrees for 45 minutes.
- *Yield: 6 servings.*

Approx Per Serving: Cal 262; Prot 12 g; Carbo 26 g;
   T Fat 13 g; 43% Calories from Fat; Chol 21 mg;
   Fiber 5 g; Sod 1088 mg

Broccoli and Rice Bake

1 cup chopped broccoli
1/2 cup chopped onion
1 1/2 cups cooked brown rice
3/4 cup shredded low-fat
    Cheddar cheese
2 egg whites, slightly beaten
1/8 teaspoon salt
1 egg
2 egg whites
1/4 cup skim milk
1/2 teaspoon Italian
    seasoning
1/8 teaspoon pepper
1/8 teaspoon salt

• Preheat oven to 375 degrees.
• Combine broccoli, onion and several tablespoons of water in microwave-safe dish. Microwave, covered, until vegetables are tender-crisp; drain.
• Combine brown rice, cheese, 2 egg whites and 1/8 teaspoon salt in bowl; mix well. Press evenly over bottom and side of 9-inch round baking dish.
• Beat egg and 2 egg whites lightly in bowl. Stir in skim milk, Italian seasoning, pepper, 1/8 teaspoon salt and broccoli mixture.
• Spoon over prepared layer.
• Bake at 375 degrees for 30 minutes or until set.
• *Yield: 4 servings.*

Approx Per Serving: Cal 188; Prot 14 g; Carbo 22 g; T Fat 5 g; 24% Calories from Fat; Chol 65 mg; Fiber 2 g; Sod 387 mg

Scalloped Cabbage

1 small head cabbage,
    chopped
3 tablespoons butter
Salt and pepper to taste
1 (8-ounce) package
    Velveeta cheese slices
3 cups saltine cracker crumbs
1 cup half-and-half
1 egg, beaten

• Preheat oven to 350 degrees.
• Cook cabbage with butter, salt and pepper in just enough water to cover in saucepan until tender; drain.
• Layer cabbage, cheese and crumbs 1/2 at a time in buttered 3-quart baking dish.
• Whisk half-and-half and egg in bowl. Pour over prepared layers.
• Bake, covered, at 350 degrees for 30 minutes; remove cover. Bake for 10 minutes longer.
• *Yield: 8 servings.*

Approx Per Serving: Cal 351; Prot 12 g; Carbo 29 g; T Fat 21 g; 54% Calories from Fat; Chol 76 mg; Fiber 2 g; Sod 894 mg

Baked Potato Chunks

1/4 cup flour
1/4 cup grated Parmesan
  cheese
3/4 teaspoon salt
1/8 teaspoon pepper
6 large potatoes, cut into
  quarters
1/3 cup butter, melted

- Preheat oven to 375 degrees.
- Mix flour, cheese, salt and pepper in large bowl with cover or plastic bag. Add potatoes; shake to coat. Arrange potatoes in butter in 9x13-inch baking pan.
- Bake at 375 degrees for 1 hour; turn once.
- *Yield: 6 servings.*

Approx Per Serving: Cal 299; Prot 6 g; Carbo 44 g; T Fat 12 g; 35% Calories from Fat; Chol 31 mg; Fiber 3 g; Sod 457 mg

Cheesy Mashed Potato and Spinach Bake

6 cups mashed potatoes
1 (10-ounce) package frozen
  chopped spinach,
  thawed, drained
1 cup sour cream with chives
1 (8-ounce) jar Cheez Whiz
1/4 cup butter
1/2 teaspoon salt
1/4 teaspoon pepper
1 cup shredded Cheddar
  cheese

- Preheat oven to 400 degrees.
- Combine all ingredients except Cheddar cheese in bowl; mix well. Spoon into greased 2-quart baking dish.
- Bake at 400 degrees for 15 minutes; sprinkle with Cheddar cheese.
- Bake for 5 minutes longer.
- *Yield: 8 servings.*

Approx Per Serving: Cal 381; Prot 13 g; Carbo 33 g; T Fat 24 g; 53% Calories from Fat; Chol 62 mg; Fiber 4 g; Sod 1178 mg

Heavenly Microwave Potatoes

2 medium potatoes, sliced
2 tablespoons sliced green
  onions
2 tablespoons chopped
  green bell pepper
1/4 cup taco sauce
1/3 cup shredded American
  cheese

- Microwave potatoes, green onions and green pepper in covered glass baking dish for 7 to 10 minutes or until tender.
- Drizzle with taco sauce; sprinkle with cheese. Microwave for 30 to 60 seconds or until cheese melts.
- *Yield: 4 servings.*

Approx Per Serving: Cal 99; Prot 4 g; Carbo 15 g; T Fat 3 g; 29% Calories from Fat; Chol 9 mg; Fiber 1 g; Sod 202 mg

Parmesan Potato Wedges

3 medium potatoes, cut into
    quarters
3 tablespoons vegetable oil
1/2 cup fine dry bread crumbs
3 tablespoons grated
    Parmesan cheese
Salt and pepper to taste

- Preheat oven to 350 degrees.
- Dip potatoes in oil; coat with bread crumbs. Sprinkle with cheese. Season with salt and pepper.
- Arrange in single layer in greased 9x13-inch baking pan.
- Bake at 350 degrees for 1 hour or until potatoes are tender.
- *Yield: 6 servings.*

Approx Per Serving: Cal 164; Prot 4 g; Carbo 19 g; T Fat 8 g; 45% Calories from Fat; Chol 2 mg; Fiber 1 g; Sod 133 mg

Potato Planks

3 medium potatoes, cut
    lengthwise into eighths
1 teaspoon salt
1/2 teaspoon sugar
1/2 teaspoon paprika
1/4 teaspoon dry mustard
1/8 teaspoon garlic powder

- Arrange potatoes in single layer in 10x15-inch baking pan sprayed with nonstick cooking spray.
- Spray potatoes with nonstick cooking spray.
- Combine salt, sugar, paprika, dry mustard and garlic powder in bowl; mix well.
- Sprinkle potatoes with 1/2 of the salt mixture.
- Broil 3 inches from heat source for 10 minutes or until potatoes begin to bubble.
- Turn potatoes; spray with nonstick cooking spray. Sprinkle with remaining salt mixture.
- Broil for 5 minutes or until brown and tender.
- *Yield: 6 servings.*

Approx Per Serving: Cal 59; Prot 1 g; Carbo 14 g; T Fat <1 g; 2% Calories from Fat; Chol 0 mg; Fiber 1 g; Sod 358 mg

Spinach and Rice Casserole

1 cup chopped onion
1 clove of garlic, minced
2 tablespoons butter
1 (10-ounce) package frozen
    spinach, thawed, drained
4 cups cooked rice
1¹/2 cups shredded Cheddar
    cheese
¹/2 cup milk
1 egg, beaten
¹/4 teaspoon pepper
Nutmeg to taste
Cayenne to taste
¹/2 cup grated Parmesan
    cheese

- Preheat oven to 350 degrees.
- Sauté onion and garlic in butter in skillet until onion is tender. Stir in spinach.
- Cook for 2 minutes, stirring frequently.
- Combine spinach mixture, rice, Cheddar cheese, milk, egg, pepper, nutmeg and cayenne in bowl; mix well.
- Spoon into 9x9-inch baking pan; sprinkle with Parmesan cheese.
- Bake at 350 degrees for 30 minutes.
- *Yield: 8 servings.*

Approx Per Serving: Cal 324; Prot 15 g; Carbo 34 g; T Fat 14 g; 39% Calories from Fat; Chol 66 mg; Fiber 2 g; Sod 390 mg

Fresh Vegetable Medley

2 cups sliced celery
2 cups green bell pepper
    strips
2 cups sugar snap peas
2 cups coarsely chopped
    tomatoes
1¹/2 cups thinly sliced onions
1¹/2 cups carrot strips
1 (8-ounce) can sliced water
    chestnuts, drained
¹/4 cup melted butter
3 tablespoons tapioca
1 tablespoon sugar
1 teaspoon salt
¹/2 teaspoon pepper

- Preheat oven to 350 degrees.
- Combine celery, green pepper, sugar snap peas, tomatoes, onions, carrots, water chestnuts, butter, tapioca, sugar, salt and pepper in bowl; mix well.
- Spoon into 2¹/2- or 3-quart baking dish.
- Bake, covered, at 350 degrees for 45 minutes; remove cover.
- Bake for 15 minutes longer.
- May add or substitute any fresh vegetables and herbs desired.
- *Yield: 8 servings.*

Approx Per Serving: Cal 146; Prot 3 g; Carbo 21 g; T Fat 6 g; 36% Calories from Fat; Chol 16 mg; Fiber 5 g; Sod 365 mg

$\mathcal{S}$low-Cooker Stuffing

Using a slow cooker to cook the stuffing allows for additional baking space in the oven for the turkey and other holiday dishes.

8 cups dry bread cubes
5 cups herb-seasoned
  stuffing
2 cups chopped onions
2 cups chopped celery
1/4 cup chopped fresh parsley
1/2 cup margarine
4 cups chicken or turkey
  broth
1 egg, beaten

- Combine bread cubes and stuffing in bowl; mix well.
- Sauté onions, celery and parsley in margarine in skillet. Pour over bread cube mixture, tossing lightly.
- Stir in broth. Add egg; mix well.
- Pack lightly into slow cooker.
- Cook, covered, on High for 45 minutes; reduce temperature to Low.
- Cook, covered, for 4 to 5 hours or until of the desired consistency.
- *Yield: 12 servings.*

Approx Per Serving: Cal 291; Prot 8 g; Carbo 41 g; T Fat 11 g; 33% Calories from Fat; Chol 18 mg; Fiber 2 g; Sod 975 mg

$\mathcal{W}$ild Rice Stuffing

12 cups bread cubes
1 cup chopped pecans
1 teaspoon sage
1 teaspoon thyme
1/2 teaspoon pepper
2 cups chopped celery
2 cups chopped onions
8 ounces mushrooms, sliced
1/2 cup butter
1 (6-ounce) package long
  grain and wild rice,
  cooked
1/2 cup butter
2 cups chicken broth

- Combine bread cubes, pecans, sage, thyme and pepper in large bowl; mix well.
- Sauté celery, onions and mushrooms in 1/2 cup butter in skillet until vegetables are tender. Stir into bread cube mixture.
- Sauté rice in 1/2 cup butter in skillet. Add broth; mix well.
- Simmer until of the desired consistency. Stir into bread cube mixture.
- May use to stuff 20- to 24-pound turkey.
- *Yield: 24 servings.*

Approx Per Serving: Cal 212; Prot 4 g; Carbo 20 g; T Fat 13 g; 55% Calories from Fat; Chol 21 mg; Fiber 2 g; Sod 399 mg

Macaroni and Cheese

2½ cups elbow macaroni, cooked, drained
1 (10-ounce) can cream of mushroom soup
2 cups shredded Cheddar cheese
1 cup milk
⅓ cup mayonnaise-type salad dressing
1 small onion, chopped
¼ teaspoon lemon and herb seasoning
1 cup herb-seasoned bread crumbs

- Preheat oven to 400 degrees.
- Combine macaroni, soup, cheese, milk, salad dressing, onion and lemon and herb seasoning in bowl; mix well.
- Spoon into 2-quart baking dish; sprinkle with bread crumbs.
- Bake at 400 degrees for 20 to 25 minutes or until brown and bubbly.
- *Yield: 6 servings.*

Approx Per Serving: Cal 507; Prot 20 g; Carbo 55 g; T Fat 23 g; 41% Calories from Fat; Chol 49 mg; Fiber 1 g; Sod 1203 mg

Tangy Pasta Nests with Vegetables

This recipe won first place in the 1995 McLeod County Foods Review.

3 tablespoons butter or margarine, melted
2 tablespoons flour
1 teaspoon grated lemon rind
Pepper to taste
¾ cup milk
2 cups frozen cauliflower, broccoli and carrots, cooked, drained
1 cup sour cream
6 ounces fettuccini, cooked, drained
1 egg, beaten
¼ cup grated Parmesan cheese

- Preheat oven to 350 degrees.
- Blend butter, flour, lemon rind and pepper in saucepan. Stir in milk. Cook until thickened, stirring constantly. Stir in vegetables and sour cream. Heat just to boiling point, stirring frequently. Spoon half the vegetable sauce into 8x12-inch baking dish.
- Toss fettuccini with egg and cheese. Using a long tined fork, twirl a few strands of fettuccini around tines; remove pasta from fork. Stand pasta upright in baking dish in shape of nest. Repeat for 6 portions of 3 nests each. Top with remaining vegetable sauce.
- Bake, covered, at 350 degrees for 20 minutes or until heated through.
- *Yield: 6 servings.*

Approx Per Serving: Cal 315; Prot 10 g; Carbo 30 g; T Fat 18 g; 49% Calories from Fat; Chol 75 mg; Fiber 2 g; Sod 201 mg

Homemade Noodles or Dumplings

2 cups flour
4 eggs, beaten
3 tablespoons water
1 teaspoon salt
2 quarts chicken broth

- Combine flour, eggs, water and salt in bowl and mix well; dough will be sticky.
- Bring chicken broth to a boil in stockpot.
- Scoop up dough 1 tablespoon at a time. Cut small pieces of dough into broth with table knife, dipping knife into broth occasionally to prevent dough from sticking to knife.
- Cook, covered, for 30 minutes or until noodles are tender.
- *Yield: 8 servings.*

Approx Per Serving: Cal 190; Prot 11 g; Carbo 25 g; T Fat 4 g; 21% Calories from Fat; Chol 106 mg; Fiber 1 g; Sod 1075 mg

Confetti Spaghetti

6 cups water
5 ounces spaghetti
1 clove of garlic, minced
2 teaspoons olive oil
1 cup thinly sliced carrot
1 teaspoon basil
1/8 teaspoon salt
Pepper to taste
1 1/2 tablespoons butter
1 cup chopped fresh broccoli
Salt to taste
Nutmeg to taste
1/3 cup chicken broth
2 tablespoons grated
    Parmesan cheese

- Bring water to a boil in saucepan. Add spaghetti; reduce heat.
- Simmer for 7 to 9 minutes or until tender; drain. Keep warm.
- Sauté garlic in olive oil in skillet until brown. Add carrots, basil, 1/8 teaspoon salt and pepper. Sauté for 2 minutes.
- Heat butter in saucepan until melted. Add broccoli, salt to taste, pepper and nutmeg.
- Sauté for 2 minutes.
- Add carrot mixture and broth; mix well.
- Simmer just until heated through.
- Place hot spaghetti on serving platter. Top with vegetable mixture; sprinkle with cheese.
- *Yield: 4 servings.*

Approx Per Serving: Cal 222; Prot 7 g; Carbo 30 g; T Fat 8 g; 33% Calories from Fat; Chol 14 mg; Fiber 2 g; Sod 248 mg

Tortellini Toss

2 cloves of garlic, minced
1/2 teaspoon olive oil
1 (14-ounce) can diced
tomatoes
1 teaspoon basil
1 (9-ounce) package cheese
tortellini, cooked, drained

- Sauté garlic in olive oil in skillet. Stir in undrained tomatoes.
- Cook over medium-high heat for 5 minutes, stirring frequently.
- Stir in basil.
- Cook for 8 minutes, stirring frequently. Stir in tortellini.
- May sprinkle with 1/4 cup grated Parmesan cheese.
- *Yield: 4 servings.*

Approx Per Serving: Cal 224; Prot 11 g; Carbo 35 g; T Fat 5 g; 21% Calories from Fat; Chol 30 mg; Fiber 1 g; Sod 398 mg

Rab-Ray Timber Wolves Wild Rice

4 cups water
1 cup wild rice
2 cups chopped celery
1 (10-ounce) can cream of
celery soup
1 (10-ounce) can cream of
chicken soup
1 (8-ounce) can sliced water
chestnuts, drained
1 onion, chopped
2 tablespoons grated
Parmesan cheese
2 tablespoons
Worcestershire sauce
2 drops of Tabasco sauce

- Preheat oven to 350 degrees.
- Combine water and wild rice in saucepan.
- Cook, covered, until wild rice is tender.
- Combine wild rice, celery, soups, water chestnuts, onion, cheese, Worcestershire sauce and Tabasco sauce in bowl; mix well.
- Spoon into 2-quart baking dish.
- Bake at 350 degrees for 45 minutes.
- May add 1/4 teaspoon liquid smoke to rice mixture. May top with French-fried onions before baking.
- *Yield: 12 servings.*

Approx Per Serving: Cal 112; Prot 4 g; Carbo 18 g; T Fat 3 g; 24% Calories from Fat; Chol 6 mg; Fiber 1 g; Sod 459 mg

Shari Sellner
Brown County

*Ch*ewy Butterscotch Candy

1 cup sugar
1/2 cup packed brown sugar
1/2 cup whipping cream
1/3 cup corn syrup
1/3 cup butter
1 teaspoon vanilla extract

- Combine sugars, cream, corn syrup and butter in large saucepan; mix well.
- Bring to a boil, stirring constantly. Cook to 246 degrees on candy thermometer, firm-ball stage, stirring constantly; remove from heat. Stir in vanilla.
- Pour onto buttered pan. Let stand until cool.
- Cut into squares; shape into twists.
- *Yield: 36 (1-piece) servings.*

Approx Per Serving: Cal 66; Prot <1 g; Carbo 10 g; T Fat 3 g; 39% Calories from Fat; Chol 9 mg; Fiber 0 g; Sod 23 mg

*Y*ummy Caramels

1 cup butter
2 1/4 cups packed brown sugar
1/8 teaspoon salt
1 cup light corn syrup
1 (14-ounce) can sweetened condensed milk
1 teaspoon vanilla extract

- Melt butter in heavy saucepan. Add brown sugar and salt; blend well.
- Stir in corn syrup and condensed milk gradually, blending well.
- Cook over medium beat for 12 to 15 minutes or to 245 degrees on candy thermometer, firm-ball stage, stirring constantly; remove from heat. Stir in vanilla.
- Pour into buttered 9x13-inch pan. Let stand until cool.
- Cut into squares with scissors.
- *Yield: 72 (1-piece) servings.*

Approx Per Serving: Cal 74; Prot <1 g; Carbo 12 g; T Fat 3 g; 35% Calories from Fat; Chol 9 mg; Fiber 0 g; Sod 45 mg

Cream Cheese Fudge

3 ounces cream cheese,
  softened
2 (1-ounce) squares baking
  chocolate, melted
1 teaspoon vanilla extract
2 cups confectioners' sugar
1/2 cup chopped walnuts

- Blend cream cheese and melted chocolate in bowl. Add vanilla; blend well.
- Add confectioners' sugar gradually, blending well. Stir in walnuts.
- Spread evenly in waxed paper-lined small pan; cover with waxed paper.
- Chill in refrigerator for 20 minutes or until firm. Cut into squares.
- *Yield: 16 (1-piece) servings.*

Approx Per Serving: Cal 119; Prot 1 g; Carbo 17 g; T Fat 6 g; 43% Calories from Fat; Chol 6 mg; Fiber 1 g; Sod 17 mg

Peanut Brittle

1 cup water
2 cups sugar
1 cup light corn syrup
2 cups raw peanuts
1 teaspoon vanilla extract
1 teaspoon butter
1 teaspoon baking soda

- Bring water to a boil in heavy 3-quart saucepan.
- Add sugar and corn syrup; reduce heat to medium-high. Boil until sugar is completely dissolved, stirring constantly.
- Cook mixture to 250 degrees on candy thermometer, hard-ball stage; do not stir.
- Add peanuts. Cook for 10 minutes or to 295 degrees on candy thermometer, stirring slowly to prevent scorching; remove from heat.
- Add vanilla and butter; mix well. Add soda; stir quickly as candy foams. Pour immediately onto 2 buttered cookie sheets; do not spread.
- Let stand until cool. Break into pieces. Store in airtight container.
- *Yield: 32 (1-ounce) servings.*

Approx Per Serving: Cal 130; Prot 2 g; Carbo 22 g; T Fat 5 g; 30% Calories from Fat; Chol <1 mg; Fiber 1 g; Sod 41 mg

Snowy Glazed Apple Squares

2¹/2 cups sifted flour
¹/2 teaspoon salt
1 cup shortening
2 egg yolks
¹/2 cup (about) milk
1¹/2 cups crushed corn flakes
5 cups sliced peeled apples
1 cup sugar
1¹/2 teaspoons cinnamon
2 egg whites
1¹/4 cups sifted
   confectioners' sugar
¹/2 teaspoon vanilla extract
3 tablespoons water

- Preheat oven to 350 degrees.
- Combine flour and salt in bowl. Cut in shortening until crumbly.
- Beat egg yolks in 1-cup measure. Add enough milk to measure ²/3 cup. Add to flour mixture; toss with fork to mix. Divide into 2 portions. Roll each to fit 10x15-inch shallow baking pan.
- Layer corn flake crumbs, apple slices and mixture of sugar and cinnamon in pastry-lined pan. Top with remaining pastry; seal edges. Beat egg whites until foamy; brush over pastry.
- Bake at 350 degrees for 1 hour or until golden brown. Spread with mixture of confectioners' sugar, vanilla and enough water to make of glaze consistency.
- Cool completely. Cut into bars.
- *Yield: 36 (1-square) servings.*

Approx Per Serving: Cal 142; Prot 2 g; Carbo 20 g; T Fat 6 g; 39% Calories from Fat; Chol 12 mg; Fiber 1 g; Sod 67 mg

Saucepan Blonde Brownies

1 cup melted margarine
2¹/2 cups packed brown sugar
4 eggs
2 teaspoons vanilla extract
3 cups flour
1 teaspoon baking powder
1 teaspoon salt
1 cup chopped pecans
1 cup semisweet chocolate
   chips

- Preheat oven to 350 degrees.
- Blend margarine and brown sugar in large heavy saucepan; remove from heat. Add eggs and vanilla; mix well. Add mixture of dry ingredients. Stir in pecans.
- Spread in greased 10x15-inch baking pan. Sprinkle with chocolate chips.
- Bake at 350 degrees for 20 minutes. Let stand until almost cool. Cut into squares.
- *Yield: 36 (1-square) servings.*

Approx Per Serving: Cal 184; Prot 2 g; Carbo 24 g; T Fat 9 g; 45% Calories from Fat; Chol 24 mg; Fiber 1 g; Sod 141 mg

*T*exas Brownies

2 cups flour
2 cups sugar
$\frac{1}{2}$ cup butter
$\frac{1}{2}$ cup shortening
1 cup strong brewed coffee
$\frac{1}{4}$ cup baking cocoa
$\frac{1}{2}$ cup buttermilk
2 eggs
1 teaspoon baking soda
1 teaspoon vanilla extract
$\frac{1}{2}$ cup butter
2 tablespoons baking cocoa
$\frac{1}{4}$ cup milk
$3\frac{1}{2}$ cups confectioners' sugar
1 teaspoon vanilla extract

- Preheat oven to 400 degrees.
- Combine flour and sugar in large bowl. Bring $\frac{1}{2}$ cup butter, shortening, coffee and $\frac{1}{4}$ cup cocoa to a boil in heavy saucepan, stirring constantly.
- Pour into flour mixture. Add buttermilk, eggs, baking soda and vanilla; mix with wooden spoon or electric mixer at high speed until well blended. Pour into buttered 11x17-inch shallow baking pan.
- Bake at 400 degrees for 20 minutes or until brownies pull from side of pan.
- Bring $\frac{1}{2}$ cup butter, 2 tablespoons cocoa and milk to a boil in heavy saucepan, stirring constantly; remove from heat.
- Blend in confectioners' sugar and vanilla. Spread warm frosting over hot brownies. Let stand until cool. Cut into squares.
- *Yield: 48 (1-square) servings.*

Approx Per Serving: Cal 145; Prot 1 g; Carbo 22 g; T Fat 6 g; 39% Calories from Fat; Chol 19 mg; Fiber <1 g; Sod 63 mg

*M*acaroon Cookie Bars

1 (2-layer) package devil's food cake mix
$\frac{1}{2}$ cup margarine, softened
1 egg
1 (14-ounce) can sweetened condensed milk
1 egg
1 teaspoon vanilla extract
1 cup chopped pecans
$1\frac{1}{4}$ cups flaked coconut

- Preheat oven to 350 degrees.
- Mix cake mix, margarine and 1 egg in bowl until crumbly. Press into greased 9x13-inch baking pan.
- Blend next 3 ingredients in bowl. Stir in pecans and 1 cup coconut. Pour over cake mix layer. Sprinkle with coconut.
- Bake at 350 degrees for 30 minutes. Cool. Cut into bars.
- *Yield: 36 (1-bar) servings.*

Approx Per Serving: Cal 157; Prot 2 g; Carbo 19 g; T Fat 8 g; 46% Calories from Fat; Chol 16 mg; Fiber 1 g; Sod 165 mg

Butter Pecan Turtle Bars

2 cups flour
1 cup packed brown sugar
1 cup pecan halves
1/2 cup butter
2/3 cup butter
1/2 cup packed brown sugar
1 cup milk chocolate chips

- Preheat oven to 350 degrees.
- Mix flour and 1 cup brown sugar in bowl. Cut in 1/2 cup butter until crumbly. Press into 9x13-inch baking pan; arrange pecan halves over top.
- Bring 2/3 cup butter and 1/2 cup brown sugar to a boil in heavy saucepan over medium heat. Boil for 30 to 60 seconds. Pour evenly over pecans.
- Bake at 350 degrees for 20 minutes.
- Sprinkle with chocolate chips. Let soften for 1 to 2 minutes; swirl chocolate over top. Cool. Cut into bars.
- *Yield: 24 (1-bar) servings.*

Approx Per Serving: Cal 226; Prot 2 g; Carbo 24 g; T Fat 14 g; 55% Calories from Fat; Chol 26 mg; Fiber 1 g; Sod 102 mg

Double Chocolate Crumble Bars

1/2 cup butter, softened
3/4 cup sugar
2 eggs
1 teaspoon vanilla extract
3/4 cup flour
2 tablespoons baking cocoa
1/4 teaspoon baking powder
1/2 cup pecans
2 cups miniature
  marshmallows
2 cups chocolate chips
1 cup peanut butter
1 1/2 cups crisp rice cereal

- Preheat oven to 350 degrees.
- Cream butter and sugar in bowl until light and fluffy. Add eggs and vanilla; mix well. Add flour, baking cocoa and baking powder; mix well. Stir in pecans. Pour into greased 9x13-inch baking pan. Bake at 350 degrees for 15 to 20 minutes.
- Sprinkle with marshmallows. Bake for 3 minutes longer. Let stand until cool.
- Melt chocolate chips with peanut butter in double boiler over hot water, stirring frequently. Mix in cereal. Spread over baked layer. Chill until firm. Cut into bars.
- *Yield: 24 (1-bar) servings.*

Approx Per Serving: Cal 245; Prot 5 g; Carbo 26 g; T Fat 16 g; 54% Calories from Fat; Chol 28 mg; Fiber 2 g; Sod 123 mg

Cranberry Cheese Bars

2 cups flour
1¹/₂ cups rolled oats
³/₄ cup packed brown sugar
1 cup butter, softened
8 ounces cream cheese, softened
1 (14-ounce) can sweetened condensed milk
¹/₄ cup lemon juice
2 tablespoons cornstarch
1 tablespoon brown sugar
1 (16-ounce) can whole cranberry sauce

- Preheat oven to 350 degrees.
- Mix first 3 ingredients in bowl. Cut in butter until crumbly. Reserve 1¹/₂ cups mixture. Press remaining mixture into greased 9x13-inch baking pan.
- Bake at 350 degrees for 15 minutes.
- Beat cream cheese in mixer bowl. Beat in condensed milk gradually. Blend in lemon juice. Spread over baked layer.
- Mix cornstarch and 1 tablespoon brown sugar in bowl. Add cranberry sauce; mix well. Spread over cream cheese layer. Sprinkle with reserved crumb mixture.
- Bake at 350 degrees for 40 minutes.
- Cool. Cut into bars. Store in refrigerator.
- *Yield: 24 (1-bar) servings.*

Approx Per Serving: Cal 266; Prot 4 g; Carbo 35 g; T Fat 13 g; 43% Calories from Fat; Chol 37 mg; Fiber 1 g; Sod 135 mg

Everything Cookies

1 cup margarine, softened
1 cup sugar
1 cup packed brown sugar
1 egg
1 teaspoon cream of tartar
1 cup rolled oats
1 cup coconut
1 cup vegetable oil
2 tablespoons vanilla extract
3 cups flour
1 teaspoon salt
1 teaspoon baking soda
1 cup crisp rice cereal
2 cups chocolate chips

- Preheat oven to 350 degrees.
- Cream margarine, sugar, brown sugar and egg in large bowl until light and fluffy.
- Add remaining ingredients in order listed, mixing well after each addition.
- Drop by spoonfuls onto ungreased cookie sheet.
- Bake at 350 degrees for 10 to 12 minutes or until golden brown. Cool on cookie sheet for 1 minute. Remove to wire racks to cool completely.
- *Yield: 84 (1-cookie) servings.*

Approx Per Serving: Cal 106; Prot 1 g; Carbo 12 g; T Fat 6 g; 53% Calories from Fat; Chol 3 mg; Fiber 1 g; Sod 67 mg

Grasshopper Bars

3/4 cup butter, softened
3/4 cup confectioners' sugar
1 tablespoon light cream
1/2 teaspoon baking powder
1/4 teaspoon mint extract
3 to 4 drops of green food
  coloring
1 1/2 cups flour
3 ounces cream cheese,
  softened
1/4 cup butter, softened
1/4 teaspoon salt
1/4 teaspoon mint extract
4 cups confectioners' sugar
3 to 4 tablespoons light
  cream
1 drop of green food coloring

- Preheat oven to 325 degrees.
- Combine 3/4 cup butter, 3/4 cup confectioners' sugar and 1 tablespoon cream in bowl; mix until smooth and creamy. Add baking powder, 1/4 teaspoon flavoring and food coloring; mix well. Add flour; mix well. Pat into ungreased 9x13-inch baking pan.
- Bake at 325 degrees for 25 to 30 minutes. Let stand until cool.
- Beat cream cheese and 1/4 cup butter in mixer bowl until well blended. Add salt and 1/4 teaspoon flavoring; blend well. Add confectioners' sugar and enough cream to make of spreading consistency. Reserve 1/2 cup of the mixture.
- Spread remaining cream cheese mixture over baked layer.
- Add a drop of food coloring to the reserved cream cheese mixture; blend well. Add enough of the remaining cream to make of glaze consistency. Spread over top.
- Chill until firm. Cut into bars. Store in refrigerator.
- *Yield: 40 (1-bar) servings.*
- **Approx Per Serving:** Cal 126; Prot 1 g; Carbo 18 g; T Fat 6 g; 42% Calories from Fat; Chol 17 mg; Fiber <1 g; Sod 72 mg

Cool cookies completely in a single layer on a wire rack before storing. Store soft and chewy cookies in an airtight container and crisp cookies in a jar with a loose-fitting lid.

Honey Jumbles

1 cup sugar
1 cup honey
3 eggs, well beaten
1/8 teaspoon salt
2 or 3 drops of anise extract
1 tablespoon baking soda
4 1/2 to 5 cups flour
2 cups (or more)
    confectioners' sugar
2 or 3 drops of anise extract
2 tablespoons (about) milk

- Combine sugar, honey, eggs, salt and 2 or 3 drops of flavoring in bowl; blend well. Add soda and flour; mix well. Chill, covered, overnight in refrigerator.
- Preheat oven to 350 degrees.
- Roll on lightly floured surface to 1/4-inch thickness. Cut with doughnut cutter. Separate holes; place on lightly greased cookie sheet. Bake at 350 degrees for 10 minutes or less or until light golden brown.
- Blend confectioners' sugar with 2 or 3 drops of flavoring and enough milk to make of spreading consistency. Frost cooled cookies.
- *Yield: 24 (1-cookie) servings.*

Approx Per Serving: Cal 219; Prot 4 g; Carbo 50 g; T Fat 1 g; 4% Calories from Fat; Chol 27 mg; Fiber 1 g; Sod 123 mg

Pecan Refrigerator Cookies

4 cups packed brown sugar
2 cups margarine, softened
3 eggs
2 1/4 teaspoons vanilla extract
1 (2-pound) package cake
    flour
3 1/4 teaspoons baking soda
2 1/4 teaspoons cream of
    tartar
2 cups chopped pecans

- Cream brown sugar, margarine, eggs and vanilla in large bowl until fluffy. Mix dry ingredients together. Add to creamed mixture; mix well. Stir in pecans.
- Press into 9x13-inch pan. Cut into strips. Cover tightly. Chill until firm.
- Preheat oven to 375 degrees.
- Slice cookie dough into thin slices; place on ungreased cookie sheet.
- Bake at 375 degrees for 8 to 10 minutes or until golden brown.
- Cool on cookie sheet for 1 minute; remove to wire rack to cool completely.
- *Yield: 130 (1-cookie) servings.*

Approx Per Serving: Cal 85; Prot 1 g; Carbo 10 g; T Fat 5 g; 52% Calories from Fat; Chol 5 mg; Fiber <1 g; Sod 80 mg

Pecan Pie Bars

2 cups flour
1/2 cup confectioners' sugar
1 cup margarine, chilled
1 (14-ounce) can sweetened
    condensed milk
1 egg
1 teaspoon vanilla extract
1 (16-ounce) package
    almond brickle chips
1 cup chopped pecans

- Preheat oven to 350 degrees.
- Combine flour and sugar in bowl. Cut in margarine until crumbly. Press into 9x13-inch baking pan.
- Bake at 350 degrees for 15 minutes.
- Blend condensed milk, egg and vanilla in bowl. Stir in brickle chips and pecans. Spread over baked layer.
- Bake at 350 degrees for 25 minutes or until golden brown.
- Cool. Cut into bars. Store in refrigerator.
- *Yield: 24 (1-bar) servings.*

Approx Per Serving: Cal 306; Prot 3 g; Carbo 32 g; T Fat 19 g; 55% Calories from Fat; Chol 21 mg; Fiber 1 g; Sod 220 mg

Snickers Cookies

1 cup butter, softened
1 cup peanut butter
1 cup sugar
1 cup packed brown sugar
2 eggs
2 teaspoons vanilla extract
3 cups flour
1 teaspoon baking powder
1 teaspoon baking soda
60 miniature Snickers bars
1 cup confectioners' sugar
2 tablespoons baking cocoa
1 tablespoon (or more) milk

- Preheat oven to 350 degrees.
- Cream butter, peanut butter and sugars in bowl. Add eggs and vanilla; mix well. Add mixture of flour, baking powder and baking soda; mix well.
- Shape a small amount of cookie dough around each candy bar, forming ball; place on ungreased cookie sheet.
- Bake at 350 degrees for 10 to 12 minutes or until golden brown. Cool on cookie sheet for 1 minute; remove to wire rack to cool completely.
- Blend confectioners' sugar, cocoa and enough milk to make of desired consistency. Drizzle over cookies.
- *Yield: 60 (1-cookie) servings.*

Approx Per Serving: Cal 178; Prot 3 g; Carbo 23 g; T Fat 9 g; 43% Calories from Fat; Chol 17 mg; Fiber 1 g; Sod 115 mg

Thumbprint Cookies

2 cups butter, softened
2 cups packed brown sugar
4 teaspoons vanilla extract
6 cups flour
2 teaspoons salt
1/2 cup milk
1 cup chocolate chips
3 cups confectioners' sugar
1 1/2 cups chocolate chips
2 tablespoons butter
1/4 cup corn syrup
2 teaspoons vanilla extract

- Preheat oven to 375 degrees.
- Cream first 3 ingredients in large bowl. Add flour and salt alternately with milk; mix well. Stir in 1 cup chocolate chips.
- Shape into 1-inch balls; place on ungreased cookie sheet. Make depression in center with thumb.
- Bake at 375 degrees for 10 minutes. Roll warm cookies several times in confectioner's sugar. Cool.
- Melt 1 1/2 cups chocolate chips with 2 tablespoons butter in saucepan over low heat. Blend in corn syrup and 2 teaspoons vanilla. Spoon into depressions in cookies.
- *Yield: 48 (1-cookie) servings.*

Approx Per Serving: Cal 237; Prot 2 g; Carbo 34 g; T Fat 11 g; 41% Calories from Fat; Chol 22 mg; Fiber 1 g; Sod 179 mg

Toffee Squares

1 cup margarine, melted
1 cup packed brown sugar
1 egg yolk, lightly beaten
1 teaspoon vanilla extract
2 cups flour
1/2 teaspoon baking soda
1/2 cup finely chopped pecans
1 1/2 cups confectioners' sugar
2 tablespoons baking cocoa
3 tablespoons margarine, softened
1 egg white
1 teaspoon vanilla extract

- Preheat oven to 350 degrees.
- Blend margarine with brown sugar in bowl. Add egg yolk and 1 teaspoon vanilla. Add mixture of flour and baking soda; mix well. Stir in pecans. Pat into rectangle on cookie sheet.
- Bake at 350 degrees for 10 to 12 minutes or until golden brown.
- Mix remaining ingredients in small bowl. Spread over hot baked layer. Let stand until cool. Cut into squares.
- *Yield: 24 (1-square) servings.*

Approx Per Serving: Cal 197; Prot 2 g; Carbo 24 g; T Fat 11 g; 50% Calories from Fat; Chol 9 mg; Fiber 1 g; Sod 129 mg

Chocolate Chip Toffee Bars

2¹/₃ cups flour
²/₃ cup packed brown sugar
³/₄ cup butter
1 egg, beaten
1¹/₂ cups semisweet
  chocolate chips
1 cup chopped pecans
1 (14-ounce) can sweetened
  condensed milk
1¹/₂ cups almond brickle
  chips
¹/₂ cup chocolate chips
¹/₄ cup almond brickle chips

- Preheat oven to 350 degrees.
- Mix flour and brown sugar in bowl. Cut in butter until crumbly. Add egg; mix well. Add 1¹/₂ cups chocolate chips and pecans; mix well. Reserve 1¹/₂ cups mixture. Press remaining mixture into greased 9x13-inch baking pan.
- Bake at 350 degrees for 10 minutes.
- Layer condensed milk, 1¹/₂ cups brickle chips, reserved crumb mixture and remaining ¹/₂ cup chocolate chips over baked layer.
- Bake at 350 degrees for 20 to 30 minutes or until golden brown. Sprinkle with ¹/₄ cup brickle chips. Cool. Cut into bars.
- *Yield: 36 (1-bar) servings.*

Approx Per Serving: Cal 243; Prot 3 g; Carbo 29 g; T Fat 14 g; 50% Calories from Fat; Chol 24 mg; Fiber 1 g; Sod 124 mg

Molasses Crunchies

2 cups packed brown sugar
1¹/₂ cups shortening
2 eggs
¹/₂ cup molasses
¹/₈ teaspoon salt
4¹/₂ cups flour
4 teaspoons baking soda
2 teaspoons cinnamon
2 teaspoons ginger
1 teaspoon cloves
1 cup (about) sugar

- Preheat oven to 350 degrees.
- Beat brown sugar, shortening, eggs and molasses in large bowl until creamy.
- Sift in dry ingredients except sugar; mix well. Chill, covered, in refrigerator.
- Shape into small balls. Dip in water; roll in sugar. Place on greased cookie sheet; flatten slightly.
- Bake at 350 degrees for 10 minutes. Cool for 1 minute; remove to wire racks.
- *Yield: 60 (1-cookie) servings.*

Approx Per Serving: Cal 112; Prot 1 g; Carbo 15 g; T Fat 5 g; 43% Calories from Fat; Chol 7 mg; Fiber <1 g; Sod 65 mg

Orange Cookies

2 cups sugar
1 cup margarine, softened
2 eggs, beaten
4 cups flour
1 teaspoon baking powder
1 teaspoon baking soda
1/2 teaspoon salt
1 cup buttermilk
Grated rind and juice of
    1 orange
2 cups confectioners' sugar
1/4 cup butter, softened
Juice of 1/2 orange

- Preheat oven to 350 degrees.
- Cream sugar and margarine in bowl until light and fluffy. Beat in eggs.
- Mix dry ingredients together. Add to creamed mixture alternately with buttermilk, mixing well after each addition. Add rind and juice of 1 orange; mix well.
- Chill, covered, in refrigerator. Drop by tablespoonfuls onto greased cookie sheet.
- Bake at 350 degrees for 5 to 10 minutes or just until brown on edges.
- Blend remaining ingredients. Frost warm cookies.
- *Yield: 90 (1-cookie) servings.*

Approx Per Serving: Cal 74; Prot 1 g; Carbo 12 g; T Fat 3 g; 33% Calories from Fat; Chol 6 mg; Fiber <1 g; Sod 58 mg

Marbled Peanut Butter Cookies

1 cup peanut butter
1 cup shortening
1 cup sugar
1 cup packed brown sugar
2 eggs
2 1/2 cups flour
1 teaspoon baking soda
1/8 teaspoon salt
1 (8-ounce) milk chocolate
    candy bar

- Preheat oven to 325 degrees.
- Beat peanut butter, shortening, sugars and eggs in bowl. Mix flour, baking soda and salt together. Add to peanut butter mixture; mix well.
- Melt half the candy bar; break remaining candy bar into pieces. Swirl melted chocolate into dough. Stir in pieces. Shape into balls; place on cookie sheet. Flatten slightly with fork.
- Bake at 325 degrees for 15 to 20 minutes or until golden brown.
- Cool on wire rack.
- *Yield: 24 (1-cookie) servings.*

Approx Per Serving: Cal 301; Prot 5 g; Carbo 33 g; T Fat 17 g; 50% Calories from Fat; Chol 20 mg; Fiber 1 g; Sod 112 mg

Holly Covington
Brown County

ℬanana Snack Cake

1 cup butter, softened
1 cup sugar
¹/₂ cup buttermilk
2 eggs
2 bananas, mashed
1 teaspoon vanilla extract
2 cups flour
1 cup rolled oats
1¹/₂ teaspoons baking soda
¹/₂ teaspoon salt
1 cup chocolate chips

- Preheat oven to 350 degrees.
- Cream butter and sugar in bowl until light and fluffy.
- Add buttermilk, eggs, bananas and vanilla; beat until well blended.
- Add flour, oats, baking soda and salt; mix well.
- Spread in greased and floured 9x13-inch cake pan. Sprinkle chocolate chips over the top.
- Bake at 350 degrees for 30 minutes or until cake tests done.
- *Yield: 15 servings.*

Approx Per Serving: Cal 323; Prot 4 g; Carbo 41 g; T Fat 17 g; 46% Calories from Fat; Chol 62 mg; Fiber 2 g; Sod 297 mg

𝒯asty Banana Cake

1 (2-layer) yellow cake mix
1¹/₄ cups banana slices
2 eggs
1 cup buttermilk
¹/₄ cup cold coffee

- Preheat oven to 350 degrees.
- Combine cake mix, banana slices, eggs, buttermilk and coffee in mixer bowl. Beat at low speed until blended. Beat at high speed for 2 minutes.
- Pour into greased and floured 12-cup bundt pan.
- Bake at 350 degrees for 40 to 50 minutes or until cake tests done.
- Cool in pan on wire rack for 45 minutes. Invert onto serving plate.
- Garnish with whipped cream and additional banana slices just before serving.
- *Yield: 12 servings.*

Approx Per Serving: Cal 219; Prot 4 g; Carbo 38 g; T Fat 6 g; 25% Calories from Fat; Chol 37 mg; Fiber 1 g; Sod 312 mg

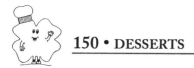

Cranberry Cake with Butter Sauce

1 cup sugar
3 tablespoons butter,
    softened
2 cups flour
1 tablespoon baking powder
1/4 teaspoon salt
1 cup milk
3 cups uncooked cranberries

- Preheat oven to 350 degrees
- Cream sugar and butter in mixer bowl. Add mixture of flour, baking powder and salt alternately with milk, mixing well after each addition. Stir in cranberries.
- Spread batter evenly in greased 8-inch square cake pan.
- Bake at 350 degrees for 35 to 40 minutes or until cake tests done.
- Serve with warm Butter Sauce over the warm cake.

Butter Sauce

1 cup sugar
1 tablespoon flour
1/2 cup butter
1/2 cup cream
1 tablespoon vinegar
1 teaspoon vanilla extract

- Mix sugar and flour in saucepan. Add butter, cream and vinegar. Bring to a boil, stirring constantly; remove from heat. Stir in vanilla.
- *Yield: 12 servings.*

Approx Per Serving: Cal 360; Prot 3 g; Carbo 54 g; T Fat 15 g; 37% Calories from Fat; Chol 45 mg; Fiber 2 g; Sod 249 mg

Make *Coconut Cream Cheese Frosting* by sautéing 2 cups shredded coconut in 2 tablespoons butter or margarine until golden brown then draining on paper towels. Cream 2 tablespoons softened butter with 8 ounces cream cheese and beat in 2 teaspoons milk, 1/2 teaspoon vanilla and 31/2 cups confectioners' sugar. Mix in 13/4 cups of the coconut, frost the cake of your choice and sprinkle with the remaining coconut.

*G*inger Cake Roll

1/2 cup flour
1 teaspoon ground ginger
1/2 teaspoon baking soda
1/2 teaspoon baking powder
1/4 teaspoon ground nutmeg
1/4 teaspoon ground cloves
4 eggs
1/2 cup sugar
1/4 cup molasses
1/2 cup confectioners' sugar
8 ounces whipped topping

- Preheat oven to 350 degrees.
- Line 10x15-inch jelly roll pan with foil; grease and flour foil.
- Sift flour, ginger, baking soda, baking powder, nutmeg and cloves together; set aside.
- Combine eggs, sugar and molasses in mixer bowl. Beat for 5 minutes or until thick and lemon-colored.
- Fold in flour mixture gently. Spread in prepared pan.
- Bake at 350 degrees for 15 minutes or until cake springs back when lightly touched.
- Sprinkle with 2 tablespoons confectioners' sugar. Invert onto tea towel sprinkled with remaining confectioners' sugar. Remove foil carefully. Roll cake in towel as for jelly roll from short side.
- Let stand until completely cool. Unroll carefully.
- Spread with whipped topping; reroll.
- Place on serving plate. Sprinkle with additional confectioners' sugar. Refrigerate until serving time.
- *Yield: 8 servings.*

Approx Per Serving: Cal 261; Prot 4 g; Carbo 40 g; T Fat 10 g; 33% Calories from Fat; Chol 106 mg; Fiber <1 g; Sod 115 mg

Make *Easy Orange Frosting* for plain or spice cakes by preparing vanilla frosting mix with orange juice instead of water or milk. Add a little grated orange rind for color and zing.

Royal Raspberry Cake

2 cups flour
1 tablespoon baking powder
1/2 teaspoon salt
1/3 cup butter, softened
1 cup sugar
1 egg, at room temperature
1 cup milk, at room
temperature
1 teaspoon vanilla extract
3 1/2 cups fresh or frozen
raspberries
1 1/2 cups confectioners' sugar
2 tablespoons milk
1 teaspoon vanilla extract

- Preheat oven to 350 degrees.
- Combine flour, baking powder and salt in bowl. Stir with wire whisk to mix. Set aside.
- Cream butter in mixer bowl. Add sugar gradually, beating well after each addition. Add egg. Beat for 1 minute.
- Add dry ingredients alternately with mixture of 1 cup milk and 1 teaspoon vanilla, beating well after each addition.
- Spread in greased and floured 9x13-inch cake pan. Spoon raspberries evenly over top of the batter.
- Bake at 350 degrees for 30 to 35 minutes or until cake tests done.
- Cool for 5 minutes.
- Blend confectioners' sugar, 2 tablespoons milk and 1 teaspoon vanilla. Drizzle over top of cake.
- Serve warm or cool. It is good as a dessert or coffee cake.
- *Yield: 15 servings.*

Approx Per Serving: Cal 226; Prot 3 g; Carbo 42 g; T Fat 5 g; 21% Calories from Fat; Chol 28 mg; Fiber 2 g; Sod 192 mg

Make *Special Holiday Cakes* as easily as every day ones:

- Make a festive Christmas cake by alternating layers of angel food cake batter with sprinkles of strawberry and lime dry gelatin in cake pan until all ingredients are used and baking as directed.
- You can make a heart-shaped cake without a special pan. Bake the batter in one 9-inch round pan and one 9-inch square pan. Cut the round layer into halves and arrange cut sides along two adjacent sides of the square layer to form a heart, trimming edges if necessary. Frost cake as desired.

$\mathscr{S}$trawberry Tunnel Cake

1 (10-inch) angel food cake
6 ounces cream cheese, softened
1 (14-ounce) can sweetened condensed milk
1/3 cup lemon juice concentrate
1 teaspoon almond extract
2 to 4 drops of red food coloring
1 cup chopped fresh strawberries
12 ounces whipped topping

- Cut top 1/2 inch from cake; set aside. Cut around outer edge and inner edge of cake, leaving 1 inch thick edge. Scoop out center, leaving 1 inch thick bottom. Tear scooped out cake into small pieces and set aside.

- Beat cream cheese in mixer bowl until fluffy. Add condensed milk gradually, beating until smooth. Beat in lemon juice, almond flavoring and food coloring. Fold in reserved cake pieces and strawberries. Fold in 1 cup whipped topping.

- Spoon strawberry mixture into cake cavity; replace cake top. Frost top and side of cake with remaining whipped topping. Chill until serving time.

- *Yield: 10 servings.*

Approx Per Serving: Cal 471; Prot 9 g; Carbo 69 g; T Fat 19 g; 35% Calories from Fat; Chol 32 mg; Fiber 1 g; Sod 586 mg

$\mathscr{C}$hocolate Chip Pie

18 graham crackers, crushed
1/2 cup melted butter
30 large marshmallows
1/2 cup milk
1 cup whipping cream, whipped
1/4 to 1/2 cup grated chocolate or miniature chocolate chips

- Mix graham cracker crumbs and butter in bowl. Press over bottom and side of 8 or 9-inch pie plate.

- Melt marshmallows in double boiler over hot water, stirring frequently. Let stand until cool.

- Fold in whipped cream. Fold in chocolate.

- Pour into prepared pie plate.

- Chill until serving time.

- *Yield: 6 servings.*

Approx Per Serving: Cal 593; Prot 5 g; Carbo 60 g; T Fat 38 g; 57% Calories from Fat; Chol 99 mg; Fiber 2 g; Sod 325 mg

Chocolate and Vanilla Tarts

1½ cups flour
3 tablespoons sugar
3 tablespoons baking cocoa
½ cup butter
2 tablespoons shortening
3 to 4 tablespoons cold water
6 ounces cream cheese,
 softened
¼ cup sifted confectioners'
 sugar
1 (8-ounce) carton vanilla
 yogurt
1 teaspoon vanilla extract
1 cup (about) whipped
 topping
2 or 3 kiwifruit, peeled,
 sliced

- Preheat oven to 400 degrees.
- Combine flour, sugar and cocoa in bowl; mix well. Cut in butter and shortening until crumbly. Sprinkle with 1 tablespoon water at time, tossing with fork until mixture forms ball.
- Roll ⅛ inch thick on lightly floured surface. Cut twelve 4½-inch circles.
- Fit circles into muffin cups; flute edges. Prick bottoms and sides with fork.
- Bake at 400 degrees for 12 minutes. Remove from pan to wire rack to cool.
- Beat cream cheese with confectioners' sugar in mixer bowl until smooth. Blend in yogurt and vanilla. Fold in whipped topping. Spoon into tart shells. Chill until serving time.
- Top with kiwifruit slices just before serving. May substitute other fresh fruit slices for kiwifruit.
- *Yield: 12 servings.*

Approx Per Serving: Cal 267; Prot 4 g; Carbo 25 g; T Fat 17 g; 57% Calories from Fat; Chol 37 mg; Fiber 1 g; Sod 135 mg

Your favorite pie filling will find new life in a different crust:
- Use gingersnaps, chocolate wafers, vanilla wafers or sugar cookies to make a crumb pie crust.
- You can substitute an equal amount of smooth or crunchy peanut butter for the shortening in your pastry recipe. It is a taste treat and handy when you have no shortening.

Cream Puff Pie

1/2 cup water
1/4 cup butter
1/2 teaspoon salt
1/2 cup flour
2 eggs
3/4 cup sugar
1/3 cup flour
1/8 teaspoon salt
2 eggs, lightly beaten
2 cups milk
1 teaspoon vanilla extract
2 cups whipping cream,
    whipped

- Preheat oven to 400 degrees.
- Bring water, butter and 1/2 teaspoon salt to a boil in large saucepan. Add 1/2 cup flour all at once. Cook until mixture forms a ball, stirring constantly; remove from heat. Beat in 2 eggs 1 at a time. Beat until mixture is smooth and shiny.
- Spread dough over bottom and halfway up side of greased 9-inch pie plate.
- Bake at 400 degrees for 35 to 40 minutes or until golden brown. Let stand until completely cooled.
- Combine sugar, 1/3 cup flour and 1/8 teaspoon salt in double boiler over simmering water. Add beaten eggs and milk; blend well.
- Cook until thickened, stirring constantly; remove from heat. Blend in vanilla. Let stand until cool.
- Fold in 1 cup whipped cream gently. Spoon into cream puff shell. Top with remaining whipped cream.
- Chill until serving time.
- Garnish with drizzle of chocolate sauce and fresh raspberries or other favorite fresh fruit.
- *Yield: 6 servings.*

Approx Per Serving: Cal 464; Prot 10 g; Carbo 43 g; T Fat 29 g; 55% Calories from Fat; Chol 227 mg; Fiber <1 g; Sod 397 mg

Always prick the bottom and side of a pie shell which is baked before filling to prevent puffing. Brush the bottom with 1 egg white beaten with 1 tablespoon water just before the shell has finished baking to keep it from becoming soggy when filled.

Sour Cream Honey Lemon Pie

1½ cups honey
5 tablespoons cornstarch
1¼ cups lemon juice
6 egg yolks, beaten
2 cups cream
¾ cup sour cream
1 baked (9-inch) pie shell
6 egg whites
¼ teaspoon cream of tartar
½ cup sugar

- Preheat oven to 350 degrees.
- Blend honey and cornstarch in large saucepan. Add lemon juice, egg yolks and cream; blend well.
- Cook over medium heat until thickened, stirring constantly. Blend in sour cream. Cook until well blended, stirring constantly; do not boil.
- Pour into baked pie shell.
- Beat egg whites with cream of tartar in mixer bowl until soft peaks form. Add sugar gradually, beating constantly until stiff peaks form.
- Spread over pie, sealing to edge.
- Bake at 350 degrees until meringue is golden brown.
- Cool on wire rack. Do not refrigerate or meringue will weep.
- *Yield: 6 servings.*

Approx Per Serving: Cal 930; Prot 11 g; Carbo 115 g; T Fat 51 g; 48% Calories from Fat; Chol 333 mg; Fiber 1 g; Sod 274 mg

Christmas Lime Parfait Pie

1 (6-ounce) package lime gelatin
2 cups boiling water
⅓ cup lime juice
1 teaspoon grated lime rind
1 quart vanilla ice cream
1 baked (10-inch) pie shell

- Dissolve gelatin in boiling water in large bowl. Add lime juice and rind.
- Add ice cream by spoonfuls, stirring until ice cream melts. May add a small amount of green food coloring if desired.
- Chill until partially set.
- Spoon gelatin mixture into pie shell. Chill until firm.
- *Yield: 8 servings.*

Approx Per Serving: Cal 349; Prot 6 g; Carbo 48 g; T Fat 16 g; 40% Calories from Fat; Chol 29 mg; Fiber 1 g; Sod 242 mg

𝒫eanut Butter Pie

18 chocolate sandwich
   cookies, crushed
2 tablespoons butter,
   softened
8 ounces cream cheese,
   softened
1 cup sugar
1 cup peanut butter
2 tablespoons melted butter
1¹/₂ cups whipping cream,
   whipped
1 tablespoon vanilla extract
¹/₂ cup semisweet chocolate
   chips
2 tablespoons butter
1 tablespoon vegetable oil

• Combine cookie crumbs and softened
  butter in bowl; mix well. Press over
  bottom and side of pie plate.
• Beat cream cheese with next 3 ingredients in mixer bowl until well blended.
  Fold in whipped cream and vanilla.
  Spread in prepared pie plate.
• Melt chocolate chips and butter in saucepan, stirring constantly. Blend in oil.
• Decorate with chocolate mixture piped
  through decorating tube or drizzled over
  top of pie. Refrigerate or freeze until
  serving time.
• *Yield: 6 servings.*

Approx Per Serving: Cal 1055; Prot 17 g; Carbo 76 g;
   T Fat 81 g; 66% Calories from Fat; Chol 154 mg;
   Fiber 4 g; Sod 637 mg

𝒜pple Rum Dum

¹/₂ cup sugar
¹/₂ cup packed brown sugar
1 egg
2 cups chopped peeled
   apples
1 cup flour
1 teaspoon baking soda
1 teaspoon ground
   cinnamon
¹/₄ teaspoon salt
¹/₂ cup chopped pecans
¹/₂ cup sugar
¹/₂ cup packed brown sugar
¹/₄ cup butter
¹/₂ cup heavy cream

• Preheat oven to 350 degrees.
• Mix ¹/₂ cup sugar, ¹/₂ cup brown sugar
  and egg in bowl. Stir in apples.
• Stir in mixture of flour, baking soda,
  cinnamon and salt. Stir in pecans. Pour
  into greased 9-inch cake pan.
• Bake at 350 degrees for 45 to 50 minutes
  or until cake tests done.
• Combine remaining ingredients in sauce-
  pan. Bring to a boil, stirring constantly.
• Serve with hot sauce and/or ice cream.
• *Yield: 8 servings.*

Approx Per Serving: Cal 418; Prot 3 g; Carbo 65 g;
   T Fat 17 g; 36% Calories from Fat; Chol 62 mg;
   Fiber 2 g; Sod 251 mg

$\mathscr{G}$rand Finale Cheesecake

1 cup graham cracker
  crumbs
1 tablespoon sugar
1 teaspoon ground
  cinnamon
2 tablespoons corn oil
  margarine, melted
4 cups low-fat cottage cheese
1 cup sugar
5 tablespoons flour
Juice of 1 lemon
2 eggs plus 2 egg whites
1 cup low-fat plain yogurt
3 cups fresh raspberries

- Preheat oven to 350 degrees.
- Combine crumbs, 1 tablespoon sugar, cinnamon and margarine in bowl; mix well. Press over bottom and halfway up side of 9-inch springform pan.
- Purée cottage cheese in food processor or blender. Add remaining ingredients except raspberries; process until smooth. Pour into prepared pan.
- Place springform pan on middle rack oven rack. Place pan with about 2 inches water on bottom rack.
- Bake at 350 degrees for 1 hour or until fairly firm. Cool on wire rack.
- Chill for 4 hours to overnight. Loosen from side of pan; remove side of pan. Top with raspberries.
- *Yield: 12 servings.*

Approx Per Serving: Cal 251; Prot 14 g; Carbo 36 g; T Fat 6 g; 20% Calories from Fat; Chol 43 mg; Fiber 2 g; Sod 423 mg

$\mathscr{N}$o-Bake Cheesecake

1 small package sugar-free
  orange gelatin
1½ cups boiling water
8 ounces light cream cheese,
  softened
6 packets artificial sweetener
8 ounces light whipped
  topping
2 (11-ounce) cans mandarin
  oranges, drained
12 graham crackers, crushed

- Dissolve gelatin in boiling water in large bowl. Chill until partially set.
- Beat cream cheese with sweetener in bowl until fluffy. Beat in whipped topping and gelatin.
- Layer crumbs, a thin layer of cream cheese mixture, ⅔ of the oranges, remaining cream cheese mixture and remaining oranges in 9-inch square dish. Chill until serving time.
- *Yield: 9 servings.*

Approx Per Serving: Cal 195; Prot 4 g; Carbo 27 g; T Fat 8 g; 37% Calories from Fat; Chol 14 mg; Fiber <1 g; Sod 162 mg

Apple Crisp

This recipe is a treasure from Edna Dallum, cook at the Minnesota State Fair 4-H Building from 1939, when the Fair opened, to 1980. For 41 years she served 4-H State Fair attendees. Edna was honored at the 1989 Fifty Year Celebration.

3 Granny Smith apples
3 tablespoons sugar
1/4 teaspoon ground
  cinnamon
1/4 teaspoon ground nutmeg
1/4 cup water
1 cup flour
1/2 cup sugar
1/2 cup packed brown sugar
2 1/4 teaspoons salt
1/2 cup butter

- Preheat oven to 350 degrees.
- Peel, core and finely chop apples. Place in buttered 9-inch square baking pan. Sprinkle with sugar, cinnamon and nutmeg. Drizzle water over top.
- Combine flour, sugar, brown sugar and salt in bowl. Cut in butter until crumbly. Sprinkle over apples.
- Bake at 350 degrees for 50 minutes or until apples are tender and topping is light brown.
- *Yield: 9 servings.*

Approx Per Serving: Cal 262; Prot 2 g; Carbo 42 g; T Fat 11 g; 35% Calories from Fat; Chol 28 mg; Fiber 1 g; Sod 641 mg

No-Bake Chocolate Eclair Dessert

1 (12-ounce) package
  graham crackers
2 (4-ounce) packages
  French vanilla instant
  pudding mix
3 cups milk
8 ounces whipped topping
2 (1-ounce) squares
  semisweet chocolate
6 tablespoons butter
3 tablespoons milk
1 1/2 cups confectioners' sugar

- Line bottom of 9x13-inch pan with graham crackers.
- Prepare pudding mix with 3 cups milk using package directions. Beat in whipped topping.
- Alternate layers of pudding mixture and graham crackers, ending with crackers.
- Melt chocolate and butter in 3 tablespoons milk in small saucepan; beat until blended. Add confectioners' sugar; beat until smooth. Spread over graham crackers.
- Refrigerate for 8 hours before serving.
- *Yield: 15 servings.*

Approx Per Serving: Cal 329; Prot 4 g; Carbo 50 g; T Fat 14 g; 36% Calories from Fat; Chol 20 mg; Fiber 1 g; Sod 404 mg

Chocolate Decadence

16 ounces semisweet
  chocolate
1/2 cup butter
1 1/2 teaspoons sugar
1 teaspoon hot water
4 egg yolks
4 egg whites
1 cup whipping cream
2 tablespoons confectioners'
  sugar
Raspberry Sauce
  (recipe below)

- Preheat oven to 425 degrees.
- Melt chocolate and butter in heavy saucepan over low heat, stirring constantly; remove from heat. Blend in sugar and hot water. Add egg yolks 1 at a time, beating well after each addition. Let stand until slightly cooled.
- Beat egg whites in mixer bowl until stiff but not dry. Fold 1/4 of the chocolate mixture gently into the egg whites. Fold in remaining chocolate mixture.
- Pour into generously buttered 8 1/2-inch springform pan.
- Bake at 425 degrees for 15 minutes; cake will look underbaked.
- Cool on wire rack. Place in refrigerator or freezer.
- Thaw cake if frozen. Loosen from side of pan; remove side of pan.
- Beat whipping cream in mixer bowl until soft peaks form. Beat in confectioners' sugar.
- Frost top of cake with whipped cream. Cut into wedges while cold.
- Let stand at room temperature for 15 minutes before serving. Top with raspberry sauce.

Raspberry Sauce

1 (10-ounce) package frozen
  raspberries, thawed
1 tablespoon confectioners'
  sugar
1/4 cup almond liqueur

- Combine all ingredients in blender container. Process until puréed; strain to remove seeds.
- *Yield: 12 servings.*

Approx Per Serving: Cal 396; Prot 4 g; Carbo 36 g;
  T Fat 28 g; 59% Calories from Fat; Chol 119 mg;
  Fiber 4 g; Sod 111 mg

Coconut Crunch

1 cup flour
1/4 cup packed brown sugar
1/2 cup butter, softened
1 cup flaked coconut
1 (6-ounce) package vanilla
  pudding and pie filling
  mix
3 cups milk
1 cup whipping cream,
  whipped

• Preheat oven to 350 degrees.
• Combine flour, brown sugar and butter in bowl; mix until crumbly. Mix in coconut. Spread in shallow baking pan.
• Bake at 350 degrees for 10 minutes or until lightly browned, stirring frequently. Let stand until cool.
• Cook pudding mix with milk using package directions.
• Sprinkle half the coconut mixture into 5x8-inch dish. Add layers of pudding, whipped cream and remaining coconut mixture. Chill overnight.
• *Yield: 8 servings.*

Approx Per Serving: Cal 460; Prot 6 g; Carbo 46 g; T Fat 29 g; 55% Calories from Fat; Chol 84 mg; Fiber 2 g; Sod 338 mg

Buster Bar Dessert

1 pound chocolate sandwich
  cookies
1/2 cup melted butter
1/2 gallon vanilla ice cream,
  softened
1 1/2 cups salted peanuts
1 1/2 cups evaporated milk
2/3 cup chocolate chips
1/2 cup butter
2/3 cup confectioners' sugar
1 teaspoon vanilla extract

• Crush cookies into crumbs. Combine with melted butter in bowl; mix well. Press into 9x13-inch dish.
• Layer ice cream and peanuts over crumbs. Freeze until firm.
• Combine evaporated milk, chocolate chips, 1/2 cup butter and confectioners' sugar in saucepan. Bring to a boil, stirring constantly. Boil for 10 minutes, stirring constantly; remove from heat. Stir in vanilla.
• Let stand for 30 minutes. Spread over ice cream and peanut layers. Freeze for 6 hours to overnight before serving.
• *Yield: 15 servings.*

Approx Per Serving: Cal 568; Prot 10 g; Carbo 53 g; T Fat 38 g; 57% Calories from Fat; Chol 72 mg; Fiber 3 g; Sod 454 mg

Orange Ice Cream

2 cups sugar
1 cup water
2 cups orange juice
2 tablespoons lemon juice
1 cup light cream, scalded
2 egg yolks, beaten
2 cups whipping cream

- Bring sugar and water to a boil in large saucepan, stirring until sugar dissolves. Boil for 8 minutes; remove from heat. Stir in juices. Cool.
- Stir a small amount of hot cream into beaten egg yolks; stir egg yolks into hot cream. Cook in double boiler over hot water until thickened, stirring constantly. Let stand until cool.
- Blend cream mixture into juice mixture. Fold whipping cream into mixture.
- Pour into 1-gallon ice cream freezer. Freeze using manufacturer's instructions.
- *Yield: 12 (1-cup) servings.*

Approx Per Serving: Cal 353; Prot 2 g; Carbo 39 g; T Fat 22 g; 54% Calories from Fat; Chol 112 mg; Fiber <1 g; Sod 24 mg

Peach Buttermilk Ice Cream

2/3 cup sugar
1 envelope unflavored gelatin
1 1/2 cups buttermilk
1 egg, beaten
3 cups whipping cream
2 teaspoons vanilla extract
1/4 teaspoon salt
1 1/2 cups chopped peaches
3 tablespoons sugar

- Mix 2/3 cup sugar and gelatin in saucepan. Stir in buttermilk. Cook over low heat until gelatin dissolves.
- Stir a small amount of hot mixture into beaten egg; stir egg into hot mixture. Cook over medium heat until thickened, stirring constantly; remove from heat. Blend in cream, vanilla and salt.
- Mix peaches with 3 tablespoons sugar. Stir into buttermilk mixture.
- Chill in refrigerator. Pour into ice cream freezer. Freeze using manufacturer's instructions.
- *Yield: 6 servings.*

Approx Per Serving: Cal 598; Prot 7 g; Carbo 44 g; T Fat 46 g; 67% Calories from Fat; Chol 200 mg; Fiber 1 g; Sod 211 mg

Ice Cream Praline Crunch

1/2 cup butter
1 cup packed brown sugar
3 cups crisp rice cereal
1/2 cup chopped pecans
1/2 cup toasted coconut
2 quarts vanilla ice cream

- Melt butter in large saucepan. Add brown sugar; mix well.
- Cook over medium heat until mixture bubbles, stirring constantly; remove from heat. Add cereal, pecans and coconut; mix well.
- Press half the mixture into 9x9-inch dish.
- Spread ice cream evenly in prepared dish. Top with remaining cereal mixture. Freeze until firm. Cut into squares.
- *Yield: 9 servings.*

Approx Per Serving: Cal 502; Prot 6 g; Carbo 58 g; T Fat 29 g; 51% Calories from Fat; Chol 79 mg; Fiber 1 g; Sod 319 mg

Fresh Plum Delight

2 cups flour
1/4 cup sugar
1 teaspoon baking powder
1/2 teaspoon salt
1/2 teaspoon grated lemon rind
1/4 teaspoon ground mace
1/2 cup margarine
1 egg, beaten
2 tablespoons cold water
2 pounds purple or red plums
3/4 cup sugar
2 tablespoons flour
1 teaspoon ground cinnamon
1 tablespoon butter
1/4 cup slivered almonds

- Preheat oven to 375 degrees.
- Combine 2 cups flour, 1/4 cup sugar, baking powder, salt, lemon rind and mace in bowl; mix well. Cut in margarine until crumbly. Add egg and water; mix until ball forms. Knead several times. Press over bottom and side of 9-inch round baking pan.
- Cut plums into halves; discard pits. Arrange plums cut side down and slightly overlapping in prepared pan.
- Combine 3/4 cup sugar, 2 tablespoons flour, cinnamon and butter in small bowl; mix until crumbly. Mix in almonds. Sprinkle over plums.
- Bake at 375 degrees for 35 minutes or until bubbly and golden brown.
- *Yield: 6 servings.*

Approx Per Serving: Cal 573; Prot 8 g; Carbo 88 g; T Fat 22 g; 34% Calories from Fat; Chol 41 mg; Fiber 4 g; Sod 443 mg

Baked Rhubarb Pudding

3 cups chopped rhubarb
³/₄ cup sugar
2 tablespoons flour
1 egg, beaten
1 cup graham cracker
   crumbs
¹/₂ cup packed brown sugar
¹/₄ cup butter

- Preheat oven to 350 degrees.
- Combine rhubarb, sugar, flour and egg in bowl; mix well. Pour into greased 8-inch square baking pan.
- Mix graham cracker crumbs, brown sugar and butter in small bowl until crumbly. Sprinkle over rhubarb mixture.
- Bake at 350 degrees for 35 to 45 minutes or until rhubarb is tender and topping is brown.
- *Yield: 6 servings.*

Approx Per Serving: Cal 341; Prot 3 g; Carbo 60 g; T Fat 11 g; 28% Calories from Fat; Chol 56 mg; Fiber 2 g; Sod 218 mg

Extra-Light Trifle

1¹/₂ cups skim milk
1 cup light sour cream
¹/₄ cup orange juice
1 (6-serving) package
   sugar-free vanilla instant
   pudding mix
1 teaspoon grated orange
   rind
1 (10-inch) angel food cake
1 quart fresh strawberries

- Combine milk, sour cream and orange juice in bowl; mix well. Add pudding mix; beat until smooth and creamy. Stir in orange rind.
- Tear cake into pieces.
- Reserve several strawberries for garnish. Slice remaining strawberries.
- Alternate layers of cake pieces, strawberry slices and pudding in large straight-sided glass bowl until all ingredients are used, ending with pudding.
- Garnish with reserved whole strawberries. Chill until serving time.
- *Yield: 15 servings.*

Approx Per Serving: Cal 156; Prot 4 g; Carbo 30 g; T Fat 3 g; 14% Calories from Fat; Chol 7 mg; Fiber 1 g; Sod 373 mg

Spring Fling Dessert

2 cups butter cracker crumbs
1/2 cup melted margarine
1/4 cup sugar
4 egg whites
1 cup sugar
1/2 teaspoon vanilla extract
11/2 cups sugar
1/3 cup cornstarch
11/2 cups cold water
3 egg yolks, beaten
1/4 cup fresh lemon juice
3 tablespoons butter
1 tablespoon grated lemon
  rind
1 cup whipping cream
1/4 cup confectioners' sugar
1 teaspoon vanilla extract

- Preheat oven to 350 degrees.
- Combine cracker crumbs, melted margarine and 1/4 cup sugar in bowl; mix well. Reserve 1/4 cup for topping. Press remaining mixture into 9x13-inch baking pan.
- Beat egg whites in mixer bowl until stiff peaks form. Beat in 1 cup sugar and 1/2 teaspoon vanilla until very stiff peaks form. Spread over crumb layer.
- Bake at 350 degrees for 18 minutes. Let stand until cool.
- Mix 11/2 cups sugar and cornstarch in saucepan. Stir in cold water. Cook over medium heat until mixture thickens and comes to a boil, stirring constantly. Boil for 1 minute, stirring constantly.
- Stir a small amount of hot mixture into beaten egg yolks; stir egg yolks into hot mixture. Cook for 1 minute, stirring constantly; remove from heat. Stir in lemon juice, 3 tablespoons butter and lemon rind.
- Let stand until cool. Spread over meringue.
- Beat whipping cream with confectioners' sugar and 1 teaspoon vanilla until soft peaks form. Spread over pudding.
- Garnish with reserved crumbs and thin lemon slices.
- Refrigerate until serving time.
- *Yield: 15 servings.*

Approx Per Serving: Cal 356; Prot 3 g; Carbo 48 g; T Fat 18 g; 44% Calories from Fat; Chol 70 mg; Fiber <1 g; Sod 199 mg

Rice Dessert

4 cups milk
1/2 cup uncooked rice
2 egg yolks
1/2 cup sugar
1/4 cup cream
1 teaspoon vanilla extract
1 teaspoon salt
1 (3-ounce) package any
    flavor gelatin
1 cup sugar
3 tablespoons cornstarch
2 1/2 cups water

• Bring milk and rice to the simmering point in saucepan, stirring frequently; do not boil. Reduce heat to low. Cook for 45 to 60 minutes or until rice is tender and mixture is thick, stirring frequently.

• Mix egg yolks, 1/2 cup sugar, cream, vanilla and salt in bowl. Stir into rice mixture. Cook until thick, stirring constantly. Pour into 9x13-inch pan. Chill in refrigerator.

• Combine gelatin, 1 cup sugar and cornstarch in saucepan; mix well. Stir in water gradually. Heat until gelatin and sugar dissolve completely and mixture is clear and thickened.

• Let stand until cool. Pour over rice layer.

• Add garnish of whipped cream just before serving.

• *Yield: 15 servings.*

Approx Per Serving: Cal 189; Prot 3 g; Carbo 35 g; T Fat 4 g; 21% Calories from Fat; Chol 43 mg; Fiber <1 g; Sod 191 mg

Swedish Cream

1 cup sugar
1 envelope unflavored
    gelatin
2 cups whipping cream
2 cups sour cream
1 teaspoon vanilla extract

• Mix sugar and gelatin in saucepan. Stir in whipping cream.

• Heat over medium-low heat until sugar and gelatin dissolve, stirring constantly; remove from heat.

• Fold in sour cream and vanilla. Pour into stemmed glasses or small glass dessert dishes. Chill until set.

• Garnish with fresh or frozen fruit.

• *Yield: 8 servings.*

Approx Per Serving: Cal 428; Prot 4 g; Carbo 29 g; T Fat 34 g; 70% Calories from Fat; Chol 107 mg; Fiber 0 g; Sod 55 mg

COOKING FOR A CROWD

Latha Rakow
Morrison County

Cooking for a Crowd

The Minnesota State Fair serves as a showcase for the activities that occur throughout the year in the 4-H program. It highlights life skills that are learned and practiced in our daily routine. "Cooking for a Crowd" is definitely a part of the 4-H experience during the State Fair. The 4-H cafeteria, located on the second floor of the 4-H Building at the State Fair, provides meal service to 4-H members, parents, support staff, judges, volunteers, and special guests. During the State Fair an average of 16,500 meals and 7,400 snacks are served totaling almost 24,000 meals.

Many special events are celebrated with food. We have shared fond memories and tender moments over the dinner tables in the 4-H cafeteria. We have also celebrated the successes and years of service that many people have devoted to the 4-H program such as the Delores L. Andol Day and the Leonard Harkness Appreciation Event. Thank you for caring about the young people of our country and join with us as we continue to showcase the leaders of the future during the State Fair.

- When planning for a large crowd, estimate 1$\frac{1}{3}$ to 1$\frac{1}{2}$ dinner rolls per guest. For fifty people, prepare six dozen rolls.
- For a cocktail party, estimate 2 to 3 drinks per person using 1$\frac{1}{2}$ of portions of liquor per drink.
- Allow 1 pound of ice per person when serving mixed drinks.
- Plan on 1 waiter per 25 guests for a large buffet.
- For a cocktail party, plan on 1 waiter per 35 guests.

*F*ormal Dinner Party Menu

Each State Fair, 4-Hers are joined by the Minnesota Extension Service Citizen's Advisory Committee for an opening-day evening meal and by the State Fair Board for a formal luncheon. The following menu is often served at the State Fair. Serve it at your next formal dinner party or for a rehearsal dinner.

Orange Glazed Chicken with Wild Rice Medley

Carrots with Sugar Snap Peas

Deluxe Dinner Salad

Assorted Dinner Rolls

Peanut Buster Fudge Cake

*O*range Glazed Chicken

50 (5-ounce) boneless
   chicken breast halves
2 to 3 cups flour
Vegetable oil for sautéing
Salt and pepper to taste
1 quart frozen orange juice
   concentrate
1 quart water
1 (16-ounce) jar orange
   marmalade

- Preheat oven to 300 degrees.
- Rinse chicken and pat dry. Coat with flour.
- Brown chicken on both sides in oil in skillet; drain. Season with salt and pepper.
- Arrange in roasting pan.
- Pour mixture of orange juice concentrate, water and orange marmalade over chicken.
- Bake, covered, at 300 degrees for 45 minutes or until chicken reaches an internal temperature of 165 degrees, basting frequently.
- *Yield: 50 servings.*

Approx Per Serving: Cal 260; Prot 34 g; Carbo 20 g; T Fat 4 g; 14% Calories from Fat; Chol 90 mg; Fiber <1 g; Sod 85 mg
Nutritional information does not include oil for sautéing.

Wild Rice Medley

1 gallon water
3 cups wild rice
3 quarts boiling water
1 pound mushrooms, sliced
4 cups long grain rice
2 cups bulgur
1 1/2 cups butter
1 cup chopped celery
1 bunch green onions, sliced
1/2 cup chicken soup base
Seasoned salt and pepper to
　taste

- Bring 1 gallon water and wild rice to a boil in stockpot; reduce heat.
- Cook until wild rice is tender; drain.
- Combine 3 quarts boiling water, mushrooms, long grain rice, bulgur, butter, celery, green onions and soup base in roasting pan; mix well.
- Bake, covered, in moderate oven for 1 hour or until rice is tender, stirring occasionally. May add additional water as needed for desired consistency.
- Stir in wild rice. Season with seasoned salt and pepper.
- *Yield: 50 servings.*

Approx Per Serving: Cal 166; Prot 3 g; Carbo 25 g; T Fat 6 g; 33% Calories from Fat; Chol 15 mg; Fiber 1 g; Sod 417 mg

Carrots with Sugar Snap Peas

8 pounds frozen baby carrots
4 cups packed brown sugar
1 pound butter
3 pounds frozen sugar snap
　peas, thawed

- Preheat oven to 325 degrees.
- Place frozen carrots in roasting pan.
- Sprinkle with brown sugar; dot with butter.
- Bake, covered, at 325 degrees for 2 1/2 hours, stirring 2 or 3 times.
- Stir in sugar snap peas.
- Bake for 10 minutes longer.
- *Yield: 50 servings.*

Approx Per Serving: Cal 167; Prot 2 g; Carbo 24 g; T Fat 8 g; 39% Calories from Fat; Chol 20 mg; Fiber 3 g; Sod 154 mg

Deluxe Dinner Salad

1 large cucumber
4 heads iceberg lettuce, torn
    into bite-size pieces
2 heads romaine, torn into
    bite-size pieces
1 cup shredded red cabbage
1 carrot, grated
1 green bell pepper, chopped
1 bunch green onions,
    chopped
8 tomatoes, cut into wedges
1 quart Italian salad dressing

- Score unpeeled cucumber with fork; cut into thin slices.
- Layer lettuce and romaine alternately with cucumber, cabbage, carrot, green pepper and green onions in 2 large serving bowls.
- Arrange tomato wedges around outer edge of bowls in shape of star.
- Pour salad dressing over salad just before serving.
- *Yield: 50 servings.*

Approx Per Serving: Cal 99; Prot 1 g; Carbo 4 g;
    T Fat 9 g; 81% Calories from Fat; Chol 0 mg;
    Fiber 1 g; Sod 153 mg

Peanut Buster Fudge Cake

2 (2-layer) packages devil's
    food cake mix
6 eggs
1 cup vegetable oil
2¹/₂ cups water
5 quarts whipped topping
1 (#10) can hot fudge ice
    cream topping
3 pounds peanuts

- Preheat oven to 350 degrees.
- Prepare cake mixes according to package directions using 6 eggs, 1 cup oil and 2¹/₂ cups water. Spoon into half sheet pan.
- Bake at 350 degrees for 25 to 30 minutes or until cake tests done.
- Let stand until cool.
- Spread with whipped topping. Swirl with ice cream topping; sprinkle with peanuts.
- *Yield: 50 servings.*

Approx Per Serving: Cal 694; Prot 13 g; Carbo 81 g;
    T Fat 40 g; 49% Calories from Fat; Chol 36 mg;
    Fiber 5 g; Sod 300 mg

*B*runch Menu

Brunches are becoming very popular. They present a leisurely approach to dining for busy schedules and often include easily prepared foods. This menu may be fun for you to prepare for family celebrations or holiday gatherings.

Fruit Medley Punch

Sausage and Cheese Puff Pastry

Toasted Ham and Cheese Muffins

Steamed Asparagus Spears

Fresh Fruit Kabobs

Orange Bowknots

*F*ruit Medley Punch

4 (16-ounce) cans frozen
    orange juice concentrate
1 (48-ounce) can pineapple
    juice
3 juice cans water
2 cups maraschino cherry
    juice

• Combine orange juice concentrate, pineapple juice, water and cherry juice in large covered container; mix well.
• Chill until serving time.
• Pour into chilled glasses.
• Garnish with orange slices or pineapple wedges.
• May substitute 1 cup grenadine for cherry juice.
• *Yield: 50 servings.*

Approx Per Serving: Cal 87; Prot 1 g; Carbo 21 g; T Fat <1 g; 1% Calories from Fat; Chol 0 mg; Fiber <1 g; Sod 3 mg

Sausage and Cheese Puff Pastry

50 puff pastry shells
10 pounds bulk pork sausage
1 tablespoon cayenne
3 pounds sharp Cheddar
  cheese, shredded
1 pound fresh mushrooms,
  chopped
18 eggs, beaten
1 bunch green onions,
  chopped

- Preheat oven to 375 degrees.
- Arrange puff pastry shells on foil-lined baking sheet.
- Bake at 375 degrees until puffed and brown; do not overbake.
- Remove to wire rack to cool. Remove top and reserve.
- Brown sausage in skillet, stirring until crumbly; drain. Season with cayenne.
- Stir in cheese, mushrooms, eggs and green onions.
- Spoon into pastry shells. Arrange on baking sheet.
- Bake for 15 minutes longer or until hot and bubbly. Remove from oven. Top with reserved tops.
- *Yield: 50 servings.*

Approx Per Serving: Cal 506; Prot 21 g; Carbo 18 g; T Fat 39 g; 70% Calories from Fat; Chol 140 mg; Fiber <1 g; Sod 923 mg

Toasted Ham and Cheese Muffins

4 dozen hard-cooked eggs,
  chopped
3 cups mayonnaise-type
  salad dressing
1/2 cup sugar
2 teaspoons prepared
  mustard
1/2 teaspoon pepper
25 English muffins, split
  into halves
50 (1-ounce) slices ham
50 (1-ounce) slices
  American cheese

- Preheat oven to 350 degrees.
- Combine eggs, salad dressing, sugar, mustard and pepper in bowl; mix well.
- Arrange muffin halves on baking sheet; top with ham.
- Spread with egg mixture; top with cheese.
- Bake at 350 degrees until cheese melts.
- *Yield: 50 servings.*

Approx Per Serving: Cal 354; Prot 22 g; Carbo 20 g; T Fat 21 g; 53% Calories from Fat; Chol 250 mg; Fiber 1 g; Sod 1075 mg

Steamed Asparagus Spears

8 pounds fresh asparagus, trimmed
1 cup melted butter
Juice of 1 lemon

- Steam asparagus in steamer until tender-crisp. Arrange on serving platter.
- Drizzle with mixture of butter and lemon juice.
- *Yield: 50 servings.*

Approx Per Serving: Cal 50; Prot 2 g; Carbo 3 g; T Fat 4 g; 63% Calories from Fat; Chol 10 mg; Fiber 1 g; Sod 39 mg

Fresh Fruit Kabobs

13 or 14 kiwifruit
3 fresh pineapple, cut into wedges
4 to 5 pints whole strawberries
2 or 3 cantaloupes, cut into 2-inch pieces
50 (12-inch) bamboo skewers

- Cut each kiwifruit into 4 slices.
- Thread kiwifruit, pineapple, strawberries and cantaloupe alternately on bamboo skewers. Arrange on serving platter.
- Chill, covered, until serving time.
- *Yield: 50 servings.*

Approx Per Serving: Cal 47; Prot 1 g; Carbo 11 g; T Fat <1 g; 7% Calories from Fat; Chol 0 mg; Fiber 2 g; Sod 5 mg

Orange Bowknots

7 (11-ounce) cans soft breadsticks
1 pound melted butter
3 cups sugar
Grated rind of 5 oranges

- Preheat oven to 350 degrees.
- Separate breadstick dough.
- Dip each breadstick in butter; roll in mixture of sugar and orange rind.
- Tie each breadstick loosely into knot. Arrange on greased baking sheet.
- Bake at 350 degrees for 15 to 20 minutes or until light brown. Remove to wire rack.
- *Yield: 50 servings.*

Approx Per Serving: Cal 228; Prot 4 g; Carbo 32 g; T Fat 10 g; 38% Calories from Fat; Chol 20 mg; Fiber <1 g; Sod 336 mg

*S*ummer Menu

The Minnesota 4-H Foundation Summer Donor Appreciation Event is held just prior to the opening of the State Fair. In the past such delicacies as Hog Roast and Barbecue Chicken with all the fixings have been served. Here are a few suggestions for your family reunion or 4-H Club summer tour or picnic.

Barbecued Turkey on a Bun

Fresh Fruit Basket

Italian Pasta Salad

Old-Fashioned Potato Salad

Crudités with Dill Dip

Texas Pecan Pie Bars

*B*arbecued Turkey on a Bun

10 pounds deli turkey
3 quarts barbecue sauce
50 sandwich buns

- Preheat oven to 250 degrees.
- Arrange turkey in baking pan.
- Bake, covered, for 1 hour; drain.
- Add barbecue sauce, stirring until well coated.
- Bake just until heated through.
- Spoon onto buns.
- May substitute deli beef for turkey.
- *Yield: 50 servings.*

Approx Per Serving: Cal 328; Prot 32 g; Carbo 30 g; T Fat 8 g; 22% Calories from Fat; Chol 69 mg; Fiber 1 g; Sod 804 mg

Fresh Fruit Basket

1 large watermelon
2 pints strawberries with
    stems
2 cantaloupes, cut into
    bite-size pieces
1 honeydew melon, cut into
    bite-size pieces
1 pound grapes, stems
    removed
3 kiwifruit, sliced

• Rinse watermelon; cut small slice from bottom for balance.
• Carve top half of watermelon in scallop or zigzag design, leaving 2-inch band in center for handle.
• Scoop out melon, leaving thin layer of pulp. Cut pulp into bite-size pieces.
• Attach strawberries to edge of basket and across handle with wooden picks.
• Fill basket with mixture of watermelon, cantaloupe, honeydew melon and grapes.
• Arrange kiwifruit and remaining strawberries over top of fruit.
• *Yield: 50 servings.*

Approx Per Serving: Cal 78; Prot 1 g; Carbo 18 g; T Fat 1 g; 9% Calories from Fat; Chol 0 mg; Fiber 2 g; Sod 8 mg

Italian Pasta Salad

2 pounds rainbow rotini,
    cooked, drained, cooled
1 bunch broccoli, cut into
    bite-size pieces
1 head cauliflower, cut into
    bite-size pieces
1 (12-ounce) package frozen
    peas and carrots
1 pint cherry tomatoes, cut
    into quarters
1 cup grated Parmesan cheese
1/2 cup sliced black olives
1/2 cup chopped green bell
    pepper
1 bunch green onions,
    chopped
3 to 4 cups creamy Italian
    salad dressing

• Combine rotini, broccoli, cauliflower, peas and carrots, tomatoes, cheese, black olives, green pepper and green onions in bowl; mix well.
• Add salad dressing, tossing to coat.
• Chill, covered, until serving time.
• May be prepared 1 day in advance and refrigerated until serving time; additional dressing may be required for desired flavor.
• *Yield: 50 servings.*

Approx Per Serving: Cal 179; Prot 4 g; Carbo 17 g; T Fat 11 g; 55% Calories from Fat; Chol 2 mg; Fiber 1 g; Sod 281 mg

Old-Fashioned Potato Salad

8 pounds potatoes, cooked,
    peeled, sliced
3¹/₂ dozen hard-cooked
    eggs, sliced
1¹/₂ cups finely chopped
    celery
1 bunch green onions, finely
    chopped
6 cups mayonnaise-type
    salad dressing
1 cup sugar
1 cup half-and-half
2 tablespoons (or more)
    prepared mustard
Salt and pepper to taste

- Combine potatoes, eggs, celery and green onions in bowl, tossing lightly.
- Stir in mixture of salad dressing, sugar, half-and-half and mustard; season with salt and pepper.
- Chill until serving time.
- Spoon into serving bowl. Place in larger bowl filled with ice to serve.
- *Yield: 50 servings.*

Approx Per Serving: Cal 265; Prot 7 g; Carbo 27 g; T Fat 15 g; 49% Calories from Fat; Chol 187 mg; Fiber 1 g; Sod 269 mg

Crudités with Dill Dip

3 cups sour cream
3 cups mayonnaise-type
    salad dressing
3 tablespoons dillweed
3 tablespoons chopped fresh
    parsley
1 tablespoon finely chopped
    onion
1 teaspoon seasoned salt
¹/₂ teaspoon pepper
¹/₂ teaspoon garlic powder
4 pounds carrots, peeled, cut
    into strips
1 bunch celery, cut into
    4-inch strips
Florets of 1 bunch broccoli
Florets of 1 head cauliflower
1 small green bell pepper,
    cut into strips or rings
1 pint cherry tomatoes

- Combine sour cream, salad dressing, dillweed, parsley, onion, seasoned salt, pepper and garlic powder in bowl; mix well.
- Chill, covered, for several hours.
- Arrange carrots, celery, broccoli, cauliflower, green pepper and cherry tomatoes on serving tray.
- Store, covered with damp paper towel, in refrigerator until serving time.
- Serve with dill dip.
- *Yield: 50 servings.*

Approx Per Serving: Cal 105; Prot 1 g; Carbo 9 g; T Fat 8 g; 64% Calories from Fat; Chol 10 mg; Fiber 2 g; Sod 155 mg

Texas Pecan Pie Bars

3 cups flour
3/4 cup butter, softened
6 tablespoons sugar
1/2 teaspoon salt
5 eggs
1 cup sugar
1 cup corn syrup
1/2 cup packed brown sugar
1/4 cup melted butter
1 1/2 teaspoons vanilla extract
2 1/2 cups chopped pecans
1 cup chocolate chips

- Preheat oven to 350 degrees.
- Combine flour, 3/4 cup butter, 6 tablespoons sugar and salt in mixer bowl.
- Beat at medium speed until crumbly.
- Press into greased half sheet pan.
- Bake at 350 degrees for 20 minutes or until brown.
- Beat eggs, 1 cup sugar, corn syrup, brown sugar, 1/4 cup butter and vanilla in mixer bowl until blended. Stir in pecans.
- Spread evenly over baked layer; sprinkle with chocolate chips.
- Bake for 25 minutes or until set.
- Loosen baked layer from sides of pan with sharp knife. Let stand until cool. Cut into bars.
- *Yield: 50 servings.*

Approx Per Serving: Cal 170; Prot 2 g; Carbo 21 g; T Fat 9 g; 47% Calories from Fat; Chol 31 mg; Fiber 1 g; Sod 74 mg

Bubbling Punch

1 (3-ounce) package cherry gelatin
1 cup hot water
8 cups cold water
1 cup sugar
1 envelope cherry instant drink mix
1 (6-ounce) can frozen lemonade concentrate
1 cup pineapple juice
1 quart lemon-lime soda

- Dissolve gelatin in 1 cup boiling water in large container; mix well.
- Add 8 cups cold water, sugar and drink mix; mix well.
- Stir in lemonade concentrate and pineapple juice. Chill until serving time.
- Pour into punch bowl. Stir in lemon-lime soda just before serving.
- Ladle into punch cups.
- *Yield: 30 servings.*

Approx Per Serving: Cal 78; Prot <1 g; Carbo 20 g; T Fat <1 g; <1% Calories from Fat; Chol 0 mg; Fiber <1 g; Sod 8 mg

Fruit Punch

2 (12-ounce) cans frozen
   pineapple juice
2 (12-ounce) cans frozen
   orange juice
1 or 2 (12-ounce) cans
   frozen berry fruit punch
1 (12-ounce) can frozen
   lemonade
5 cups sugar
4 or 5 envelopes fruit punch
   drink mix
4 gallons water
4 to 6 quarts lemon-lime
   soda or ginger ale

- Thaw all frozen juices. Combine in
  5-gallon pail.
- Add sugar and drink mix. Add water;
  mix until sugar dissolves.
- Freeze a portion of the mixture in
  molds or ice cube trays. Chill the
  remaining punch.
- Place ice molds in punch bowl. Pour
  punch into bowl.
- Add soda just before serving; stir gently.
- *Yield: 125 (²/₃-cup) servings.*

Approx Per Serving: Cal 82; Prot <1 g; Carbo 21 g;
   T Fat <1 g; <1% Calories from Fat; Chol 0 mg;
   Fiber <1 g; Sod 9 mg

Traverse County 4-H Chili

2¹/₂ pounds ground beef
2 cups chopped onions
1¹/₂ cups chopped celery
1 tablespoon salt
¹/₂ teaspoon pepper
1 (46-ounce) can tomato
   juice
¹/₂ gallon dark kidney beans
¹/₂ gallon chili beans, drained
1¹/₂ cups catsup
1¹/₂ tablespoons chili powder
1 teaspoon dry mustard
¹/₂ cup water

- Brown ground beef in stockpot, stirring
  until crumbly; drain. Stir in onions,
  celery, salt and pepper. Cook until
  onions are tender, stirring frequently.
- Add tomato juice, undrained kidney
  beans, chili beans, catsup, chili powder
  and dry mustard; mix well.
- Rinse tomato juice can with water; pour
  into chili.
- Cook over low to medium heat for
  several hours or until of the desired
  consistency, stirring occasionally.
- *Yield: 20 servings.*

Approx Per Serving: Cal 336; Prot 22 g; Carbo 37 g;
   T Fat 12 g; 32% Calories from Fat; Chol 51 mg;
   Fiber 10 g; Sod 1698 mg

Vegetable Beef Soup

9 pounds beef stew meat
5 pounds potatoes, coarsely
    chopped
3 pounds onions, chopped
3 gallons plus 1 cup water
2 to 3 (16-ounce) packages
    frozen mixed vegetables
3 (46-ounce) cans tomato
    juice
1½ (32-ounce) packages
    pearled barley
3½ cups chopped carrots
3½ cups sliced celery
1 (16-ounce) package frozen
    corn
1 rutabaga, chopped
1 large head cabbage,
    chopped
9 bay leaves

- Combine stew meat, potatoes, onions, water, mixed vegetables, tomato juice, barley, carrots, celery, corn, rutabaga, cabbage and bay leaves in large bowl; mix well.
- Spoon into 3 large stockpots.
- Cook until beef and vegetables are tender and mixture is of the desired consistency, stirring occasionally.
- Discard bay leaves. Ladle into soup bowls.
- May add minced garlic to soup.
- *Yield: 75 servings.*

Approx Per Serving: Cal 164; Prot 13 g; Carbo 21 g; T Fat 4 g; 21% Calories from Fat; Chol 33 mg; Fiber 4 g; Sod 303 mg

Confirmation Salad

5 pounds cooked turkey, cut
    into bite-size pieces
24 to 30 ounces shell pasta,
    cooked, drained
1 (20-ounce) can crushed
    pineapple, drained
12 hard-cooked eggs,
    chopped
16 to 20 ounces frozen peas
1 bunch celery, chopped
1 (2-ounce) jar pimento,
    drained, chopped
1 onion, finely chopped
4 cups mayonnaise-type
    salad dressing
1½ cups western dressing

- Combine turkey, pasta, pineapple, eggs, frozen peas, celery, pimento and onion in bowl; mix well.
- Stir in mixture of salad dressing and western dressing.
- Chill, covered, until serving time.
- *Yield: 50 servings.*

Approx Per Serving: Cal 281; Prot 18 g; Carbo 22 g; T Fat 13 g; 43% Calories from Fat; Chol 95 mg; Fiber 1 g; Sod 303 mg

Fruit Salad

5 (4-ounce) packages lemon pudding and pie filling mix
Juice of 2 lemons
3 cups whipping cream, whipped
2 gallons fruit cocktail, drained
1 gallon pineapple chunks, drained
3 pounds green grapes
2 (16-ounce) cans mandarin oranges, drained
6 red apples, chopped
1 (28-ounce) jar maraschino cherries, drained
3 (10-ounce) packages miniature marshmallows

- Prepare pudding using package directions.
- Let stand until cool.
- Stir in lemon juice. Fold in whipped cream.
- Combine fruit cocktail, pineapple, grapes, mandarin oranges, apples, cherries and marshmallows in large bowl; mix well. Fold in pudding mixture.
- Chill, covered, for 8 to 10 hours.
- *Yield: 100 servings.*

Approx Per Serving: Cal 197; Prot 1 g; Carbo 43 g; T Fat 3 g; 15% Calories from Fat; Chol 33 mg; Fiber 2 g; Sod 41 mg

Potato Salad

14 pounds potatoes, cooked, peeled, chopped
12 hard-cooked eggs, chopped
1 cup chopped onion
1 cup chopped celery
1½ quarts mayonnaise-type salad dressing
1 cup cream
½ cup vinegar
½ cup sugar
¼ cup prepared mustard
¼ cup dillweed
Salt and pepper to taste

- Combine potatoes, eggs, onion and celery in bowl; mix well.
- Stir in mixture of salad dressing, cream, vinegar, sugar, mustard, dillweed, salt and pepper.
- May add additional cream for desired consistency.
- Chill, covered, until serving time.
- *Yield: 50 servings.*

Approx Per Serving: Cal 274; Prot 5 g; Carbo 37 g; T Fat 13 g; 41% Calories from Fat; Chol 65 mg; Fiber 2 g; Sod 242 mg

*B*etter Than Potato Salad

1 cup long grain rice
2 cups mayonnaise-type
   salad dressing
4 teaspoons prepared
   mustard
1/2 teaspoon salt
2 cups chopped celery
1 medium onion, finely
   chopped
4 hard-boiled eggs, chopped
8 radishes, sliced

- Cook rice using package directions. Let stand until cool.
- Combine salad dressing, mustard and salt in bowl; mix well.
- Combine cooled rice, celery, onion, eggs and radishes in large bowl. Add salad dressing; mix well. Chill until serving time.
- *Yield: 15 servings.*

Approx Per Serving: Cal 194; Prot 3 g; Carbo 19 g; T Fat 12 g; 55% Calories from Fat; Chol 65 mg; Fiber 1 g; Sod 343 mg

*S*crambled Eggs

7 dozen eggs
2 teaspoons salt
2 cups milk
2/3 cup Wondra flour
2 quarts milk, heated
1 pound butter
1 pound ham, chopped

- Preheat oven to 400 degrees.
- Beat eggs and salt in mixer bowl until blended.
- Combine 2 cups milk and flour in bowl; mix well.
- Add to egg mixture; mix well. Add hot milk gradually, stirring constantly.
- Heat butter in baking pan until melted. Pour in egg mixture; sprinkle with ham.
- Bake at 400 degrees for 20 minutes. Turn eggs with spatula.
- Bake for 10 minutes longer.
- Keep eggs warm in electric roaster set on Low; do not keep eggs warm in aluminum pans.
- *Yield: 50 servings.*

Approx Per Serving: Cal 240; Prot 15 g; Carbo 5 g; T Fat 18 g; 68% Calories from Fat; Chol 388 mg; Fiber <1 g; Sod 410 mg

Barbecued Hamburgers

18 pounds lean ground beef
15 onions, chopped
5 cups catsup
4 cans tomato soup
1/2 cup prepared mustard
1/4 cup salt
3 tablespoons chili powder
2 tablespoons pepper

- Crumble ground beef into large electric roaster.
- Add onions, catsup, soup, mustard and seasonings; mix well.
- Bake, covered, at 350 degrees for 1 1/2 hours, stirring frequently.
- Adjust seasonings if necessary.
- Ladle ground beef onto buns.
- Keep ground beef mixture warm in the roaster turned to a very low setting or for easier serving ladle the mixture into a slow cooker set on Low.
- *Yield: 120 servings.*

Approx Per Serving: Cal 173; Prot 16 g; Carbo 6 g; T Fat 10 g; 51% Calories from Fat; Chol 51 mg; Fiber 1 g; Sod 456 mg

Western Sloppy Joes

2 pounds ground beef
1 cup chopped onion
1 cup chopped celery
1 green bell pepper, chopped
2 cups water
1 (16-ounce) can chili beans
3/4 cup catsup
1/4 cup cider vinegar
2 tablespoons brown sugar
1 tablespoon prepared
    mustard
1 tablespoon
    Worcestershire sauce
1 teaspoon each salt, paprika
    and chili powder
1/2 teaspoon pepper

- Brown ground beef in large skillet, stirring until crumbly. Drain, reserving 1 tablespoon of pan drippings. Remove ground beef to bowl.
- Sauté onion, celery and green pepper in reserved pan drippings in skillet until soft. Return ground beef to skillet.
- Add water, undrained chili beans, catsup, vinegar, brown sugar, mustard, Worcestershire sauce, salt, paprika, chili powder and pepper; mix well.
- Simmer for 1 hour or until thickened, stirring frequently.
- *Yield: 15 servings.*

Approx Per Serving: Cal 192; Prot 16 g; Carbo 10 g; T Fat 10 g; 47% Calories from Fat; Chol 50 mg; Fiber 2 g; Sod 509 mg

$\mathscr{C}$how Mein

1 (1-gallon) can bean sprouts
5 bunches celery, chopped
4 cups chopped onions
1 (1-gallon) can chop suey
   vegetables
1 (1-gallon) can cooked
   pork, drained
2 cups soy sauce
2 envelopes onion soup mix
1/3 cup (or more) cornstarch
Kitchen Bouquet to taste

• Drain bean sprouts, reserving liquid.
• Mix reserved liquid, celery and onions in stockpot. Simmer until vegetables are tender, stirring occasionally. Add bean sprouts, chop suey vegetables, pork, soy sauce and soup mix; mix well.
• Dissolve cornstarch in a small amount of water. Stir into bean sprout mixture. Add Kitchen Bouquet. Cook until thickened, stirring constantly.
• Simmer for 30 minutes or until of the desired consistency.
• *Yield: 100 servings.*

Approx Per Serving: Cal 126; Prot 5 g; Carbo 4 g;
   T Fat 10 g; 71% Calories from Fat; Chol 21 mg;
   Fiber 1 g; Sod 911 mg

$\mathscr{M}$eat Loaf

12 pounds lean ground beef
3 cups dry bread crumbs
2 cups chopped onions
6 eggs, beaten
2 tablespoons salt
1/2 teaspoon pepper
6 (8-ounce) cans tomato
   sauce
2/3 cup water

• Preheat oven to 350 degrees.
• Combine first 6 ingredients in large bowl; mix well. Shape into 4 to 6 loaves; place in large baking pans.
• Bake at 350 degrees for 1 1/2 hours.
• Drain and reserve drippings. Let meat loaf and drippings stand for several minutes. Skim drippings. Measure 2/3 cup or more of the skimmed drippings; pour into saucepan. Add tomato sauce and water to drippings; mix well. Heat to serving temperature.
• Place meat loaves on serving plates; slice as desired. Spoon sauce over sliced meat loaves or serve over slices.
• *Yield: 50 servings.*

Approx Per Serving: Cal 282; Prot 26 g; Carbo 7 g;
   T Fat 16 g; 52% Calories from Fat; Chol 106 mg;
   Fiber 1 g; Sod 538 mg

*B*aked Bean Casserole

2 pounds ground beef
8 (28-ounce) cans baked
  beans
3 (16-ounce) cans kidney
  beans
1 pound bacon, crisp-fried,
  crumbled
1 (12-ounce) jar molasses
1 cup packed brown sugar

- Brown ground beef in skillet, stirring until crumbly; drain.
- Combine ground beef, baked beans, kidney beans, bacon, molasses and brown sugar in stockpot; mix well.
- Cook just until heated through or of the desired consistency, stirring occasionally.
- *Yield: 75 servings.*

Approx Per Serving: Cal 163; Prot 9 g; Carbo 25 g; T Fat 4 g; 21% Calories from Fat; Chol 17 mg; Fiber 7 g; Sod 451 mg

*T*en Thousand Chocolate Chip Cookies

From the kitchen cookbook of a World War II aircraft carrier.

100 pounds sugar
87 pounds shortening
75 pounds brown sugar
12 pounds butter
500 eggs
165 pounds flour
1½ pounds baking soda
3 cups salt
1 quart water
3 cups vanilla extract
112 pounds chocolate chips

- Cream sugar, shortening, brown sugar and butter in mixer bowl until smooth.
- Add eggs, beating until blended.
- Add mixture of flour, baking soda and salt; mix well.
- Beat in water and vanilla until blended.
- Stir in chocolate chips.
- Drop by teaspoonfuls onto cookie sheet.
- Bake in moderate oven until light brown.
- Remove to wire rack to cool.
- *Yield: 10,000 servings.*

Nutritional information for this recipe not available.

Make *Lemonade Pies For a Crowd* with 1 gallon softened vanilla ice cream and two (12-ounce) cans frozen lemonade concentrate. Spoon into 6 graham cracker pie shells and freeze until firm. Garnish with whipped cream and lemon slices.

$\mathcal{Q}$uantities to Serve 100

Beverages

Carbonated beverages . . . . 12 (2-liter) bottles
Coffee, ground . . . . 3 pounds
Frozen fruit juice concentrate . . . . 9 (12-ounce) cans
Punch . . . . 4 gallons

Dairy

Butter . . . . 3 pounds
Cheese . . . . 1³/₄ pounds
Ice Cream . . . . 4 gallons
Milk . . . . 6 gallons

Beef, Pork, Poultry and Fish

Bacon . . . . 12 pounds
Beef . . . . 40 pounds
Beef, sliced for sandwiches . . . . 10 pounds
Chicken salad . . . . 12¹/₂ quarts
Frankfurters . . . . 25 pounds
Ground beef . . . . 30 to 36 pounds
Ham . . . . 40 pounds
Roast pork . . . . 40 pounds
Shrimp, peeled . . . . 24 pounds
Shrimp in shell . . . . 40 pounds
Turkey, to roast . . . . 70 to 80 pounds

Salads and Relishes

Cabbage for slaw . . . . 20 pounds
Carrot strips . . . . 12¹/₂ pounds
Celery strips . . . . 12¹/₂ pounds
Lettuce . . . . 20 heads
Pickles . . . . 4 quarts
Potato salad . . . . 13 quarts
Vegetable salad . . . . 20 quarts

*Q*uantities to Serve 100

Vegetables and Grains

Asparagus, fresh	40 pounds
Baked beans	5 gallons
Beets	30 pounds
Carrots	26 pounds
Cauliflowerets	26 pounds
Frozen vegetables	20 (16-ounce) packages
Green beans, fresh	13 pounds
Macaroni	9 pounds
Noodles	96 ounces
Potatoes	35 pounds
Potatoes, scalloped	5 gallons
Spaghetti	9 pounds
Sweet potatoes	50 pounds

Miscellaneous

Bread	10 loaves
Cakes	8 (9-inch) layers
Cake mixes	6 to 8 packages
Fruit cocktail	1 gallon
Pies	18 (9-inch)
Ice for tea	100 pounds
Olives	1³/₄ pounds
Potato chips	6 pounds
Pudding	24 (4-ounce) packages

Andrea Hammel
Washington County

Contributors

Blair Aakre
Karen Aakre
Jenna Aanden
Kristen Ackerman
Lisa Ackerman
Carissa Adams
Mark Adelmann
Michele Adelmann
Kandy Ahlers
MerlLynda Ahlers
Sarah Ahlfs
Ila M. Akkerman
Caroline Alberg
Abby Alleman
Cheryl Allen
Patricia Almquist
Cara Almquist-Plews
Becky Alper
Dawn Alsleben
Tiffany Alsleben
JoAnn Ammann
Becky Amundson
Brandon Amundson
Eric Amundson
Michael Amundson
Tony Amundson
Connie Anderson
Jane Anderson
Jessica Anderson
Nathan and Brannon
   Anderson
Ryan Anderson
Timothy Anderson
Delores L. Andol
Angela Anno
Durene Anno
Amber Appel
Cheri Appel
Donna Appel
Rose Appel
Terrilyn Arends
Rhonda Arneson
Becky Asp
Ryan Aspelund
Terry Anne Aspelund
Jerritt Aune
Tyler and Samantha Auspos
Crystal Bailey
Jane Bailey
Julianne Bailey

Karen Ball
Luke Barker
Kelly Lynn Barlau
Jan Barthelemy
Matthew Baudino
Mary Catherine Bauer
Sara Baumetz
Sonia Baumetz
Judy Beck
Rhonda and Angela Becker
Shari Becklund
Darryn and Kendell
   Beckstrom
Kaylee Beito
Luther Bell
Mary Ann Bell
Naomi Bell
Rachel Bell
Ruth Bell
Sarah Bell
Jenifer Benes
Lisa Benes
Barb Bening
Linda L. Benson
Marsha Benson
Allay Beraki
Ashley Berg
Lynn Bernstetter
Betsy Bianchi
Beth A. Bielen
Big Bend Aces 4-H Club
Betty Bigger
Tara Jean Bisek
Bill Bloedow
Laura Bloedow
Betty Bly
Beverly Bode
Becky Bodurtha
Jill Boettcher
Mindy Boettcher
Joanne Bolland
Cynthia Borchert
Matthew Borchert
Wilma Bosch
Joel and Jared Botzek
Ryan Boyer
Jeff Boyle
Trisha Boyle
Sandra Brandt
Willa Bratsch

Julie Bratvold
Nancy Bratvold
Randy Bratvold
Robert Bratvold
Karen Braulick
Lucy Braulick
Sarah Braulick
Kris Braulizk
Jennifer Brausen
Galen Brelie
Gerald and Julie Briese
Emily Brinker
Meg Brinker
Bethany Broberg
Patricia Broberg
JoAnn Brockberg
Maxine Broderius
Jeremy Brogaard
Preston Brogaard
Pete Brokaw
Jennifer Bronson
Justin Bronson
Sandy Bronson
Debbie Broughten
Jenny Brown
Nancy Brown
Aaron Brownlee
Kira Brownlee
LuAnn Bruns
Valerie Bryce
Christy A. Bubolz
Mary Ann Bucher
Mary Buck
Char Buckentin
David Edwin Burgstaler
Burlington Cubs 4-H Club
Staci Busch
Brigette Buss
Tamitha L. Buxengard
Richard Byrne
Susan Cadieux
Katie Capistran
Anita Cardinal
Aaron Carlson
Bonnie Irene Carlson
Brad Carlson
Donald Edwin Carlson
Dustin Carlson
Sheila Carlson
Raeann Carpentier

Shawna Carpentier
John Cavanaugh
Sally Cavanaugh
Cynthia Celander
Heidi Chapel
Ken Chapel
Gail Cherne
Elaine Christiansen
Christa Cichoski
Kim Cichoski
Sharon Cichosz
Elisabeth Clark
Ruth Clark
Seth Clark
Tom Clark
Amy Cleveland
Cloverdale 4-H Club
Craig Coil
Curt Coil
Jenny Coleman
Kathy Conrad
Mandy Cota
Country Bumpkins 4-H
    Club
Anna Covington
Holly Covington
Kathy Covington
Bettina Crawford
Erin Crawford
Isaac Crawford
Lance Crawford
Natasha Cronen
Dorene Cyr
Brigette Dahl
Kristina Dahl
Allison Dahlgren
Aron Dahlgren
Grace Dahlgren
Teresa Dahlgren
Patty Appel Dahlke
Annamarie Daley
Edna Dallum
Dane Prairie 4-H Club
Alexis Danielson
Amanda Dauna
Carol David
Gus David Family
Rachelle David
Sarah David
Vito David
Ashley Ann Davison
Barbara Davison
Chad Davison
Chris Davison

Carla Dean
Gail Dean
Naomi Dean
Darrell DeHart
Joel Dehne
Karen Dellwo
Delton Doers 4-H Club
Marie DeMars
Rachelle DeMars
Dustin Lee Denzer
Kevin Denzer
Sarah M. Diehn
Christy Diel
Marcia Dischinger
Jodie Dobratz
Julie Dobratz
Wendy Dodge
Janet Dolezal
Kari Dolezal
Sarah Domoradzki
Cynthia Dorau
Amber Dostal
Chris Dostal
Denise Dostal
Josh Dostal
Matthew Dostal
Nicole Dostal
Randy Dostal
Ryan Dostal
Allison Dotzenrod
Garrett Doucette
Katherine Dreher
Randy Drinkall Family
Carol Duchene
Diane Duchene
Jaclyn Duesterhoeft
Duin Family
Katie Dumphy
Becky Dunham
Lori Dunham
Jan Dzwonkowski
Julie Eastvold
Theresa and Daniel Eaton
Anna Ebbesen
Betty Edgren
Helen Edwards
Kimberly and Kari Edwards
Marjorie Ehlers
Tammie Ehlers
Christy Eichers
Danessa Eide
Diane Eide
Rachel Eidet
Sarah Eidet

Jacob Ekola
Marcine Elder
Kurtis Ellefson
Seth Ellefson
M. Kathi Ellis
Joan Enderle
Arla Engelkes
Jill Engelmann
Katie Engelmann
Megan Enninga
Jennifer Enter
Beth Erdmann
Hilda Erickson
Justine Erickson
Roxanne Erickson
Jule Erjavec
Jeanie Evans
Mary Evans
Nicollet Farber
Kelsey Fasteland
Maggie Fasteland
Martha Fasteland
Mickenzie Fasteland
Rachel Fasteland
Mindy Ferrie
Lisa Fest
Sharon Fey
Kristi Finnell
Debra L. Fischer
Lois Fischer
Molly Fischer
Chris Flynn
David Flynn
Elizabeth Flynn
Ryan Flynn
Amanda Fogelson
Ryan Fogelson
Angie Foix
Bea Foix
Diana Fradette
Laurie Fredin
Andrea Froehlich
Vicki Froehlich
Amanda Fugelson
Judy Gaebel
Ingrid Gangestad
Elaine Garding
LeAnn Garding
Colleen Doucette Garrett
Adriane Gehl
Kindel Gehl
Paige Gehl
Jaclyn Gehrke
Tony Gehrke

Carrie Genser
Kathy Genser
Michelle Genser
Darci Gerard
Dianne Gerard
Heath Gerard
Jason Geving
Mary Lou Gillette
Monica Gjevre
Janelle Glady
Kathleen Glady
Margaret Glady
Lorna Glesne
Agnes Goblirsch
Janette Goette
Ruby Goldberg
Donna Golly
Keith Golly
Linda Golly
Dawn Gordon
Hannah Gordon
Rebecca Gordon
Carol and Kristi Gottwalt
Eleanor Gottwalt
Sara Gottwalt
Andi Grams
Anna Greenberg
Gretchen Greenberg
J. D. Greenberg
Nate Greenberg
Amber Gregg
Kristy Greminger
Shannon Griffen
Kevin Griffin
Mary R. Griffin
Julietta Grimes
Bobby Groenewold
Brenda Groenewold
Jennifer Gronfeld
Julie Gronfeld
Melissa Gronfeld
Paula Gross
Nancy Grunhovd
Amber Gullickson
Andrea Gullickson
Jenny Haake
Justin Haake
Niki Haake
Hackensack Hustlers 4-H
    Club
Jan Haeg
Andrew Hagen
Brent Hagen
Melissa Hagen

Chelsi Haider
Sadie Haider
Todd Halbersma
Sue Mattson Halena
Adriana Hall
Ashley Hall
Gina Hall
Jean Halvorson
Andrea Hammel
DeAnn Hammer
Dawn Hanson
Heather Hanson
Happy Highlanders 4-H
    Club
Happy Hollow Hustlers
    4-H Club
Alex Hard
Brian Hard
Dede Hard
Megan Hard
Maxine Harkness
Harmony 4-H Club
Charlotte Harms
Becky Harrington
Erin Haspel
Gregory Haubrich
Matthew Haubrich
Susan Haubrich
Sue Haugen
Penny Hawkins
Amanda Hedlund
Garrett Hedlund
Nathaniel Hedlund
Peggy Hedman
Eric Heimark
Katrina Heimark
Jackie Helget
Jodi Helget
Kayla Helget
Leona Hellesvig
Heidi Hendrickson
Edgar Hendrickx Family
Tanya Herber
Tricia Herber
Kathy Kearney Herberg
Linda Hermann
Phillip Hermann
Alyssa Herrig
Angela Herrig
Lois Herrig
Amanda Hettver
Bev Hettver
Caryn Hewitt
Brian Hicks

Michelle Hicks
Heather C. Hill
Bonnie Hintz
Kara Hippe
Janet Hipple
Jan Hively
Woody Hobart
Deb Hodapp
Nichole Hodapp
Jena Hoefs
Ruth Hoefs
Shane Hoefs
Hokah Chiefs 4-H Club
Lenne Holland
Jason Hollerman
Matt Hollerman
Alisha Holm
Connie Holm
Katie Holmen
Linda Holmgren
Kevin Holt
Todd L. Holt
Cleo Holtberg
Lynn Shimota Honnold
Lynn Hruby
Jill Huber
Cara Hubly
Tracy Hunt
Aliq Hussain
Kim Hussain
Kortney Ihnen
Abby Illa
Diane Illa
Carla Ingebretsen
Irlbeck Family
Angela Irlbeck
Arlene Isder
Cheryl Isder
Melissa Isder
Alisha Iverson
Ashley Iverson
Doreen Iverson
Stacy Iverson
Beth Rynders Jacobs
Joyce Jacobs
Laura Jacobs
Randy Jacobs
Bev Jacobsen
Marlys Jacobson
Jill Jacoby
Karen Janku
Jane and Bonnie Janski
Aaron Jax
Anne Jefferson

Jim Jefferson
Karin Jergenson
Kristin Jergenson
Susanna Johns
Amber Johnson
Carol Johnson
Carole A. Johnson
Cory Johnson
Elizabeth Johnson
Jana Johnson
Joan Johnson
Judy Johnson
Lacey, Chris and Brittney
   Johnson
Maren Johnson
Margaret Johnson
Marlene Johnson
Melanie Johnson
Nicholas Johnson
Paul Johnson
Shirley Johnson
Susanne Johnson
Tonia and Ashley Johnson
Judy Johnston
Brian Jokela
Stella M. Jones
Danielle Jonsgaard
Sue Josephson
Angela Judes
Kris Jurgens
Wayne Jurgens
Maxine Kaehler
Beth Kahn
Danielle Kahn
Jesse Kahn
Mary Kahn
Lisa Kaiser
Megan Kappers
Ryan Kappers
Dale Karels
Derek Karels
Sandra Toenies Keating
Adriane Keierleber
Candi Keierleber
Deb Keierleber
Robin Keierleber
Tammy Keierleber
Kaycee Keller
Lindsey Keller
Elsie Kelly
Jim Kemp
Barb Kern
Sally Kern
Alyssa Kics

Elizabeth Kietzer
Kathy Kiffmeyer
Amy Kitchell
Diane Klaus
Gretchen Klaus
Nathan Klaus
Zachary Klaus
Audrey Kleespies
Kurt Kleespies
Nancy Klein
Melissa Klingberg
Merle Klouse Family
Danielle Knopik
Joanne Knopik
Martina Harjes Knowles
Pam Knutson
Kendra Koch
Kirsten Koch
Mark Koch
Rachael Koester
Jacob E. Kola
Karin Kolzow
Orma Kraai
Edna Kraayenbrink
Travis Krahn
Trent Krahn
Jennifer Kral
Elaine Kramer
Kelly Krause
Angie Krohn
Sara Krohn
Zac Krohn
Cornelia Kryzer
Jacob Kunert
Joseph Kunert
Nicole Kvittem
Stephan Lacey
Kevin and Evie Ladd
Megan Ladd
Anne Laehn
Julia LaFleur
Ann Lakeberg
Ashley Lakeberg
Mary Fran Lamison
Katie Lammers
Peter Lammers
Jake Lampert
Kim Lampert
Luke Lampert
Virginia and Elizabeth
   Landkammer
Sarah Laney
Linda Langness
Debra B. Larson

Kalyn Maninga Larson
Marian Larson
Randy Larson Family
Sarah Larson
Mary Lauer
Emma LaVoie
Jacob Ledding
Michelle Ledding
Marcia Leddy
Mary O. Lee
Marie Lee-Rude
Meghan Lentsch
Michael Lentsch
Justine Leslie
Connie Lewis
Evelyn Lewis
Jim Lewis
Aimee Lien
Elsie Liepitz
Kristie Lind
Amy Lindahl
Judy Lindahl
Heidi Lindelof
Anna Lindgren
Brita Lindgren
Janet Lindgren
Krista Lindgren
Rodger Lindgren
Svea Lindgren
Greta Lippert
Jenni Lippitt
Portia Lippitt
Joanna Lisell
Sandra Burfeind Livermore
Jane Lockwood
Laura Lockwood
Ericka Loebertmann
Jamie and Samantha Loock
Justin Lopau
Kirsten Lopau
Wendy Lopau
Stephanie Morken Lucas
Linette Lundeen
Irene D. Lundell
Linda Luschen
Stefanie Luschen
Lisa Lux
Camey Maland
Larry Malone Family
Heidi Jo Maltzan
Trudy Maninga
Angela Mannila
Aaron Marquette
Craig Marquette

Barb Marthaler
Sarah Marthaler
Melissa Martin
Bertie Martinez
Dawn Marx
Carolyn Matz
Anna Maurer
Alice Mayers
Elizabeth McCabe
Jonathan McCabe
Matt McCabe
Patty Jo McCabe
Mary E. McCarte
Bryan McCoy
Melissa McCoy
Crystal McDevitt
Anne McDonald
Kathy McFadden
Rachal McKuskey
Donna McLouth
Tressa McLouth
Shannon McMarten
Hannah Meacham
Ellen Meier
Brionna Meisner
Dielle Meisner
Monica Meschke
Carisa Meulehroeck
Allison Meyer
Jessica Meyer
Lucas Meyer
Melanie Meyer
Bonnie Mickelson
Elizabeth P. Mickelson
Jonathan Mickelson
Linda W. Mickelson
Kaaren Mikus
Cindy Millar
Carol Miller
Kristine Miller
Martha and Amy Modrynski
Kjersten Moe
Doris Moeller
Kristle Moen
Mandi Moen
Sharon Moenkhaus
Laura Molden
Michelle Molden
Elsa Moluf
Stefan Moluf
Henry Montplaisir
Korey Montplaisir
Meghan Moore
Mary Mootz

Barbara Morken
Kimberly Morken
Anna Mueller
Helen K. Mueller
Brandon Mullenbach
Linda Murch
Tara, Lindsey and Betsy
    Murphy
Heda Najmaie
Dan Nare
Brenda Nash
Jadon Nash
Amanda Nathe
Dan Nave
Marlys Neldner
Megan Neldner
Molly Neldner
Will Neldner
Becky Nelson
Brent Nelson
Christopher and Miranda
    Nelson
Cody Nelson
Crystal Lee Nelson
Jenny Nelson
Karin Nelson
Teresa Nelson
Sophia Nequse
Andy Nere
Anne Nere
LuAnn M. Nere
Ashley Nesburg
Cynthia Nesburg
Tara Nesburg
Jan Nice
Robert Nicko
Dorothy Nicolai
Andrew Nielsen
Heather Nielsen
Krista Nielsen
Amy Niemann
Tyler Niemeyers
Beef Noll
Chuck Noll
Deb Noll
Judy Noll
Peter Noll
Kylee Noren
Debbie Norling
Marie Norton
Brenda Notch
Carol Notch
Derrick Nyhus
Jeannie Nytes

Ruth Ann Nytes
Dan O'Connell Family
Heidi Olehiser
Eric Olmscheid
Joan Olmscheid
Diana, Missy and Scott
    Olsen
Gudrun Olsen
Lars Olsen
Sonja Olsen
Janelle Olson
Jean Olson
Joseph Olson
Judy Olson
Justine Olson
Katherine Olson
Dawn Oltmans
Carrie Onerheim
Jim Onerheim
Kari Osmondson
Anne Osowski
Wendy Osowski
Karen Ostlie
Kevin Ott
Mary Ott
Katie Otto
Lynn M. Otto
Samantha Oxborough
Jamaica Oyster
Allison Page
Stephanie Palm
Ardis Palmer
Jimmie Palmer
Mary Palmer
Kimberly Pangrac
Mary Ann Papke
Mike Parker
Jennifer Parrish
Melissa Parrish
Beth Patterson
Jared and Joel Patterson
Heather Paulson
Marianne Paulson
Nick Paulson
Ruth Paulson
Jan Pavlisich
Shirley Peak
Chris Pearson
Kathi Kraai Pearson
Elaine Pease
Jeremy Pease
Weston Pease
Cheryl Pederson
Elizabeth Peeters

Pelican 4-H Club
Hilary Penner
Janine Penner
Marissa Penner
Brittany Pennings
Steven Pennings
Sue Pennings
Mary Beth Perdie
Evelyn Perron
John and Beth Peter
Adam Peterson
Amy Peterson
Arlin Peterson
Kelsey J. Peterson
Kristen Peterson
Stephanie Peterson
Vegas Peterson
Joyce and Terri Petron
Sarah M. Pfeffer
Becky Phillips
Philles Phillips
Sheila Phillips
Alicia Piechowski
Bernice Piechowski
Cassie Piechowski
Micole Piechowski
Sandy Piechowski
Cindy, Gary and Glen Piehl
Ellie Piehl
Erin Piehl
LeAnna M. Pierson
Dairn Jay Pieti
Lisa Pietig
Melissa Pietila
Jim and Justin Pizzella
Angi and Jacki Popp
Mary Nell Preisler
Kassandra Prodoehl
Amanda Proulx
Heather Proulx
Katie Proulx
Kim Proulx
Kris Proulx
Kurtis Proulx
Toni Przybylski
Kelly Purdy
Jennifer Putnam
JoAnna Putnam
Alicia Qualley
Amanda Rabehl
Anna Rabehl
Kimberly Rabehl
Marilyn Rabehl
Elaine Radloff

Latha Rakow
Brandon Rakstad
Ryan Rakstad
Sandy Rand
Brian Rangaard
Jeremy Rangaard
Camille Rasmussen
Colleen Rasmussen
Grant Rasmussen
Lindsey Rauenhorst
Lucas and Katy Ravdabargh
Dan Rechtzigel
Michelle Reding
Juanita J. Reed-Boniface
Adam Regnier
Kyle Regnier
Kristin Reiman
Jackie Reineke
Laurn Reinke
Pam, Jason and Kim Reistad
Judy Relf
Kathy Remme
Gloria Rettig
Naomi Rettig
Bonny Reynolds
Megan Rhodd
Quinn Rhodd
Joyce Rife
Adrienne Ritchie
Anna Rivard
Kathy Rivard
Peter Robey
Carlota Robinson
Betty Rochel
Lorna Rockstad
Joanna Roeschlein
Lorraine Roiger
Delphine Rolf
Kathryn Rolf
Mildred Rosenhammer
Phyllis Rossow
Halie C. Rostberg
Heidi Rostberg
Hillary Rostberg
Suzette Rowen
Laura Rueckert
Michael Rueckert
Sara, Sonia, Becky and Cody
    Runke
Emily Rusch
Seth Rusch
Teryl Rusch
Trisha Rust
Jessie Rustad

Nancy Rustad
Katie Ruter
Michelle Rygh
Tara Rygh
Barbara Rynders
John Rynders
Valerie Ryti-Cunningham
Karen Sakry
Mark Sakry
Faustino Salgado
Maria Salgado
Karen, Chris and Sarah
    Salmela
Angela Sanborn
Anthony Sanborn
Stephanie Sanborn
Becky Sander
Cassie Sander
Holly Sander
Reid Sander
Angela N. Sangster
Mary Ann Sarja
Jan Sawatzke
Tammy Sawatzke
Cheryl Schaefer
Jared Schaefer
Anna Schafer
Jeffrey Schaffer
Sharon Schaffer
Marcy Schewe
Jan Schilmoeller
Chandra Schlagel
Linda Schlauderaff
Clarice Schmidt
Linda Schmiesing
Angela and Randy
    Schoenrock
Laurie Schroeder
Chelsey Schrupp
Nickolas Schrupp
Dean Schuette Family
Kyle Schulz
Carol Schwartau
Casandra Schwartau
Chuck Schwartau
Corinne Schwartau
Craig Schwartau
Ron and Connie Schwartau
Becky Schweich
Shirley Segner
Charlie Sehr
Constance Sehr
Debb Sehr
Cheryl Seibert

Becky Seidl
Leona A. Seidl
Steve and Barb Seifert
Annette Seitz
Cathy Seitz
Barb Sellner
Celeste Sellner
Christopher Sellner
Karen Sellner
Laura Sellner
Lisa Sellner
MaDonna Sellner
Shannon Sellner
Shari Sellner
Theresa Sellner
Jacob Serfling
Keith Severson
Vince Sexton Family
Lanette Shaffer
Norma Shaffer
Karen Share
Kathy Shearon
William D. Shearon
Sarah Shimota
Shannon Shimota
Debbie Shoekmeen
James M. Simon
Jill Sirek
Brandon Sis
Nathan Sis
Wanda Sis
AnnaMarie Sjol
Janet Sjol
Alice Skarsten
Emily Skoien
Amber Smith
Gregory Smith
Heather Smith
Jodi Smith
LaVonne Smith
Nathan Smith
Phyllis Smith
Sharon Smith
Teffeny A. Smith
Alyssa Soderholm
Stacy Soderstrom
Erin Solom
Mary Solom
Jean Solsrud
Adam Sorum
Ashley Sorum
Justin Sorum
Summer Sorum
Spang 4-H Club

Marge Speer
Donna Speltz
Joe Speltz
Amanda Sprick
Ken Stangler
Anne Stangler
Jill Stangler
Mary Jo Stangler
Anita Stark
Leilani Stauffer
Ben Staven
Rebecca Steffen
Peggy Steinkamp
Anthony Stevens
Sheldon Stevermer
Rena Stigen
Amy Stocker
Robin Stoffel
Sandy Stoffel
Amy L. Struthers
Andrew D. Struthers
Anna M. Struthers
ChrysMarie Suby
Brian Suckow
Janet Suckow
Matthew Suckow
Faith Sullivan
Penny Summer
Sunnyside 4-H Club
Peggy Svendsen
Barbara Svoboda
Lori Svoboda
Kim Swanson
Brett Swap
Daniel Swenson
Gwendolyn Swenson
Karl Swenson
Katherine Swenson
Kurt Swenson
Larry Noel Swenson
Mike Swenson
Chip Sylva
Justin Sylva
Valerie Sylva
Jamie Tanata
Barb Thalacker
Jeremy Thalacker
Reason Thalacker
Alex Thom
Jiles Thomas
Judy Thomas
Justin Thomas
Kathy Thomas
Morgan Thomas

Deb Thomforde
Kyle Thomforde
Dawn Thompson
Jill Thompson
Julie Thompson
Karen Thompson
Laura Thompson
Linda Thompson
Lisa Thompson
Diane Thorson
Betty Thurston
Tibbets Brook Flyers 4-H
   Club
Doris Tibbetts
Korey Tibbetts
Pam Timmerman
Terry Timmerman
Traci Timmerman
Mary Tobolaski
Bonnie Toenies
Cheryl Tomnitz
Kari Torgerson
Mary Totland
David Trana
Kevin Trana
Kristy Trana
Traverse County 4-H
   Federation
Tijuana Triangles
Bruce Turner
Carol Turner
Jean Ann Tweeten
Karen Tweeten
Kati Tweeten
Brent Tyrrell
Jakin Tyrrell
Nichole Tyrrell
Troy Tyrrell
Amy Uhlenkamp
Cindy Uhlenkamp
Anderew Ulrich
Debbie Ulrich
Jessica Ulrich
Andrew Umphrey
Miranda Umphrey
Bradley Urieze
Kris Williams Uter
Gabrielle VanDyk
Nichole VanDyk
Kelsie Vangness
Glenyce Peterson Vangsness
Tracy VanMoorlehem
Cheryl Vantlorn
Becky VanWesten

Stacy VanWesten
Christy Vastenhout
Nicole Vastenhout
Kristen Vatthauer
Andrew Velishek
Brian Velishek
Jon Velishek
Tom Velishek
Tracy Velishek
Wayne Velishek
Melissa and Jennifer Viaene
Joan M. Vievering
Robby Visker
Ryan Visker
Susan Visker
Krista Voge
Kimberley Voges
Emma Volker
Molly Votava
Kristin Wagner
Wahkon Willing Workers
   4-H Club
Andy Walker
George Walker
Jacob Walker
Jared Walker
Joyce Walker
Karen Walker
Kim Walker
Shaina Walker
Elaine Walter
Joyce Warner
Kati and Anne Warner

David Warren
Bev Watie
Jill Wavra
Melissa Wavra
Michelle Wavra
Susan Wavra
Janice Rising Weaver
April Weinreich
Grace Weinreich
Hannah Weinreich
Jacob Weinreich
Jean P. Weiske
M. Eileen Welsh
Hilary Weness
Christy Wensauer
Jonathan Werth
Teresa Werth
Lori West
Megan West
Ashley Westbury
Karen Weyer
Marlys Wheeler
Cheryl White
Victor White
Martin Wigert
Roxy Wigton
Matt Wilberding
D. Jay Willert
Darlene Willert
T. J. Williams
Yvonne Williams
Brandon Wilson
Dillon Wilson

Karin L. Winscher-Ihnen
Scott Wiste
Shannon Wiste
Kathy Wobig
Scott Ross Woizeschke
Woodland 4-H Club
Shirley Worms
Douglas Wosick
Krischauna Wosick
Sharon Wright
Cara Wubbenhorst
Carole and Fred Wurst
Donna Yokiel
Katie Yokiel
Scott Yokiel
Stacie Yokiel
Karen Younk
Julie Zachariason
Laura Zachariason
Lindsay Zachariason
Shirley Zehnder
Melissa Zeig
Rosie Zeig
Ann M. Zick
Sheldon L. D. Zick
Diane Zilmer
Heather Zilmer
Ellen Zipp
Jennifer Zipp
Maria Zipp
Melanie Zipp
Marjorie Springer Zluticky

Special Thanks To ...

Richard A. W. Byrne, Director of the Center for 4-H Youth Development
Elaine Christiansen, Cookbook Committee, 4-H Foundation Board of Trustees
Edna Dallum, retired cook at the 4-H Building at the State Fair 1939–1980
Molly Fischer, Cookbook Committee, Director of the 4-H Cafeteria at the 4-H Building
Dede Hard, Cookbook Committee, Assistant Director of the 4-H Cafeteria at the 4-H Building
Leonard Harkness, retired State 4-H Leader of Minnesota and his wife, Maxine
Mary Fran Lamison, Cookbook Committee Member and retired MES Staff member
Marian Larson, Cookbook Committee Member and retired MES Staff member
James Lewis, Executive Director of the Minnesota 4-H Foundation
Debra Noll, Development Associate of the Minnesota 4-H Foundation
Sara Thoms, Cookbook Committee, 4-H Foundation Board of Trustees
Joyce Walker, Youth Development Educator, Center for 4-H Youth Development, 4-H
   Foundation Board of Trustees

County Extension Offices

Contact your local County Extension office for more information on 4-H.

Aitkin Co. Ext. Office
Courthouse
209 2nd St. NW
Aitkin, MN 56431-1257
Phone: (218) 927-7321

Anoka Co. Ext. Office
Anoka Co. Activity Center
550 Bunker Lake Blvd. NW
Anoka, MN 55304-4199
Phone: (612) 755-1280

Becker Co. Ext. Office
AG Service Center
809 8th St. SE
Detroit Lakes, MN
56501-2842
Phone: (218) 847-3141

Beltrami Co. Ext. Office
815 15th St. NW
Bemidji, MN
56601-2501
Phone: (218) 759-0038

Benton Co. Ext. Office
Courthouse Building
531 Dewey St.
Foley, MN 56329-0247
Phone: (612) 968-6254

Big Stone Co. Ext. Office
20 SE 2nd St.
Ortonville, MN
56278-1544
Phone: (612) 839-2518

Blue Earth Co. Ext. Office
Govt Ctr., 410 S. 5th St.
P.O. Box 8608
Mankato, MN
56002-8608
Phone: (507) 389-8325

Brown Co. Ext. Office
300 2nd Ave. SW
Sleepy Eye, MN
56085-1402
Phone: (507) 794-7993

Carlton Co. Ext. Office
310 Chestnut Street
P.O. Box 307
Carlton, MN 55718-0307
Phone: (218) 384-3511

Carver Co. Ext. Office
609 West First Street
Waconia, MN 55387-1204
Phone: (612) 442-4496

Cass Co. Ext. Office
Courthouse
P.O. Box 3000
Walker, MN 56484-3000
Phone: (218) 547-3300

Chippewa Co. Ext. Office
Courthouse, 629 N. 11th St.
Montevideo, MN
56265-1685
Phone: (612) 269-6521

Chisago Co. Ext. Office
38694 Tanger Drive
North Branch, MN
55056-9500
Phone: (612) 257-2982

Clay Co. Ext. Office
Courthouse
807 11th St. N.
Moorhead, MN 56560-1500
Phone: (218) 299-5020

Clearwater Co. Ext. Office
Clearwater County Bldg.
RR 1 Box 18
Bagley, MN 56621-9103
Phone: (218) 694-6151

Cook Co. Ext. Office
Community Center Bldg.
P.O. Box 1150, 317 West 5th
Grand Marais, MN
55604-1150
Phone: (218) 387-9031

Cottonwood Co. Ext. Office
235—9th Street
Windom, MN 56101-1642
Phone: (507) 831-4022

Crow Wing Co. Ext. Office
County Service Bldg.
322 Laurel St.
Brainerd, MN 56401-3578
Phone: (218) 828-3980

Dakota Co. Ext. Office
Fairgrounds
4100 220th St. W.
Farmington, MN 55024-9539
Phone: (612) 463-3302

Dodge Co. Ext. Office
42 E. Main St.
P.O. Box 159
Dodge Center, MN
55927-0159
Phone: (507) 374-6435

Douglas Co. Ext. Office
Courthouse
305 8th Ave. W.
Alexandria, MN
56308-1785
Phone: (612) 762-2381

Faribault Co. Ext. Office
412 N. Nicollet St.
P.O. Box 130
Blue Earth, MN 56013-0130
Phone: (507) 526-6240

Fillmore Co. Ext. Office
P.O. Box 318
Preston, MN 55965-0310
Phone: (507) 765-3896

Freeborn Co. Ext. Office
Courthouse—Room 222
411 S. Broadway
Albert Lea, MN 56007-1147
Phone: (507) 373-1475

Goodhue Co. Ext. Office
Courthouse—Room 105
509 W. 5th St.
Red Wing, MN 55066-2540
Phone: (612) 385-3100

Grant Co. Ext. Office
411 First St. SE
P.O. Box 1099
Elbow Lake, MN 56531-1099
Phone: (218) 685-4820

Hennepin Co. Ext. Office
1525 Glenwood Ave.
Minneapolis, MN
55405-1264
Phone: (612) 374-8400

Houston Co. Ext. Office
419 Foltz Drive
P.O. Box 228
Caledonia, MN 55921-0228
Phone: (507) 724-5807

Hubbard Co. Ext. Office
Courthouse
301 Court St.
Park Rapids, MN
56470-1483
Phone: (218) 732-3391

Isanti Co. Ext. Office
555—18th Ave. SW
Cambridge, MN
55008-9386
Phone: (612) 689-1810

Itasca Co. Ext. Office
Courthouse, 123–4th St. NE
Grand Rapids, MN
55744-2600
Phone: (218) 327-2849

Jackson Co. Ext. Office
419 Main St., P.O. Box 309
Lakefield, MN 56150-0309
Phone: (507) 662-5293

Kanabec Co. Ext. Office
Courthouse, 18 North Vine
Mora, MN 55051-1351
Phone: (612) 679-3010

Kandiyohi Co. Ext. Office
905 W. Litchfield
P.O. Box 977
Willmar, MN 56201-0977
Phone: (612) 235-1485

Kittson Co. Ext. Office
Courthouse, P.O. Box 369
Hallock, MN 56728-0369
Phone: (218) 843-3674

Koochiching Co. Ext. Office
Courthouse Complex
701 4th St. W.
Intl. Falls, MN 56649-2486
Phone: (218) 283-6282

Lac Qui Parle Co. Ext. Office
Courthouse, 600 6th St.
Madison, MN 56256-1295
Phone: (612) 598-3325

Lake Co. Ext. Office
Courthouse
601 3rd Ave.
Two Harbors, MN
55616-1517
Phone: (218) 834-8377

Lake of the Woods Co. Ext.
Office
Courthouse
P.O. Box 598
Baudette, MN 56623-0598
Phone: (218) 634-1511

Le Sueur Co. Ext. Office
88 S. Park
Lecenter, MN 56057-1620
Phone: (612) 357-2251

Lincoln Co. Ext. Office
402 N. Harold, P.O. Box 130
Ivanhoe, MN
56142-0130
Phone: (507) 694-1470

Lyon Co. Ext. Office
AG Service Center
1400 East Lyon Street
Marshall, MN 56258-2529
Phone: (507) 537-6702

McLeod Co. Ext. Office
840 Century Ave., Suite B
Hutchinson, MN 55350-0144
Phone: (612) 587-0770

Mahnomen Co. Ext. Office
P.O. Box 477
Mahnomen, MN
56557-0477
Phone: (218) 935-2226

Marshall Co. Ext. Office
Courthouse
208 E. Colvin Ave.
Warren, MN 56762-1698
Phone: (218) 745-5232

Martin Co. Ext. Office
104 Courthouse
201 Lake Ave.
Fairmont, MN 56031-1845
Phone: (507) 235-3341

Meeker Co. Ext. Office
305 N. Sibley Ave.
P.O. Box 562
Litchfield, MN 55355-0562
Phone: (612) 693-2801

Mille Lacs Co. Ext. Office
635 Central Avenue N.
Milaca, MN 56353-1743
Phone: (612) 983-8317

Morrison Co. Ext. Office
Govt Center, 213 First Ave. SE
Little Falls, MN 56345-3100
Phone: (612) 632-0161

Mower Co. Ext. Office
Courthouse, 201 NE 1st St.
Austin, MN 55912-3475
Phone: (507) 437-9552

Murray Co. Ext. Office
County Courts Building
P.O. Box 57
Slayton, MN 56172-0057
Phone: (507) 836-6148

Nicollet Co. Ext. Office
Courthouse
501 S. Minnesota Ave.
St. Peter, MN
56082-2533
Phone: (507) 931-6800

Nobles Co. Ext. Office
Courthouse Basement
P.O. Box 758
Worthington, MN
56187-0758
Phone: (507) 372-8210

Norman Co. Ext. Office
101 W. Third Ave.
Ada, MN 56510-1200
Phone: (218) 784-7183

Olmsted Co. Ext. Office
1421 SE 3rd Ave.
Rochester, MN 55904-7947
Phone: (507) 285-8250

Otter Tail E. Co. Ext. Office
222 Second Ave. SE
Perham, MN 56573-1719
Phone: (218) 346-5750

Otter Tail W. Co. Ext. Office
Courthouse
121 W. Junius Ave.
Fergus Falls, MN
56537-2544
Phone: (218) 739-2271

Pennington Co. Ext. Office
Courthouse, P.O. Box 616
Thief River Falls, MN
56701-0616
Phone: (218) 681-2116

Pine Co. Ext. Office
105 Fire Monument Road
P.O. Box 370
Hinckley, MN 55037-0370
Phone: (612) 384-6156

Pipestone Co. Ext. Office
Municipal Bldg.
119 SW 2nd Ave., Suite 2
Pipestone, MN 56164-1684
Phone: (507) 825-5416

Polk East Co. Ext. Office
P.O. Box 69
McIntosh, MN 56556-0069
Phone: (218) 563-2465

Polk West Co. Ext. Office
U Teaching & Outreach Ctr.
P.O. Box 556
Crookston, MN 56716-0556
Phone: (218) 281-8696

Pope Co. Ext. Office
Courthouse
130 Minnesota Ave. E.
Glenwood, MN 56334-1628
Phone: (612) 634-5735

Ramsey Co. Ext. Office
2020 White Bear Avenue
St. Paul, MN 55109-3795
Phone: (612) 777-8156

Red Lake Co. Ext. Office
Courthouse
P.O. Box 279
Red Lake Falls, MN
56750-0279
Phone: (218) 253-2895

Red Lake Nation
P.O. Box 279
Red Lake, MN 56671-0279
Phone: (218) 679-3959

Redwood Co. Ext. Office
Courthouse, P.O. Box 130
Redwood Falls, MN
56283-0130
Phone: (507) 637-8323

Renville Co. Ext. Office
Renville Co. Office Bldg.
500 E. Depue Ave.
Olivia, MN 56277-1396
Phone: (612) 523-2522

Rice County Ext. Office
Courthouse
218 3rd Street NW
Faribault, MN 55021-5146
Phone: (507) 332-6109

Rock Co. Ext. Office
311 West Gabrielson
P.O. Box 898
Luverne, MN 56156-0898
Phone: (507) 283-4446

Roseau Co. Ext. Office
308 Center St. West
Roseau, MN 56751-1499
Phone: (218) 463-1052

St. Louis Co. Ext. Office
Courthouse
1810 E. 12th Ave.
Hibbing, MN 55746-1680
Phone: (218) 262-0144

St. Louis Co. Ext. Office
109A Washburn Hall
2305 E. 5th St.
Duluth, MN 55812-2420
Phone: (218) 726-7512

St. Louis Co. Ext. Office
Northland Office Center
307 1st St. S., Suite 114
Virginia, MN 55792-2668
Phone: (218) 749-7120

Scott Co. Ext. Office
123 First St. E.
Jordan, MN 55352-1580
Phone: (612) 492-2370

Sherburne Co. Ext. Office
Sherburne Co. Govt Ctr.
P.O. Box 311—13880 Hwy. 10
Elk River, MN 55330-0311
Phone: (612) 241-2720

Sibley Co. Ext. Office
Courthouse, P.O. Box 207
Gaylord, MN 55334-0207
Phone: (612) 237-5531

Stearns Co. Ext. Office
Midtown Square
3400 First St. N. #400
Saint Cloud, MN
56303-4000
Phone: (612) 255-6169

Steele Co. Ext. Office
County Admin. Annex
590 Dunnell Dr., P.O. Box 890
Owatonna, MN 55060-0890
Phone: (507) 451-8040

Stevens Co. Ext. Office
Colonial Square
208 Atlantic Ave.
Morris, MN 56267-1321
Phone: (612) 589-7423

Swift Co. Ext. Office
Courthouse, P.O. Box 305
Benson, MN 56215-0305
Phone: (612) 843-3796

Todd Co. Ext. Office
Courthouse Annex
119 3rd St. S.
Long Prairie, MN
56347-1354
Phone: (612) 732-4435

Traverse Co. Ext. Office
Courthouse, P.O. Box 457
Wheaton, MN 56296-0457
Phone: (612) 563-4515

Wabasha Co. Ext. Office
611 Broadway Ave. #40
Wabasha, MN 55981-1613
Phone: (612) 565-2662

Wadena Co. Ext. Office
Courthouse
415 S. Jefferson Ave.
Wadena, MN 56482-1594
Phone: (218) 631-2332

Waseca Co. Ext. Office
300 North State St. #1
Waseca, MN 56093-2933
Phone: (507) 835-0600

Washington Co. Ext. Office
Suite 202
1825 Curve Crest Blvd.
Stillwater, MN 55082-6054
Phone: (612) 439-0101

Watonwan Co. Ext. Office
Courthouse, P.O. Box 68
St. James, MN 56081-0068
Phone: (507) 375-1275

Wilkin Co. Ext. Office
421 Nebraska Ave.
Breckenridge, MN
56520-1415
Phone: (218) 643-5481

Winona Co. Ext. Office
202 W. 3rd St.
Winona, MN 55987-3115
Phone: (507) 457-6440

Wright Co. Ext. Office
Room 130
10 2nd St. NW
Buffalo, MN 55313-1186
Phone: (612) 682-7394

Yellow Medicine Co. Ext.
1004 10th Ave., P.O. Box 128
Clarkfield, MN
56223-0128
Phone: (612) 669-4471

$\mathcal{I}$ndex

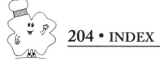

$\mathcal{O}$rder Form

Minnesota 4-H Recipes
340 Coffey Hall, 1420 Eckles Avenue
St. Paul, Minnesota 55108

Make checks payable to the Minnesota 4-H Foundation.

Name:_____

Address: _____

City/State/Zip:_____

Please send _____ copies   @ $12.95 each   _____

Postage and handling   @ $ 2.50 each   _____

Total $ _____

See reverse side for gift card information.

$\mathcal{O}$rder Form

Minnesota 4-H Recipes
340 Coffey Hall, 1420 Eckles Avenue
St. Paul, Minnesota 55108

Make checks payable to the Minnesota 4-H Foundation.

Name:_____

Address: _____

City/State/Zip:_____

Please send _____ copies   @ $12.95 each   _____

Postage and handling   @ $ 2.50 each   _____

Total $ _____

See reverse side for gift card information.

$\mathcal{O}$rder Form

Minnesota 4-H Recipes
340 Coffey Hall, 1420 Eckles Avenue
St. Paul, Minnesota 55108

Make checks payable to the Minnesota 4-H Foundation.

Name:_____

Address: _____

City/State/Zip:_____

Please send _____ copies   @ $12.95 each   _____

Postage and handling   @ $ 2.50 each   _____

Total $ _____

See reverse side for gift card information.

Gift Card Information

Enclosed gift card to read:

_____

_____

_____

_____

All copies of *Minnesota 4-H Recipes* will be sent to same address unless otherwise specified. If you wish one or more books sent as gifts, furnish a list of names and addresses of recipients. If you wish to enclose your own gift card with each book, please write name of recipient on outside of the envelope, enclose with order, and we will include it with your gift.

Gift Card Information

Enclosed gift card to read:

_____

_____

_____

_____

All copies of *Minnesota 4-H Recipes* will be sent to same address unless otherwise specified. If you wish one or more books sent as gifts, furnish a list of names and addresses of recipients. If you wish to enclose your own gift card with each book, please write name of recipient on outside of the envelope, enclose with order, and we will include it with your gift.

Gift Information

Enclosed gift card to read:

_____

_____

_____

_____

All copies of *Minnesota 4-H Recipes* will be sent to same address unless otherwise specified. If you wish one or more books sent as gifts, furnish a list of names and addresses of recipients. If you wish to enclose your own gift card with each book, please write name of recipient on outside of the envelope, enclose with order, and we will include it with your gift.